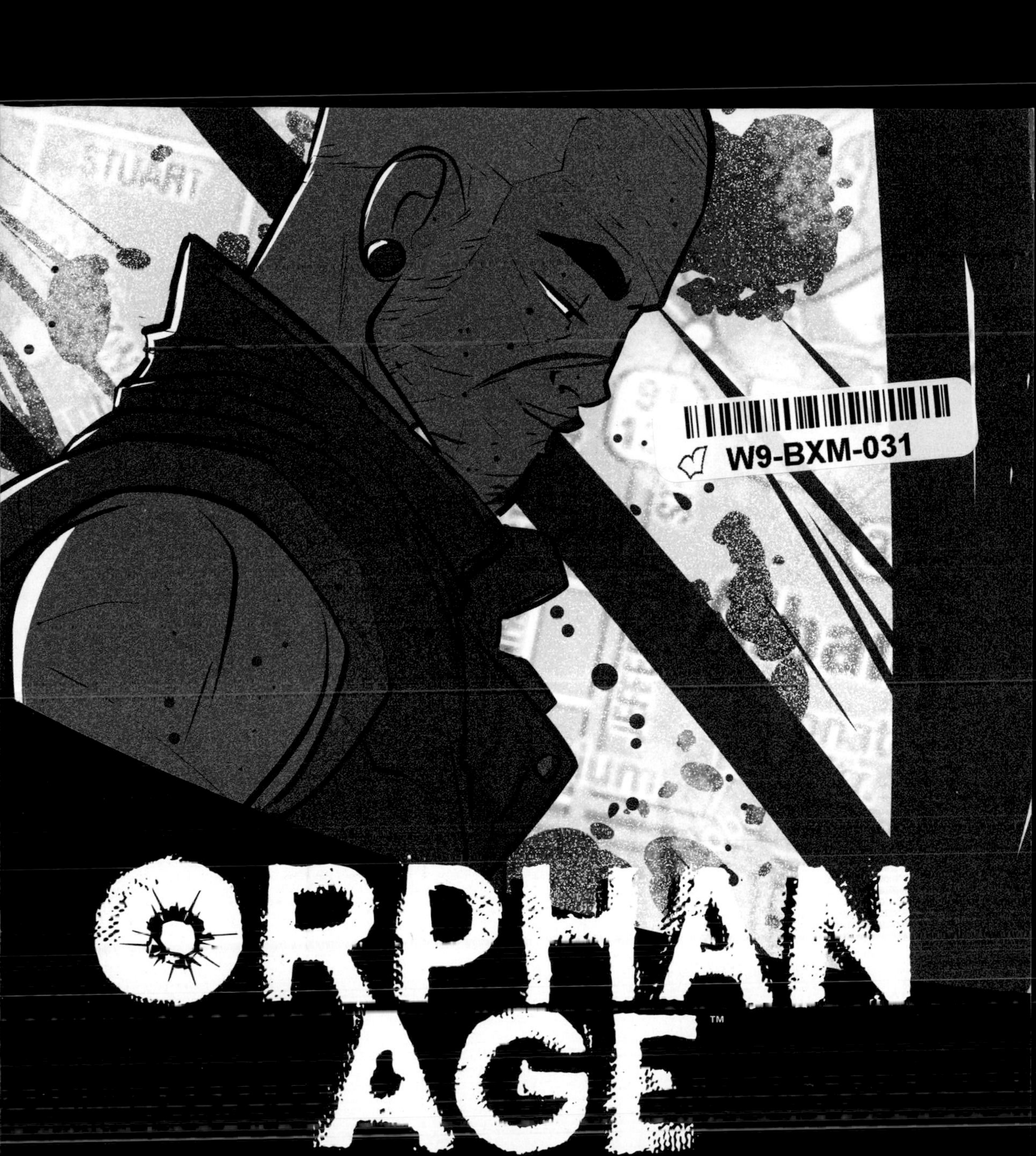
STUART

ORPHAN AGE™

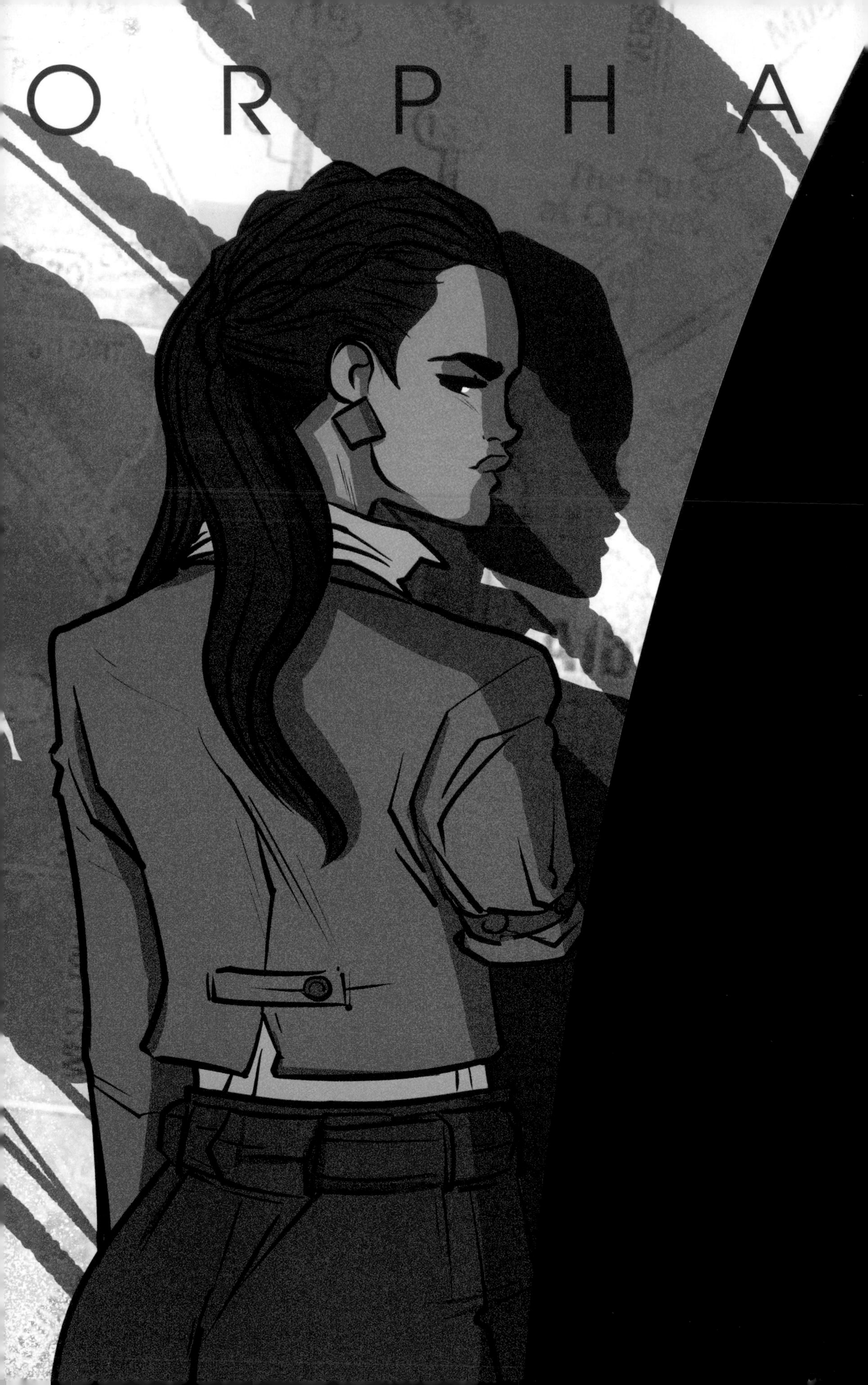
O R P H A

N A G E ™

TED ANDERSON co-creator & writer

NUNO PLATI co-creator & artist

JOÃO LEMOS & NUNO PLATI colorists

MARSHALL DILLON letterer

NUNO PLATI front & original covers

JUAN DOE variant cover

JARED K. FLETCHER logo designer

COREY BREEN book designer

MIKE MARTS editor

AFTERSHOCK™

MIKE MARTS - Editor-in-Chief • JOE PRUETT - Publisher/CCO • LEE KRAMER - President • JON KRAMER - Chief Executive Officer
STEVE ROTTERDAM - SVP, Sales & Marketing • DAN SHIRES - VP, Film & Television UK • CHRISTINA HARRINGTON - Managing Editor
MARC HAMMOND - Sr. Retail Sales Development Manager • RUTHANN THOMPSON - Sr. Retailer Relations Manager • KATHERINE JAMISON - Marketing Manager
BLAKE STOCKER - Director of Finance • AARON MARION - Publicist • LISA MOODY - Finance • RYAN CARROLL - Development Coordinator
JAWAD QURESHI - Technology Advisor/Strategist • CHARLES PRITCHETT - Comics Production • COREY BREEN - Collections Production
TEDDY LEO - Editorial Assistant • STEPHANIE CASEBIER & SARAH PRUETT - Publishing Assistants

AfterShock Logo Design by COMICRAFT
Publicity: contact AARON MARION (aaron@publichausagency.com) & RYAN CROY (ryan@publichausagency.com) at PUBLICHAUS
Special thanks to: IRA KURGAN, MARINE KSADZHIKYAN, ANTONIA LIANOS & STEPHAN NILSON

Originally published as Orphan Age #1-5. PRINTED IN KOREA.
First Printing: November 2019. 10 9 8 7 6 5 4 3 2 1

AFTERSHOCKCOMICS.COM Follow us on social media

I N T R O D U C T I O N

ORPHAN AGE is a post-apocalyptic story, which means it's really a story about our current worries and fears, as seen in a world that gives them free rein.

An apocalypse clears the decks from a storytelling standpoint, giving a creator the chance to tell a story that focuses on a group outside the normal rules and restrictions of society. Often the conflict comes down to whether there can even be a continuation of society in the face of zombie hordes or unnatural disasters, or whether society must completely redefine itself in response. The material supports of society—the roads, buildings, farms, phone networks, fire trucks—are often destroyed or rendered inoperable, forcing a radical reevaluation of what is necessary for survival. As the world crumbles around our heroes, we the audience are meant to ask: how would we act if we lost our tools for survival? How can society continue under such conditions?

With ORPHAN AGE, I wanted to invert this question, as it were: what if all the physical materials of society were still present, but the people who knew how to make use of them were gone? What if society had to be rebuilt by those who don't yet understand it? What if there could be no continuity of the world as we know it?

In other words, what if the children were suddenly in charge?

And so ORPHAN AGE is *actually* about children: how we raise them, how we teach them, what they know, what they *think* they know. How does a child believe the world works? How does a child think the world *should* work? And how would they try to build that world?

ORPHAN AGE is not an entirely accurate extrapolation of what a world without grown-ups would look like. But that's never the point of stories like these. The point of a post-apocalyptic story is to ask questions of ourselves *today*, to interrogate the way we live now. These stories aren't meant to be a roadmap or a crystal ball, because they can't be. The future will arrive, one way or another, and one day our children *will* be in charge.

We must try to teach them well.

TED ANDERSON
November 2019

1

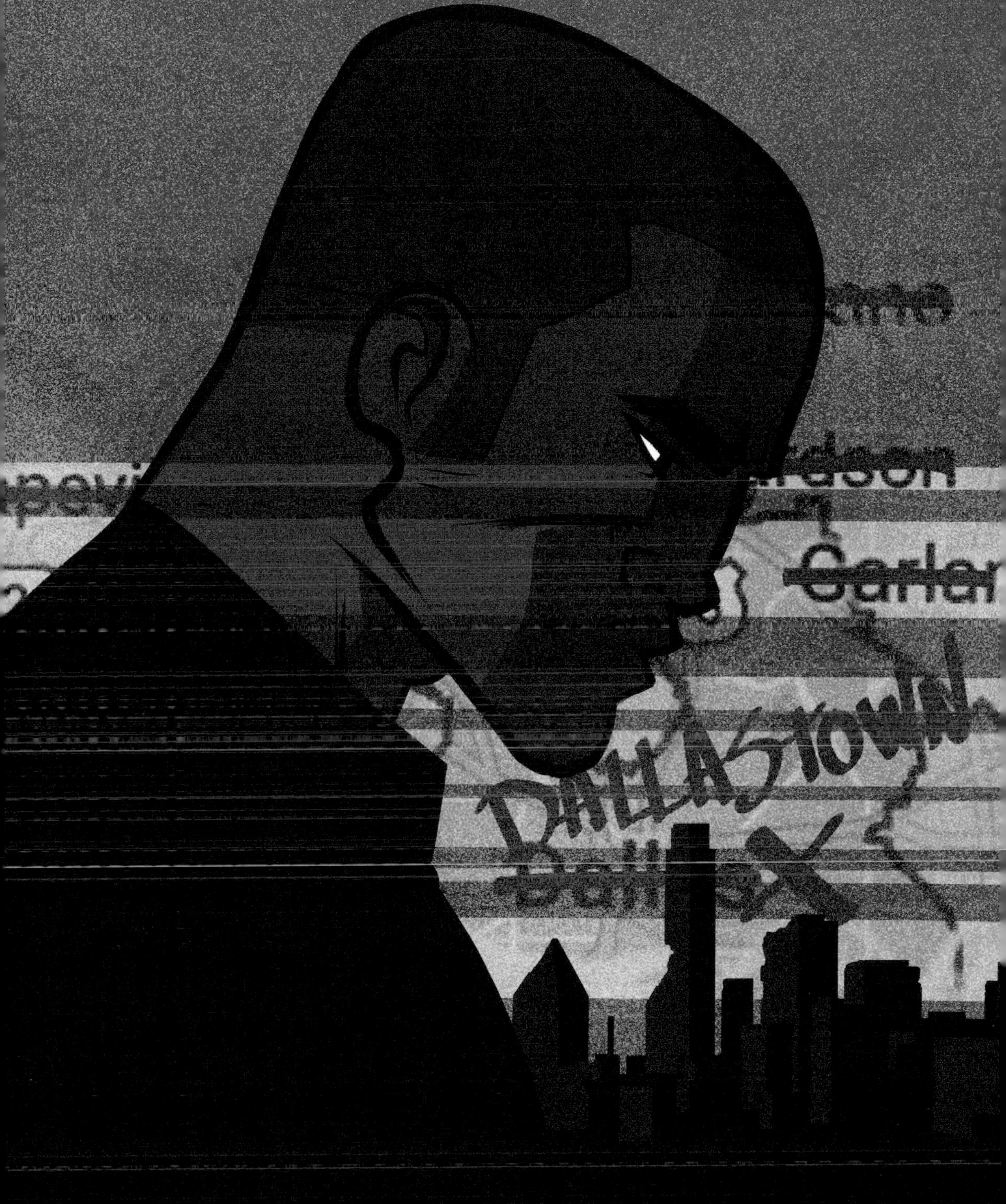

CHILDHOOD

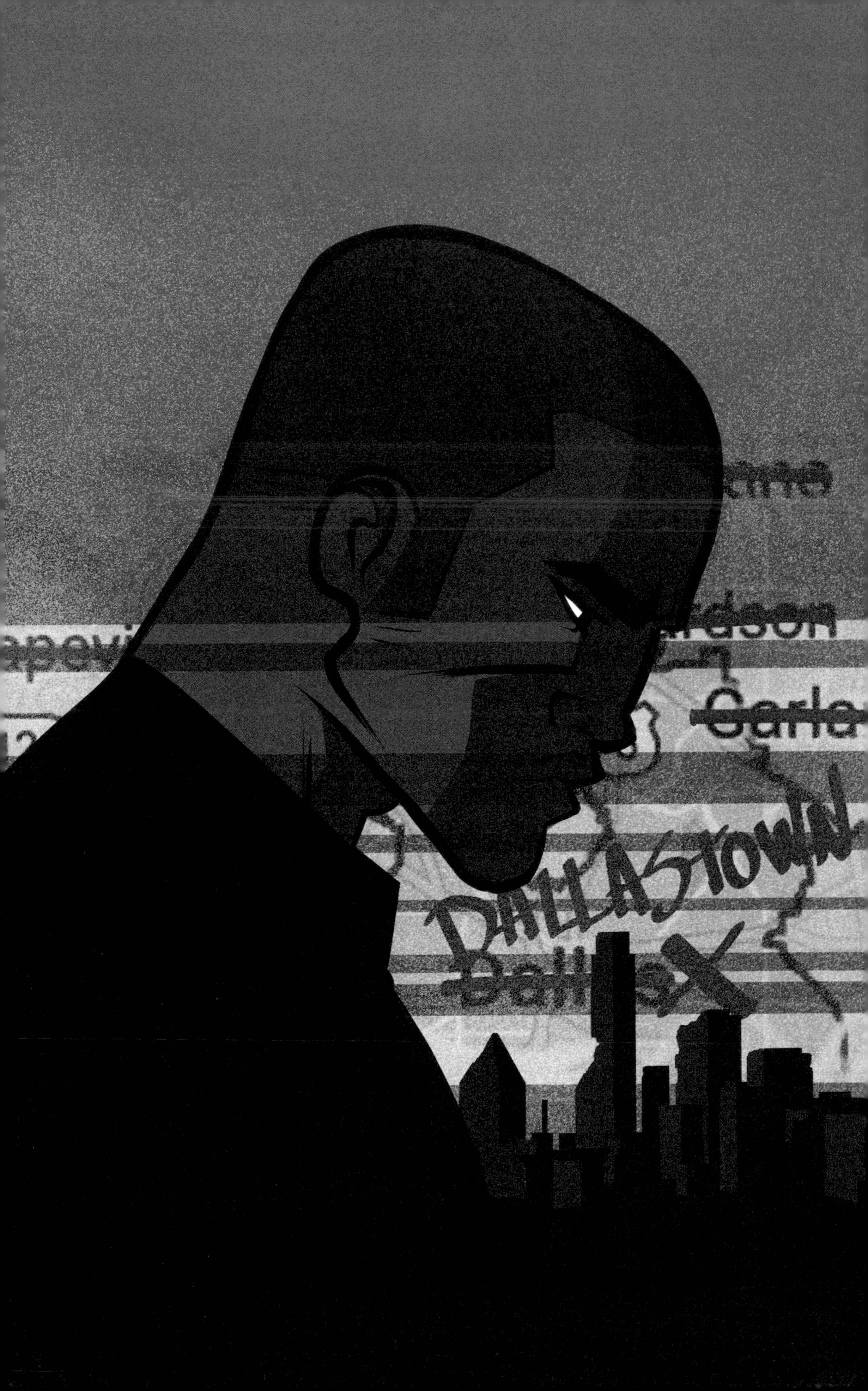
Carla
DALLASTOWN

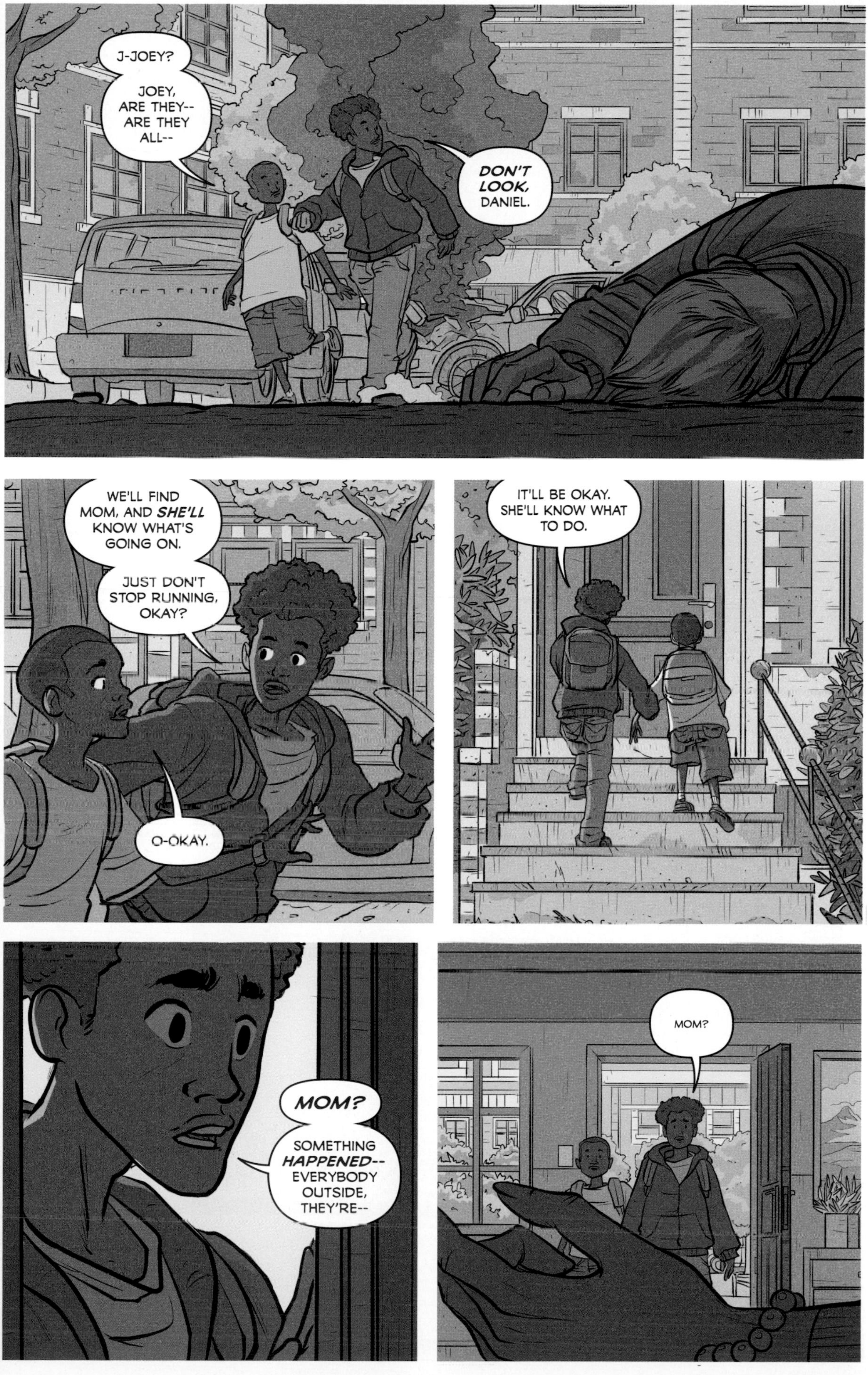
J-JOEY?
JOEY, ARE THEY-- ARE THEY ALL--
DON'T LOOK, DANIEL.
WE'LL FIND MOM, AND SHE'LL KNOW WHAT'S GOING ON.
JUST DON'T STOP RUNNING, OKAY?
O-OKAY.
IT'LL BE OKAY. SHE'LL KNOW WHAT TO DO.
MOM?
SOMETHING HAPPENED-- EVERYBODY OUTSIDE, THEY'RE--
MOM?

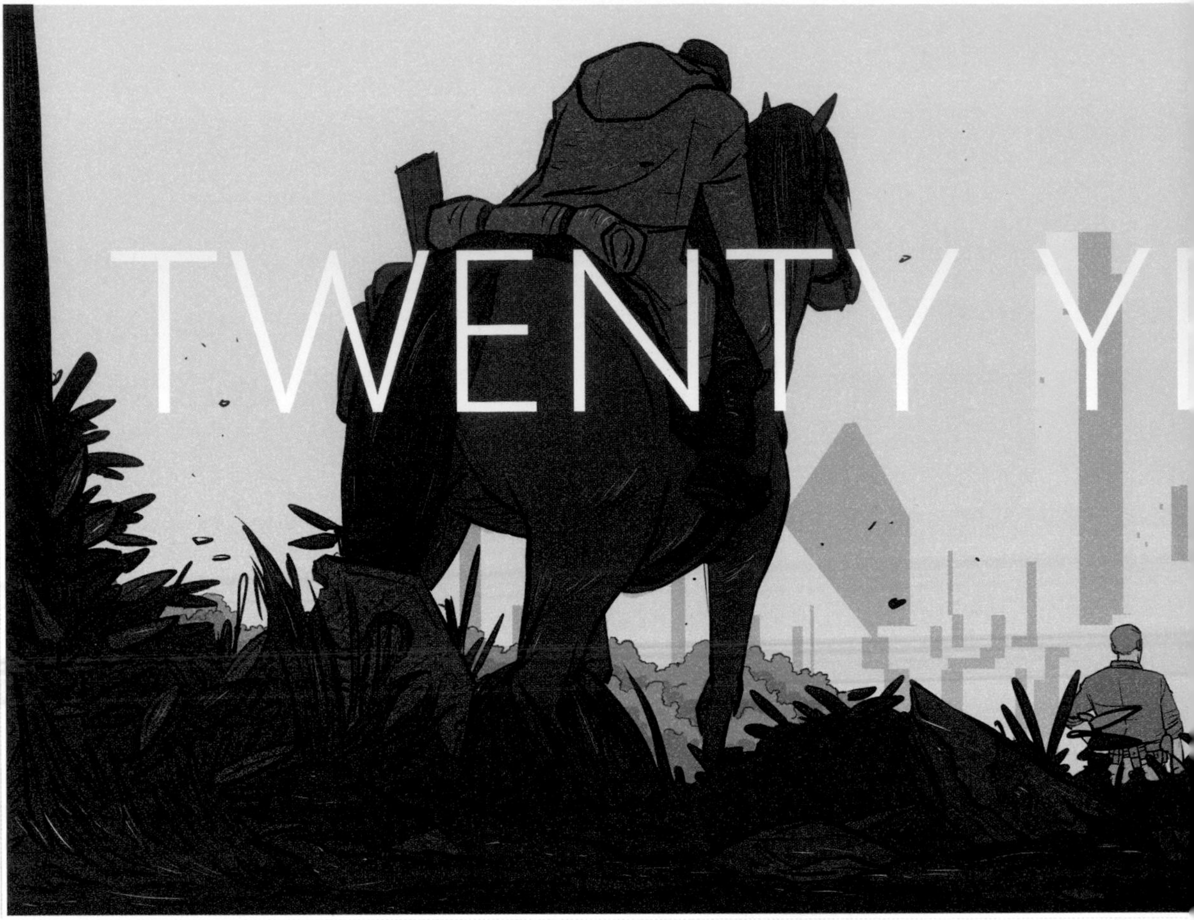
TWENTY Y

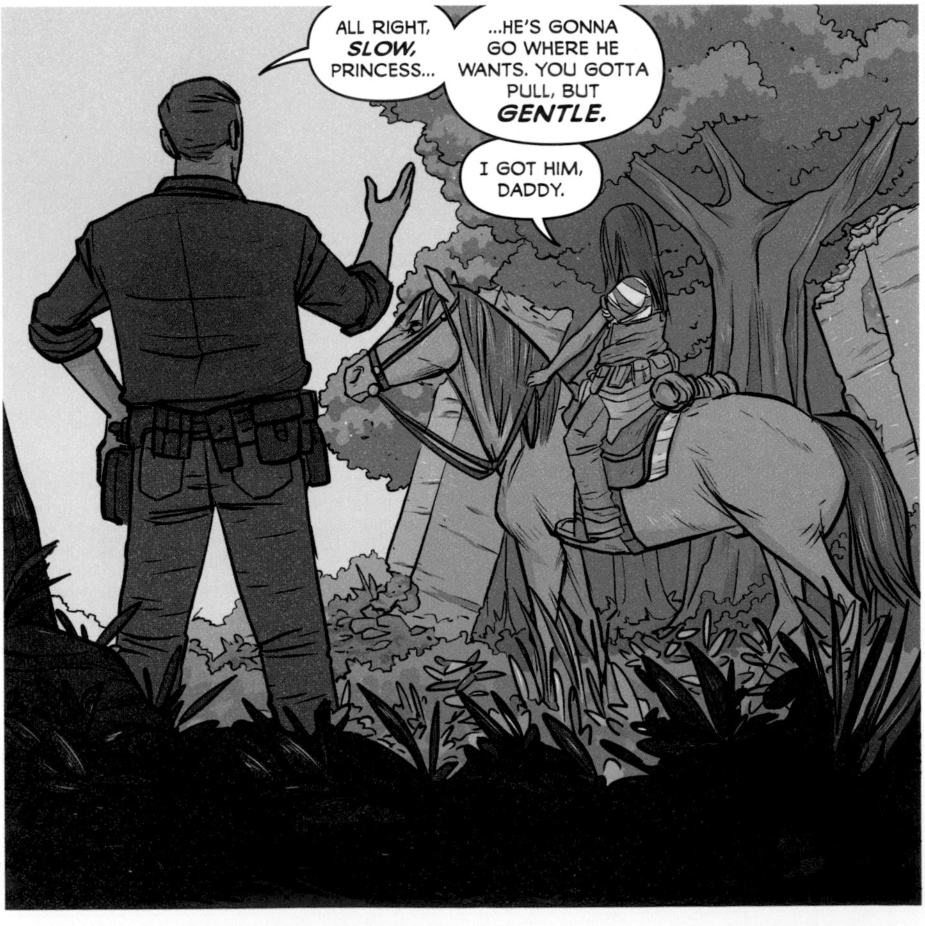
ALL RIGHT, **SLOW,** PRINCESS...
...HE'S GONNA GO WHERE HE WANTS. YOU GOTTA PULL, BUT **GENTLE.**
I GOT HIM, DADDY.

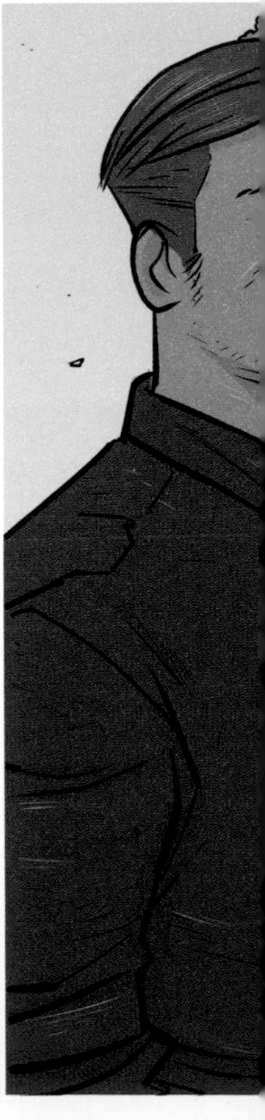

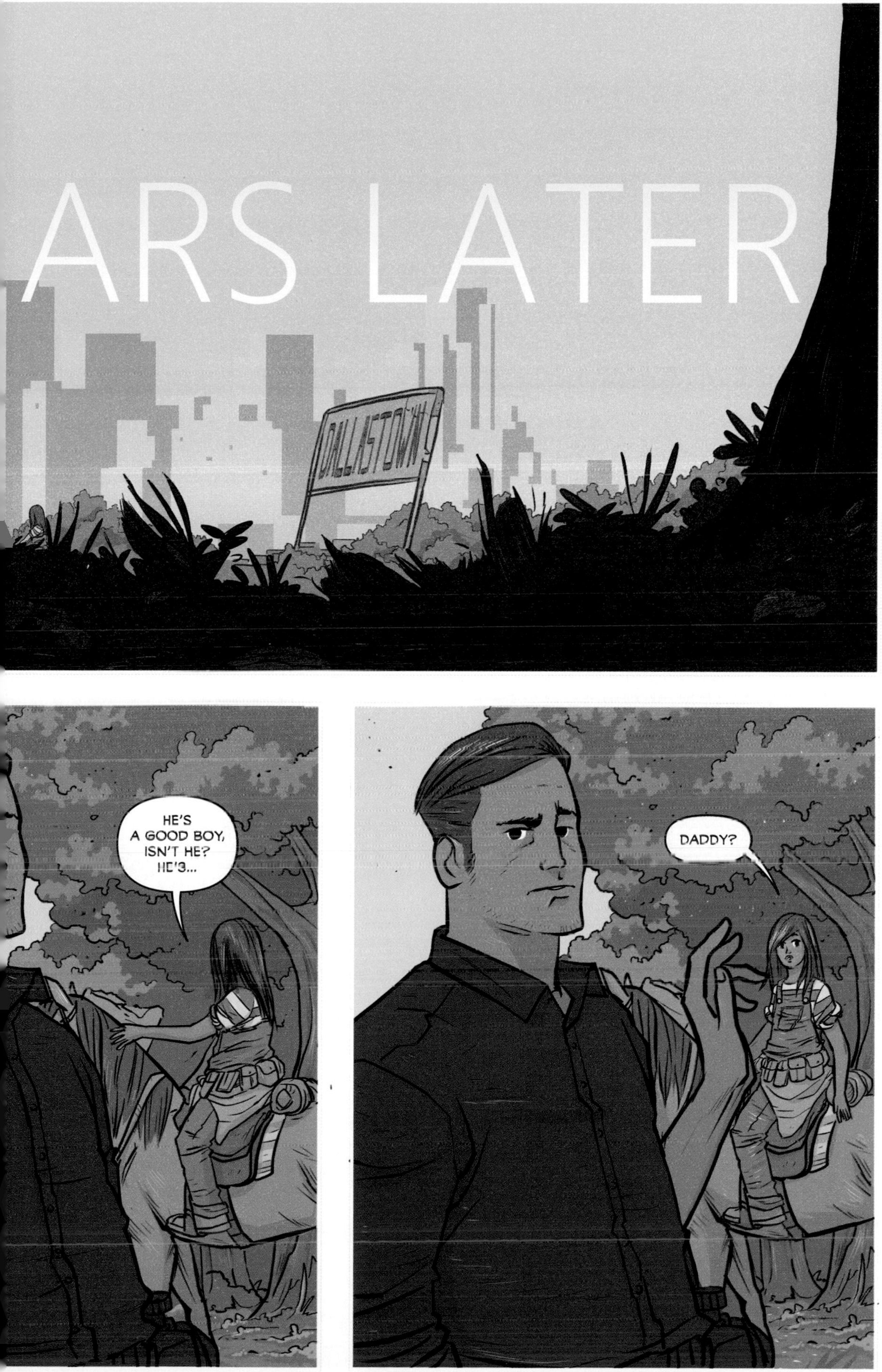
ARS LATER
DALLASTOWN
HE'S A GOOD BOY, ISN'T HE? HE'S...
DADDY?

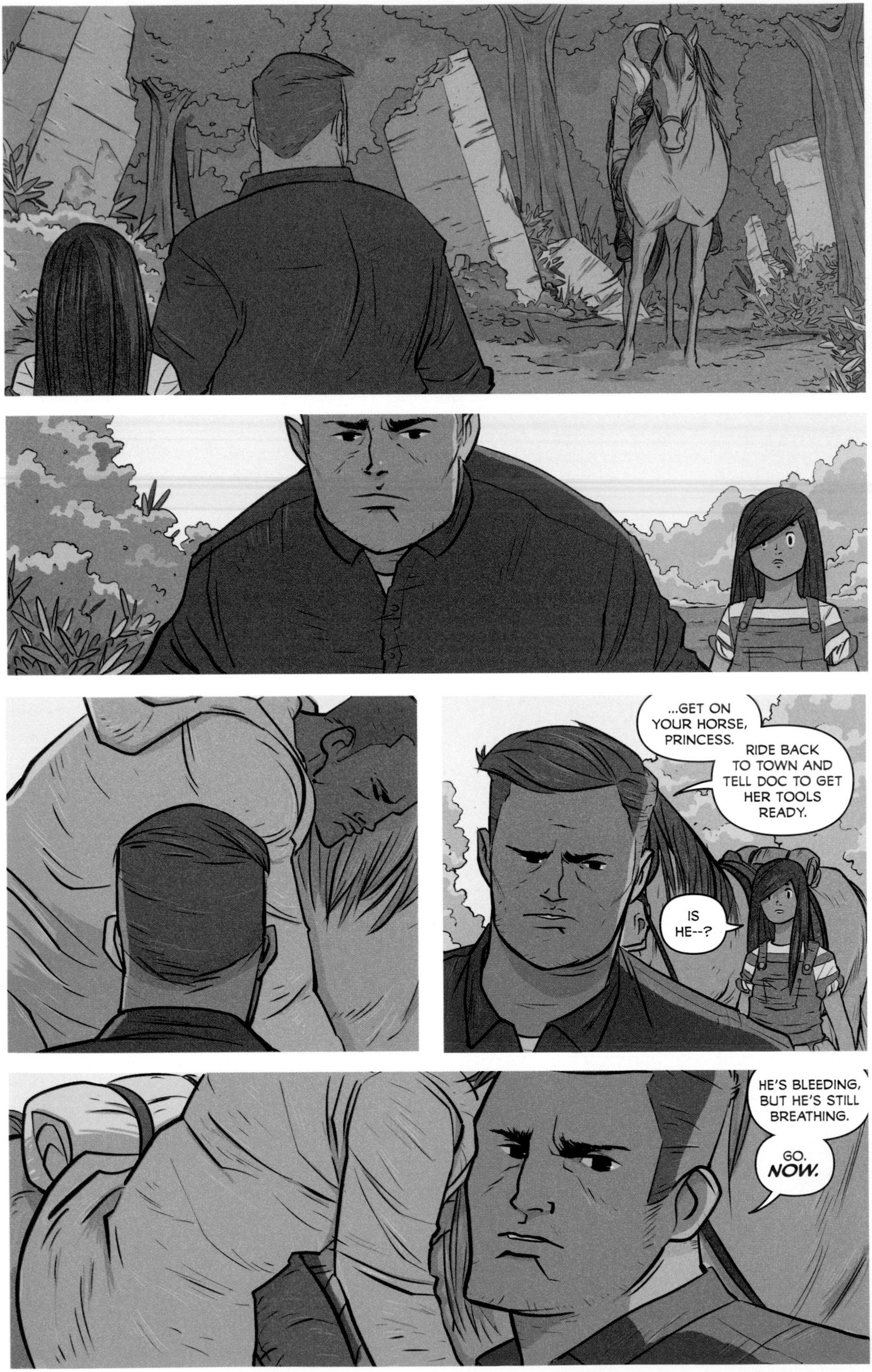
...GET ON YOUR HORSE, PRINCESS.
RIDE BACK TO TOWN AND TELL DOC TO GET HER TOOLS READY.
IS HE--?
HE'S BLEEDING, BUT HE'S STILL BREATHING.
GO. *NOW.*

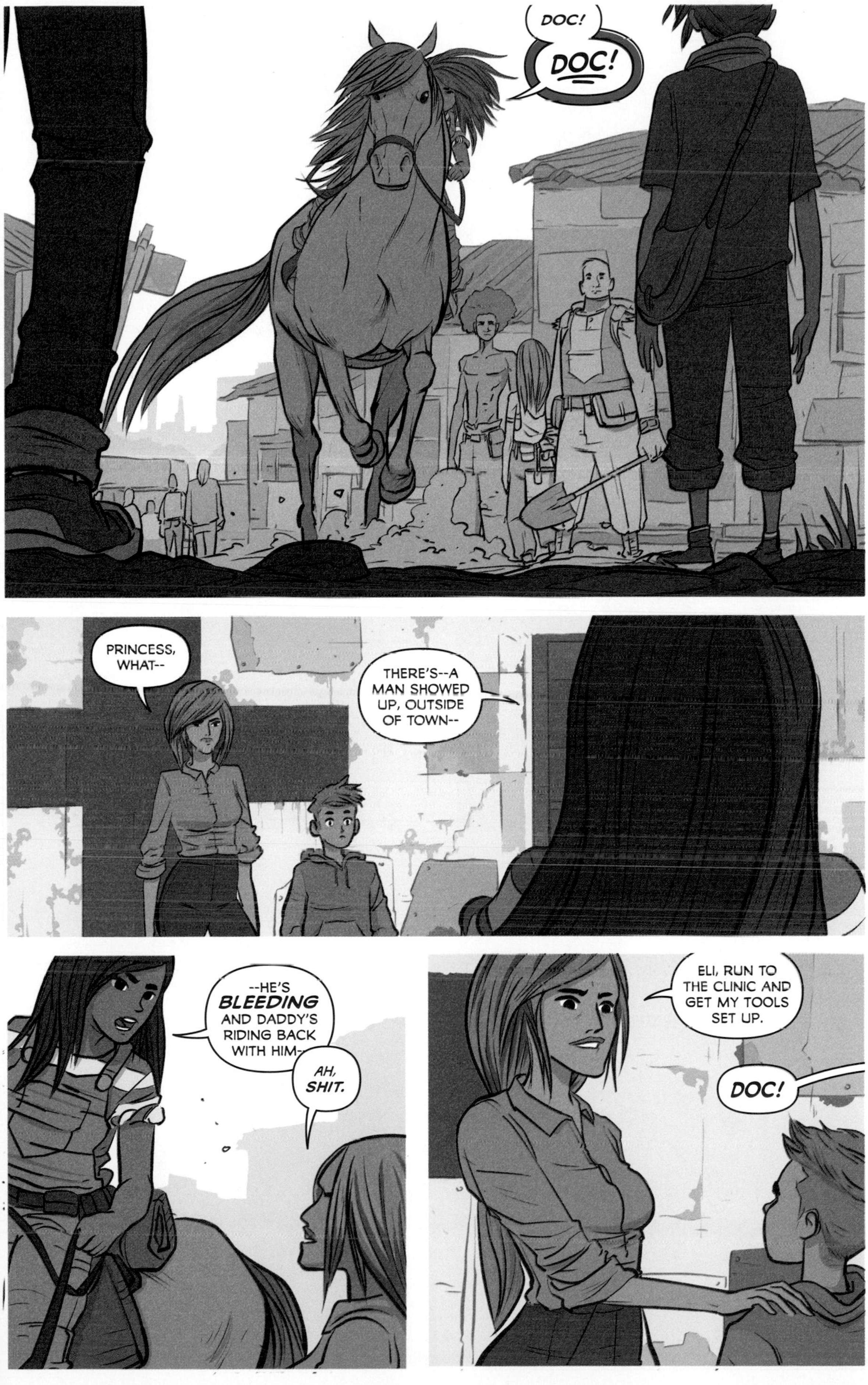
DOC!
DOC!
PRINCESS, WHAT--
THERE'S--A MAN SHOWED UP, OUTSIDE OF TOWN--
--HE'S BLEEDING AND DADDY'S RIDING BACK WITH HIM--
AH, SHIT.
ELI, RUN TO THE CLINIC AND GET MY TOOLS SET UP.
DOC!

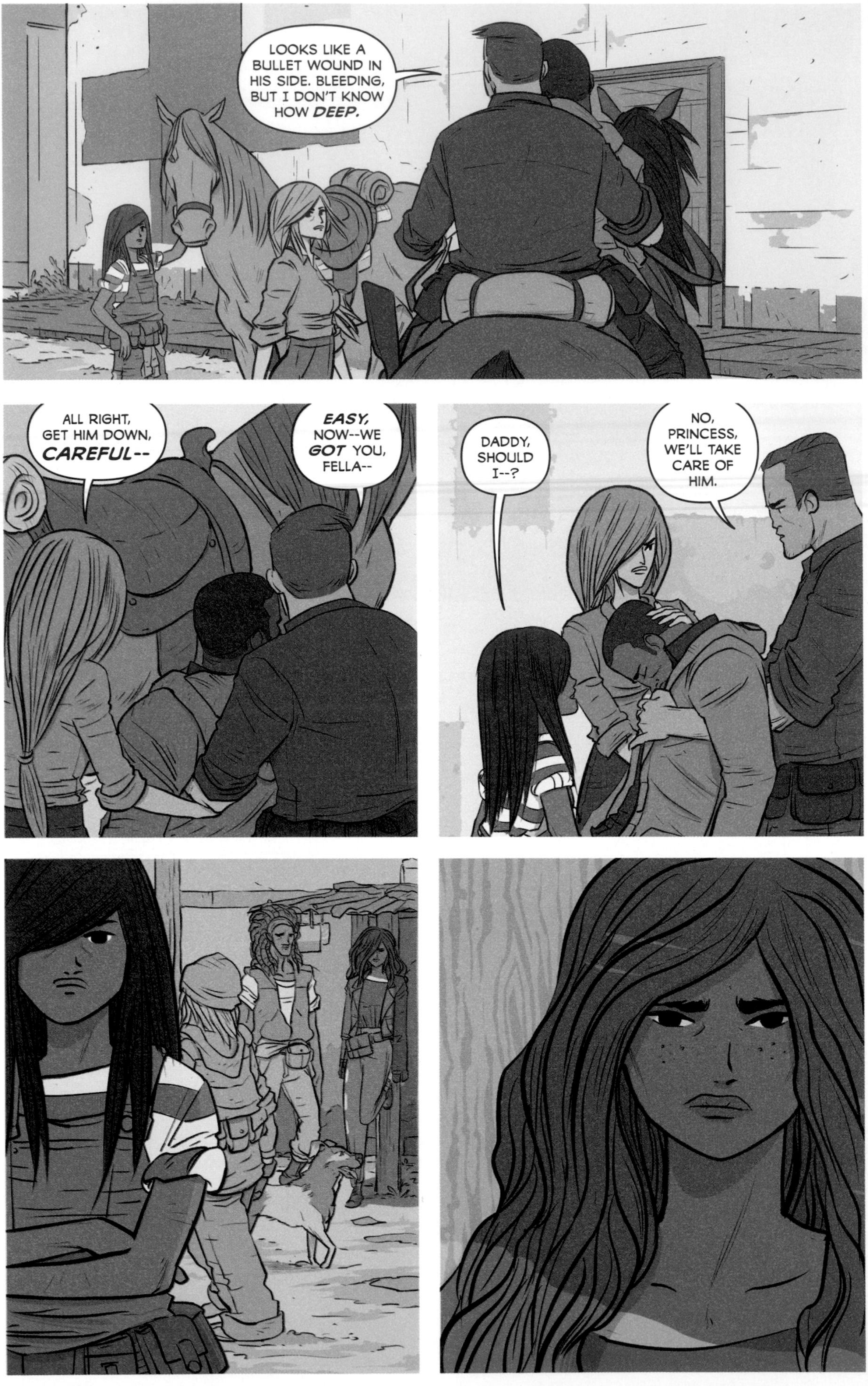
LOOKS LIKE A BULLET WOUND IN HIS SIDE. BLEEDING, BUT I DON'T KNOW HOW *DEEP.*
ALL RIGHT, GET HIM DOWN, *CAREFUL--*
EASY, NOW--WE *GOT* YOU, FELLA--
DADDY, SHOULD I--?
NO, PRINCESS, WE'LL TAKE CARE OF HIM.

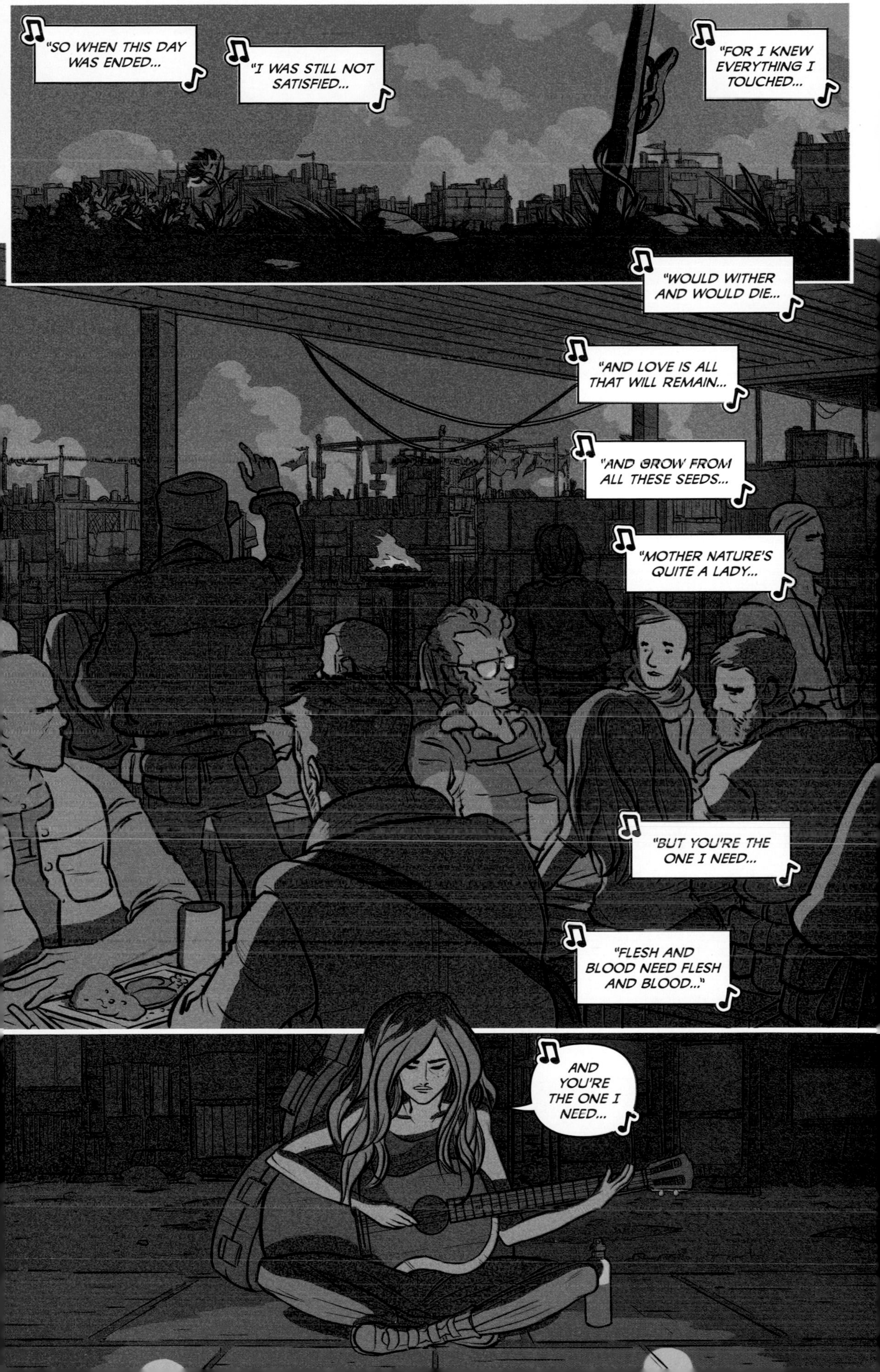
"SO WHEN THIS DAY WAS ENDED...
"I WAS STILL NOT SATISFIED...
"FOR I KNEW EVERYTHING I TOUCHED...
"WOULD WITHER AND WOULD DIE...
"AND LOVE IS ALL THAT WILL REMAIN...
"AND GROW FROM ALL THESE SEEDS...
"MOTHER NATURE'S QUITE A LADY...
"BUT YOU'RE THE ONE I NEED...
"FLESH AND BLOOD NEED FLESH AND BLOOD..."
AND YOU'RE THE ONE I NEED...

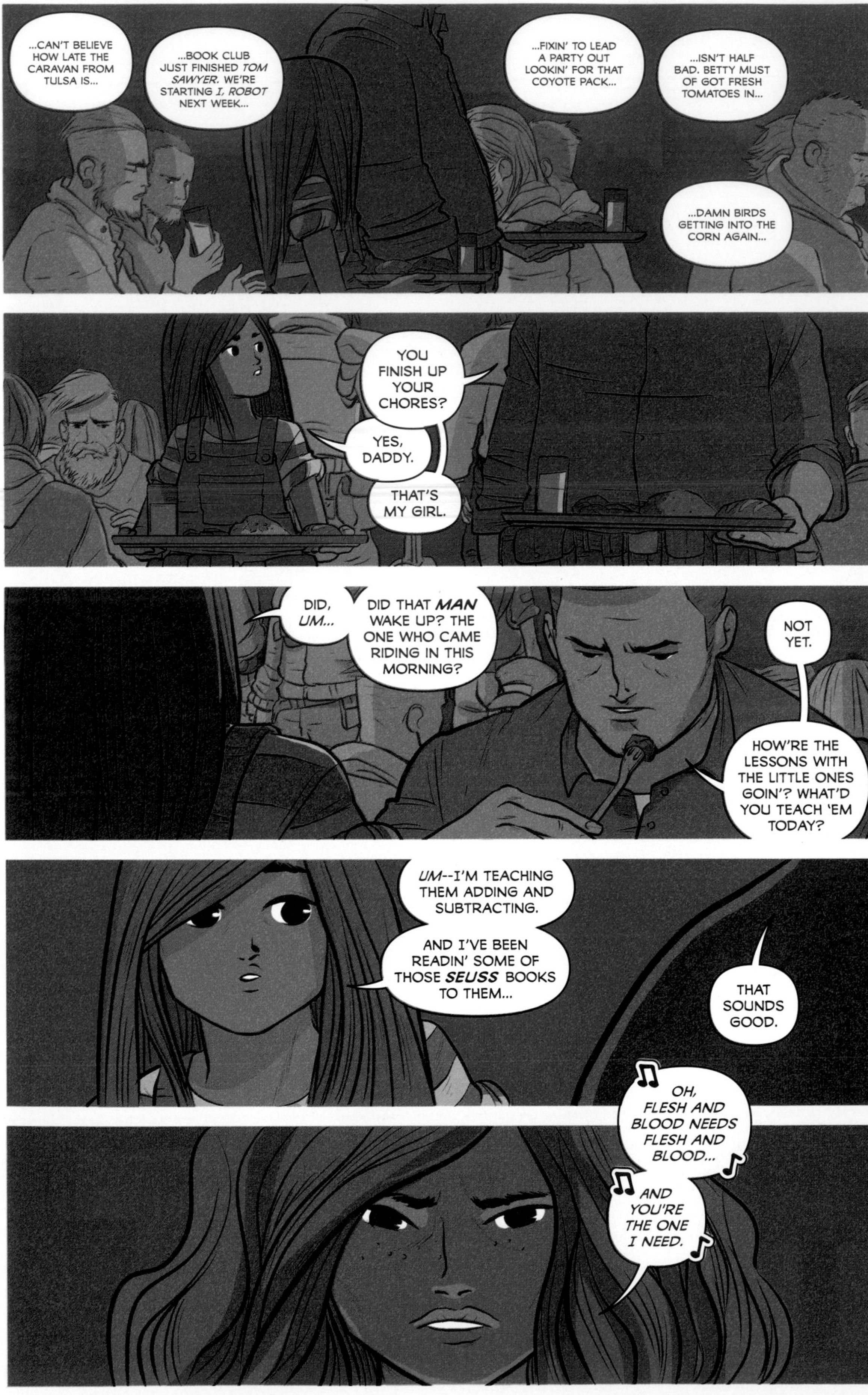
...CAN'T BELIEVE HOW LATE THE CARAVAN FROM TULSA IS...
...BOOK CLUB JUST FINISHED *TOM SAWYER.* WE'RE STARTING *I, ROBOT* NEXT WEEK...
...FIXIN' TO LEAD A PARTY OUT LOOKIN' FOR THAT COYOTE PACK...
...ISN'T HALF BAD. BETTY MUST OF GOT FRESH TOMATOES IN...
...DAMN BIRDS GETTING INTO THE CORN AGAIN...
YOU FINISH UP YOUR CHORES?
YES, DADDY.
THAT'S MY GIRL.
DID, *UM...*
DID THAT ***MAN*** WAKE UP? THE ONE WHO CAME RIDING IN THIS MORNING?
NOT YET.
HOW'RE THE LESSONS WITH THE LITTLE ONES GOIN'? WHAT'D YOU TEACH 'EM TODAY?
UM--I'M TEACHING THEM ADDING AND SUBTRACTING.
AND I'VE BEEN READIN' SOME OF THOSE ***SEUSS*** BOOKS TO THEM...
THAT SOUNDS GOOD.
♫ *OH, FLESH AND BLOOD NEEDS FLESH AND BLOOD...* ♪
♫ *AND YOU'RE THE ONE I NEED.* ♪

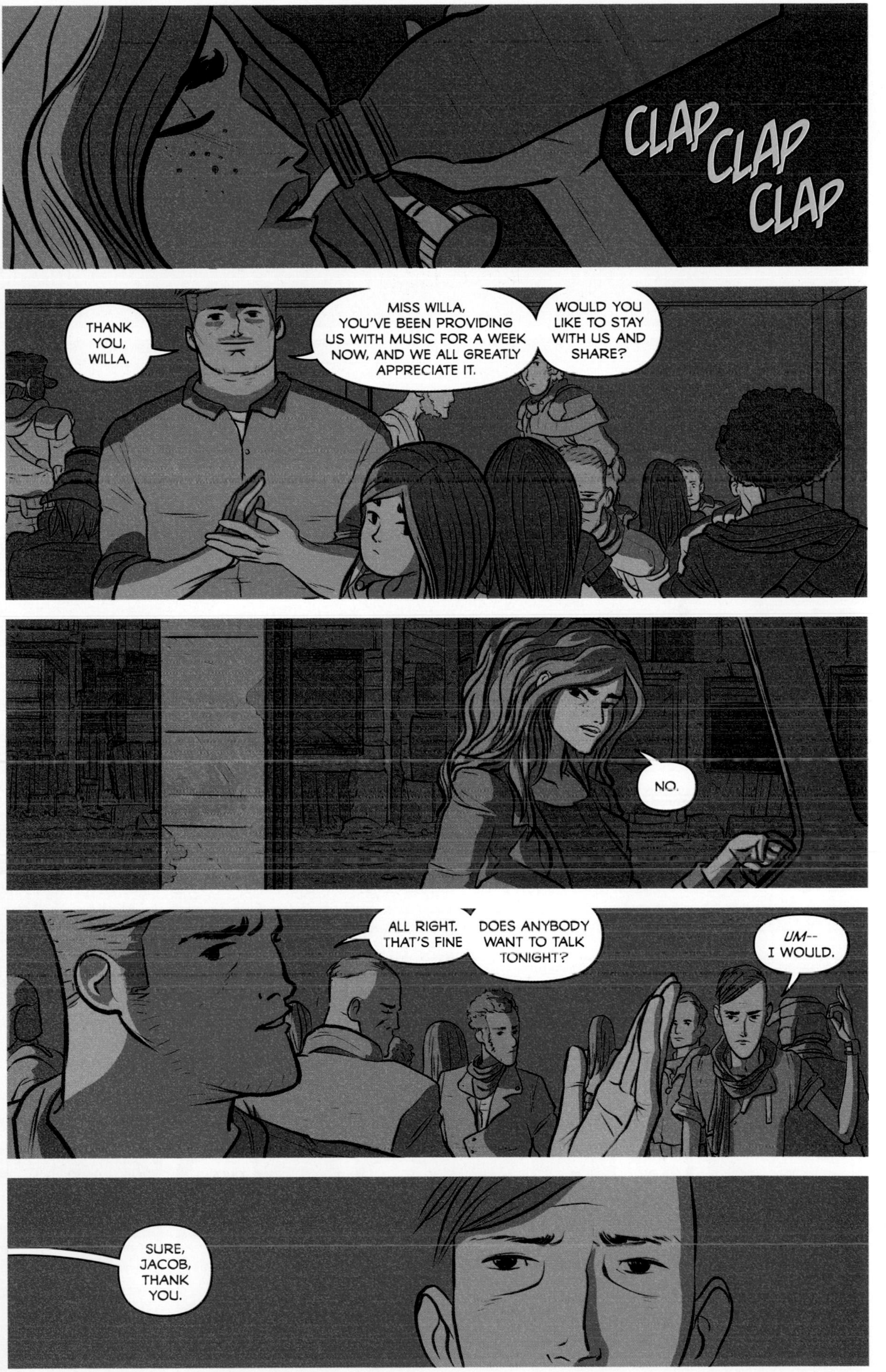
CLAP CLAP CLAP
THANK YOU, WILLA.
MISS WILLA, YOU'VE BEEN PROVIDING US WITH MUSIC FOR A WEEK NOW, AND WE ALL GREATLY APPRECIATE IT.
WOULD YOU LIKE TO STAY WITH US AND SHARE?
NO.
ALL RIGHT. THAT'S FINE
DOES ANYBODY WANT TO TALK TONIGHT?
UM-- I WOULD.
SURE, JACOB, THANK YOU.

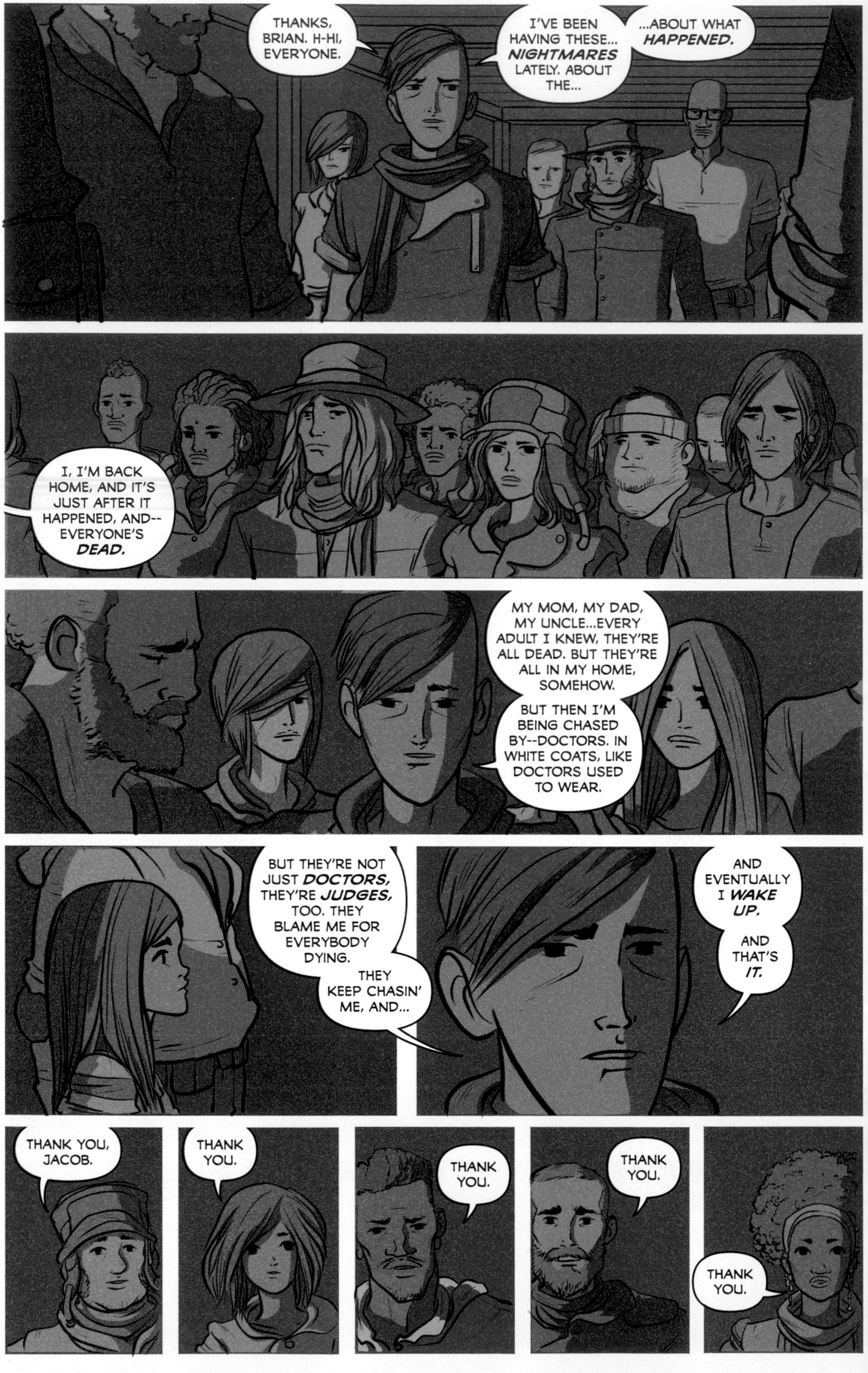
THANKS, BRIAN. H-HI, EVERYONE.
I'VE BEEN HAVING THESE... NIGHTMARES LATELY. ABOUT THE...
...ABOUT WHAT HAPPENED.
I, I'M BACK HOME, AND IT'S JUST AFTER IT HAPPENED, AND-- EVERYONE'S DEAD.
MY MOM, MY DAD, MY UNCLE...EVERY ADULT I KNEW, THEY'RE ALL DEAD. BUT THEY'RE ALL IN MY HOME, SOMEHOW.
BUT THEN I'M BEING CHASED BY--DOCTORS. IN WHITE COATS, LIKE DOCTORS USED TO WEAR.
BUT THEY'RE NOT JUST DOCTORS, THEY'RE JUDGES, TOO. THEY BLAME ME FOR EVERYBODY DYING.
THEY KEEP CHASIN' ME, AND...
AND EVENTUALLY I WAKE UP.
AND THAT'S IT.
THANK YOU, JACOB.
THANK YOU.
THANK YOU.
THANK YOU.
THANK YOU.

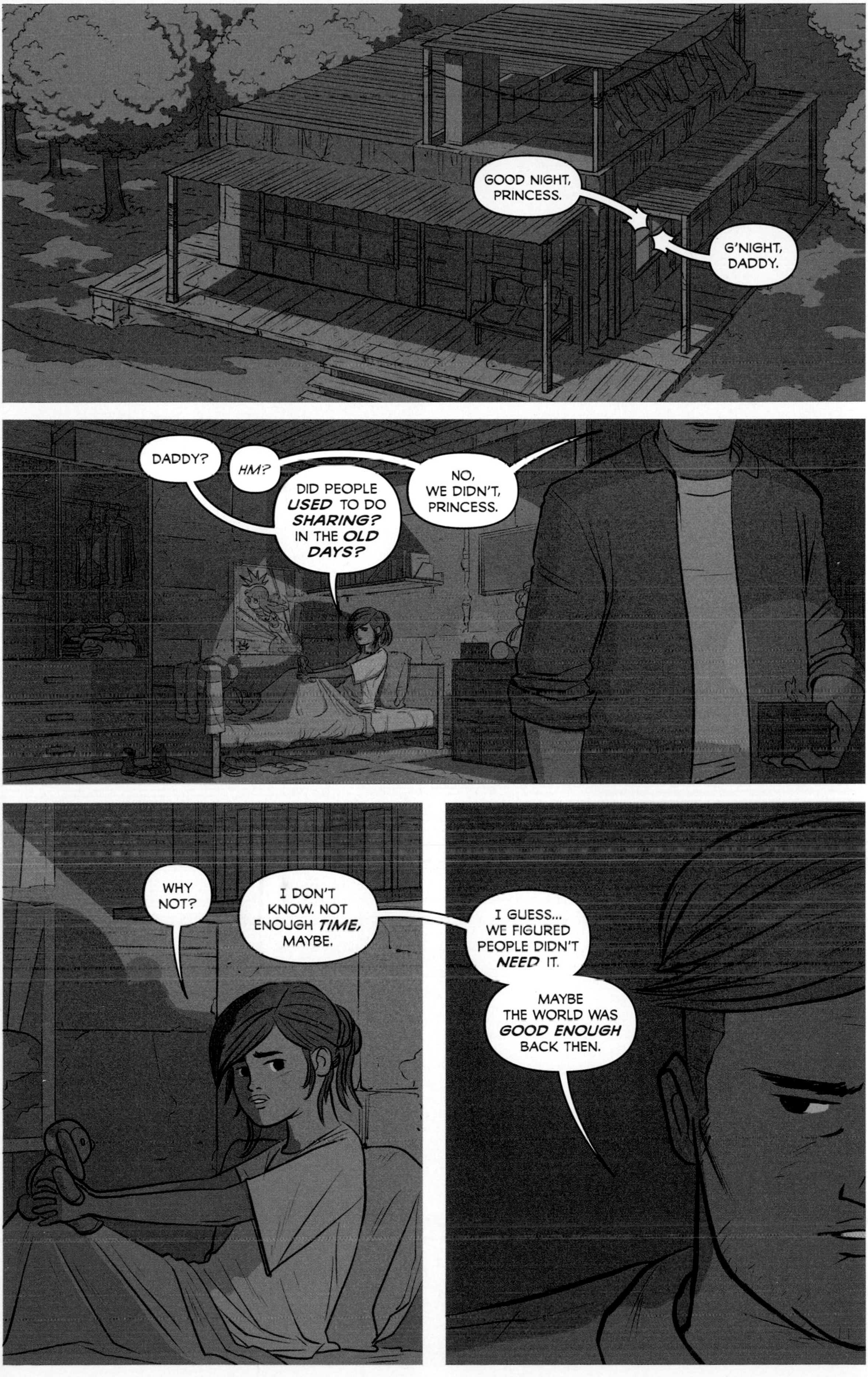
GOOD NIGHT, PRINCESS.
G'NIGHT, DADDY.
DADDY?
HM?
DID PEOPLE USED TO DO SHARING? IN THE OLD DAYS?
NO, WE DIDN'T, PRINCESS.
WHY NOT?
I DON'T KNOW. NOT ENOUGH TIME, MAYBE.
I GUESS... WE FIGURED PEOPLE DIDN'T NEED IT.
MAYBE THE WORLD WAS GOOD ENOUGH BACK THEN.

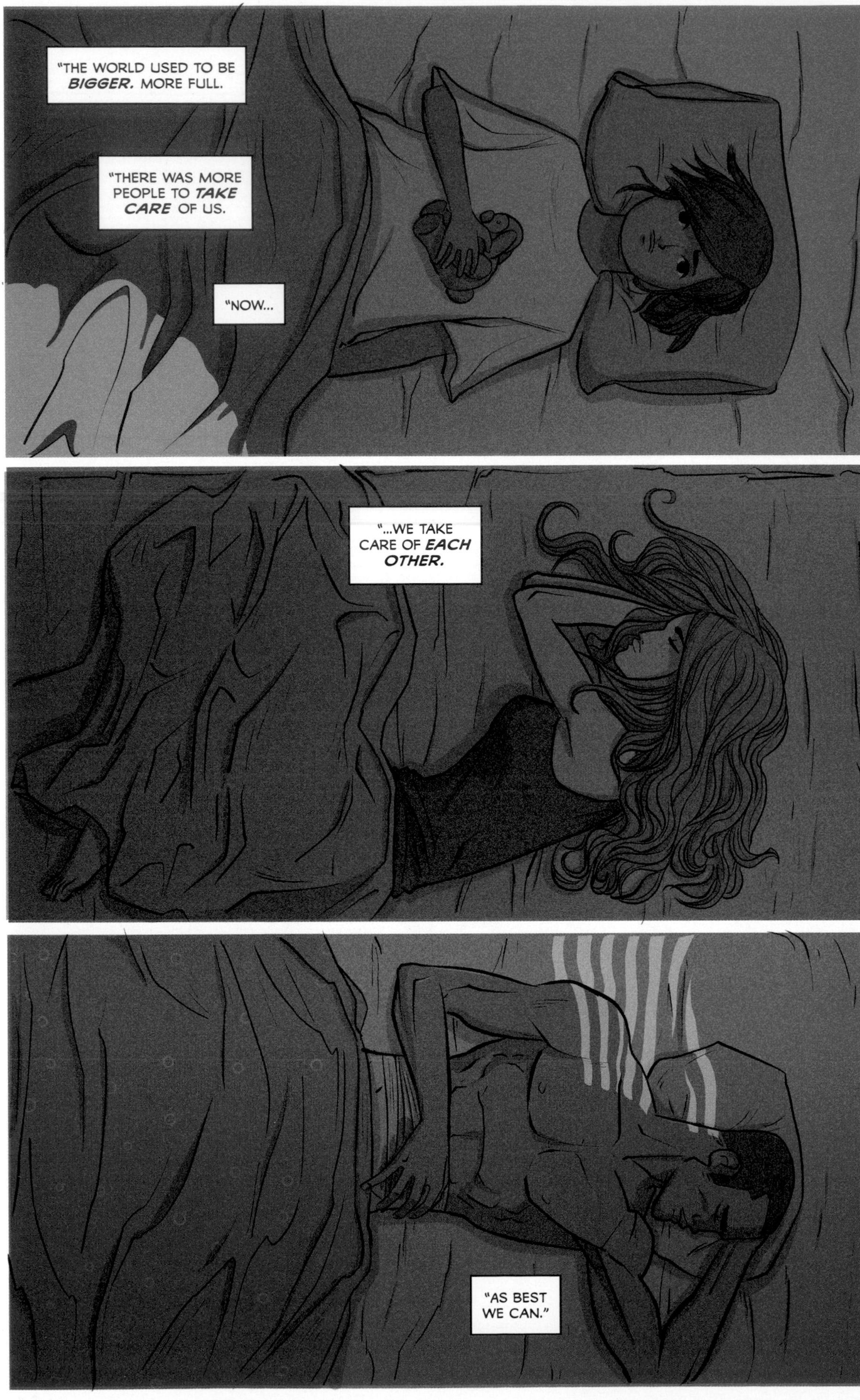
"THE WORLD USED TO BE *BIGGER.* MORE FULL.
"THERE WAS MORE PEOPLE TO *TAKE CARE* OF US.
"NOW...
"...WE TAKE CARE OF *EACH OTHER.*
"AS BEST WE CAN."

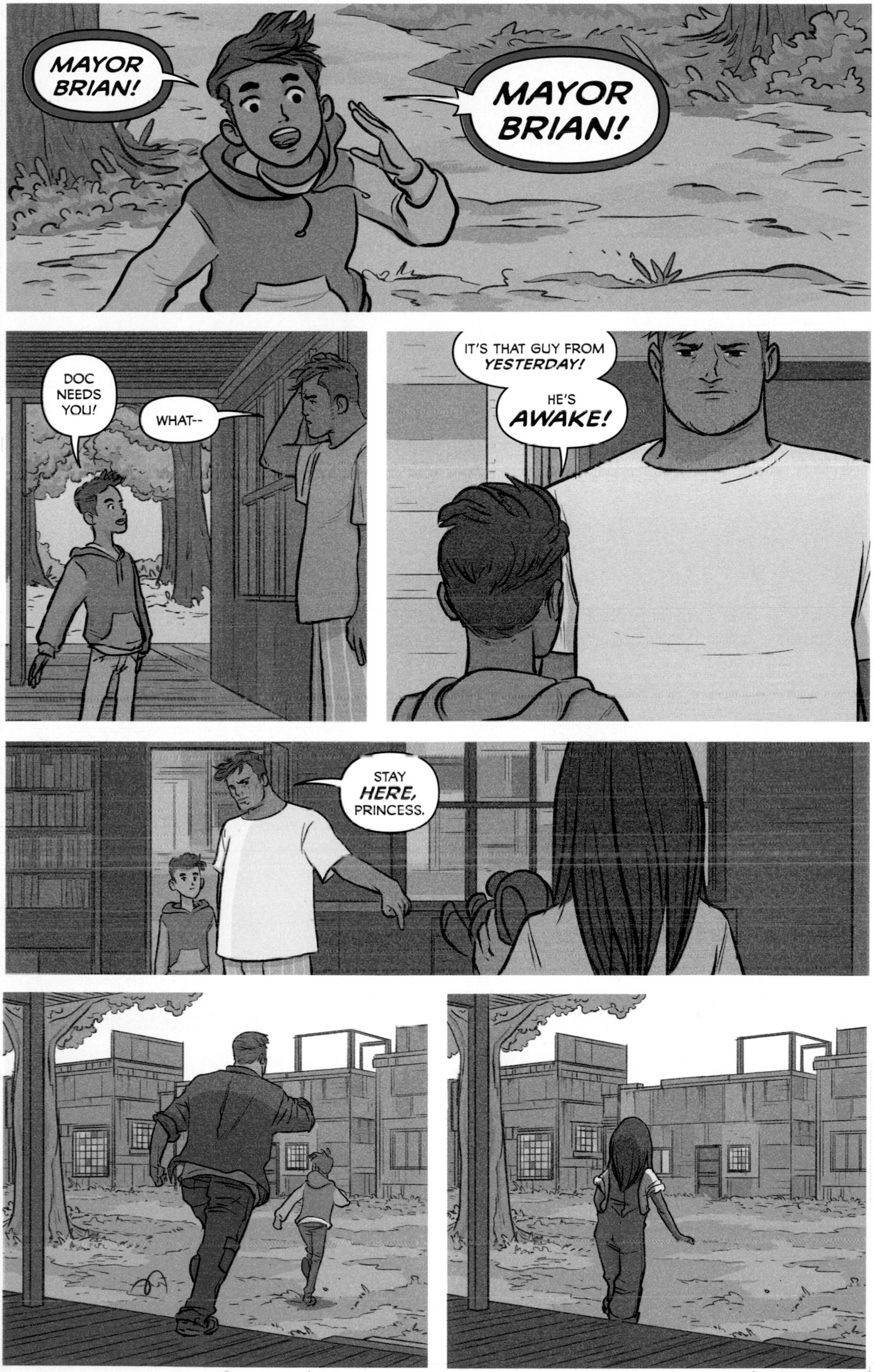
MAYOR BRIAN!
MAYOR BRIAN!
DOC NEEDS YOU!
WHAT--
IT'S THAT GUY FROM YESTERDAY!
HE'S AWAKE!
STAY HERE, PRINCESS.

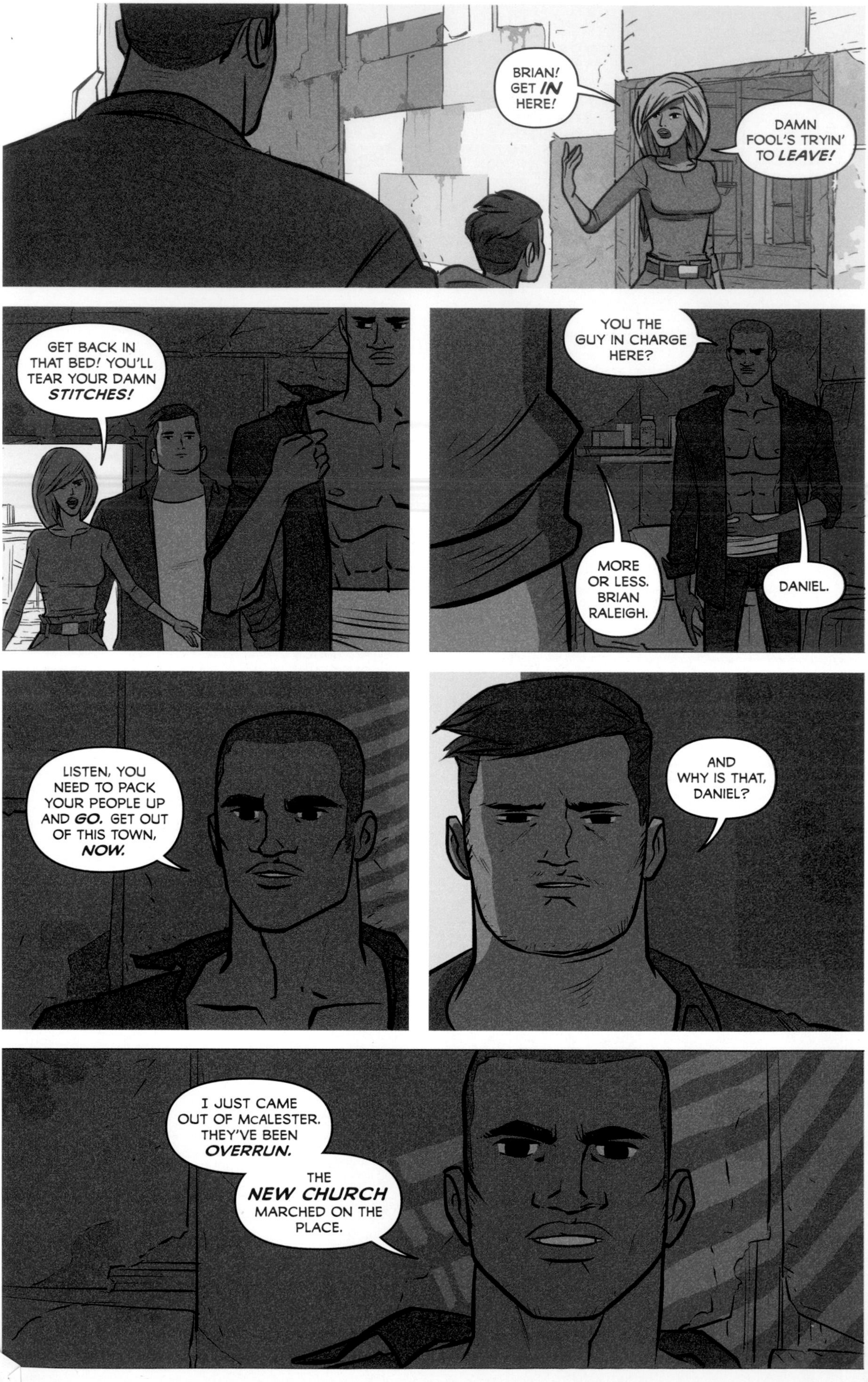
BRIAN! GET IN HERE!
DAMN FOOL'S TRYIN' TO LEAVE!
GET BACK IN THAT BED! YOU'LL TEAR YOUR DAMN STITCHES!
YOU THE GUY IN CHARGE HERE?
MORE OR LESS. BRIAN RALEIGH.
DANIEL.
LISTEN, YOU NEED TO PACK YOUR PEOPLE UP AND GO. GET OUT OF THIS TOWN, NOW.
AND WHY IS THAT, DANIEL?
I JUST CAME OUT OF McALESTER. THEY'VE BEEN OVERRUN.
THE NEW CHURCH MARCHED ON THE PLACE.

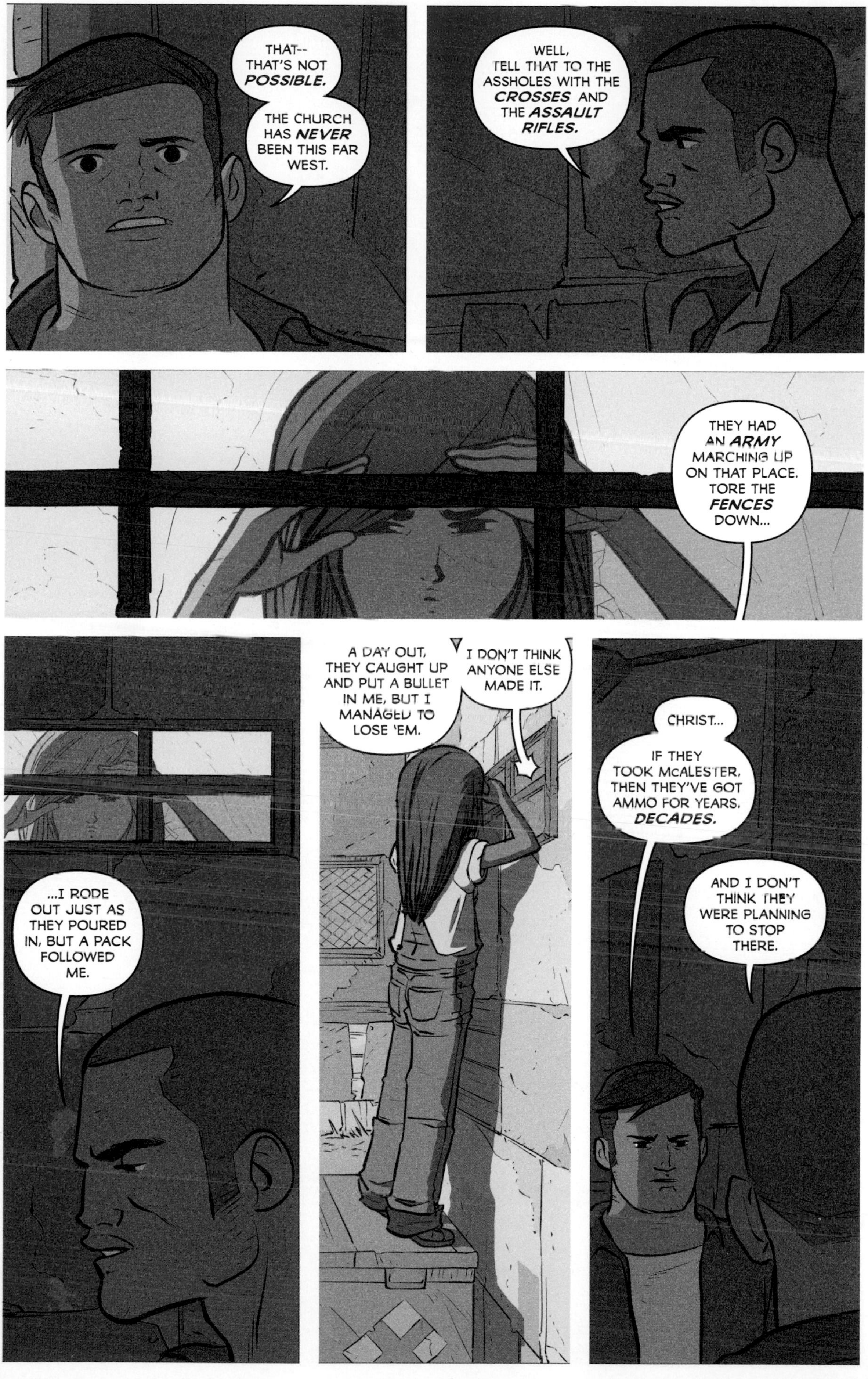
THAT-- THAT'S NOT *POSSIBLE.*
THE CHURCH HAS *NEVER* BEEN THIS FAR WEST.
WELL, TELL THAT TO THE ASSHOLES WITH THE *CROSSES* AND THE *ASSAULT RIFLES.*
THEY HAD AN *ARMY* MARCHING UP ON THAT PLACE. TORE THE *FENCES* DOWN...
...I RODE OUT JUST AS THEY POURED IN, BUT A PACK FOLLOWED ME.
A DAY OUT, THEY CAUGHT UP AND PUT A BULLET IN ME, BUT I MANAGED TO LOSE 'EM.
I DON'T THINK ANYONE ELSE MADE IT.
CHRIST...
IF THEY TOOK McALESTER, THEN THEY'VE GOT AMMO FOR YEARS. *DECADES.*
AND I DON'T THINK THEY WERE PLANNING TO STOP THERE.

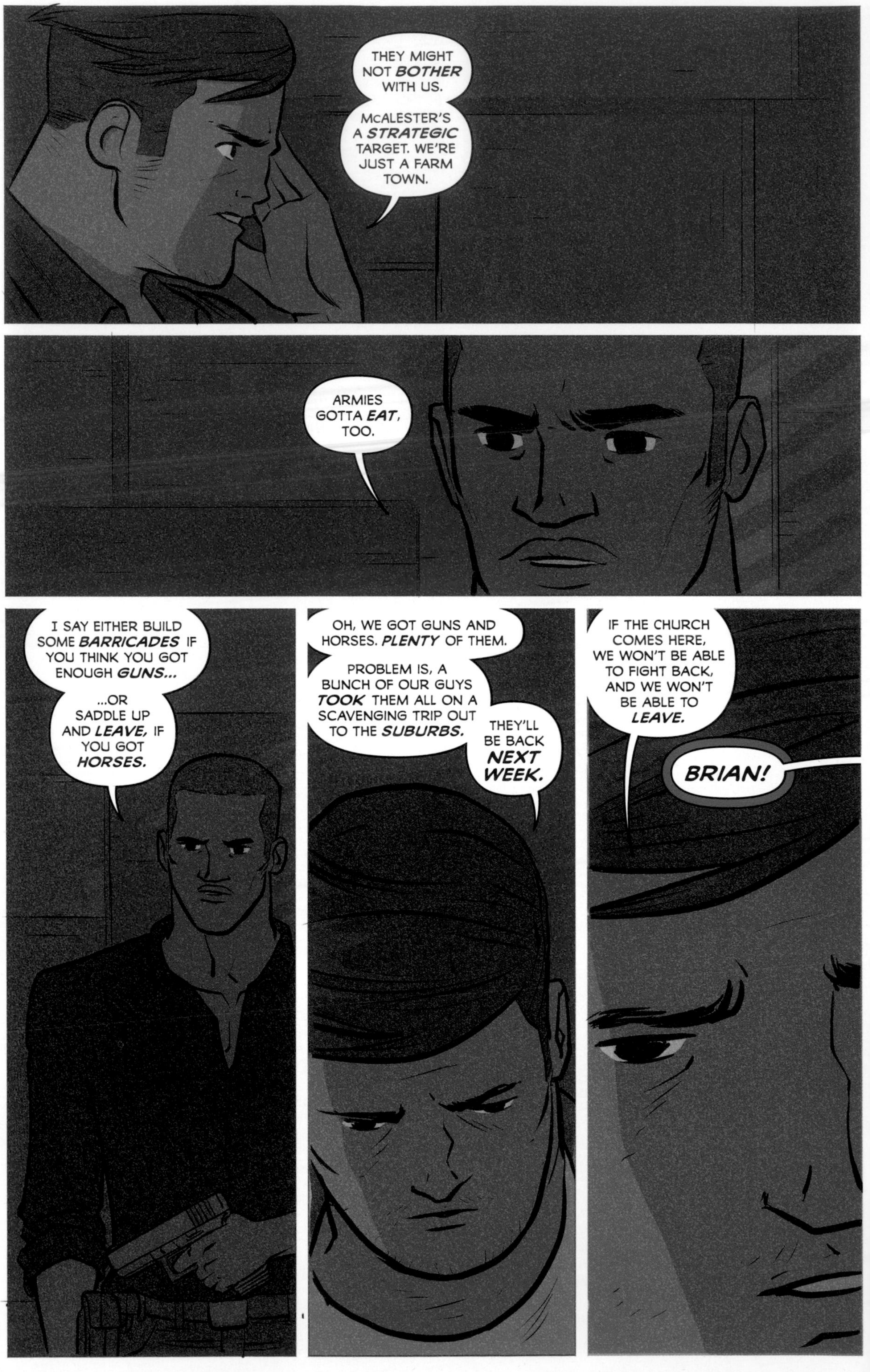
THEY MIGHT NOT BOTHER WITH US.
McALESTER'S A STRATEGIC TARGET. WE'RE JUST A FARM TOWN.
ARMIES GOTTA EAT, TOO.
I SAY EITHER BUILD SOME BARRICADES IF YOU THINK YOU GOT ENOUGH GUNS...
...OR SADDLE UP AND LEAVE, IF YOU GOT HORSES.
OH, WE GOT GUNS AND HORSES. PLENTY OF THEM.
PROBLEM IS, A BUNCH OF OUR GUYS TOOK THEM ALL ON A SCAVENGING TRIP OUT TO THE SUBURBS.
THEY'LL BE BACK NEXT WEEK.
IF THE CHURCH COMES HERE, WE WON'T BE ABLE TO FIGHT BACK, AND WE WON'T BE ABLE TO LEAVE.
BRIAN!

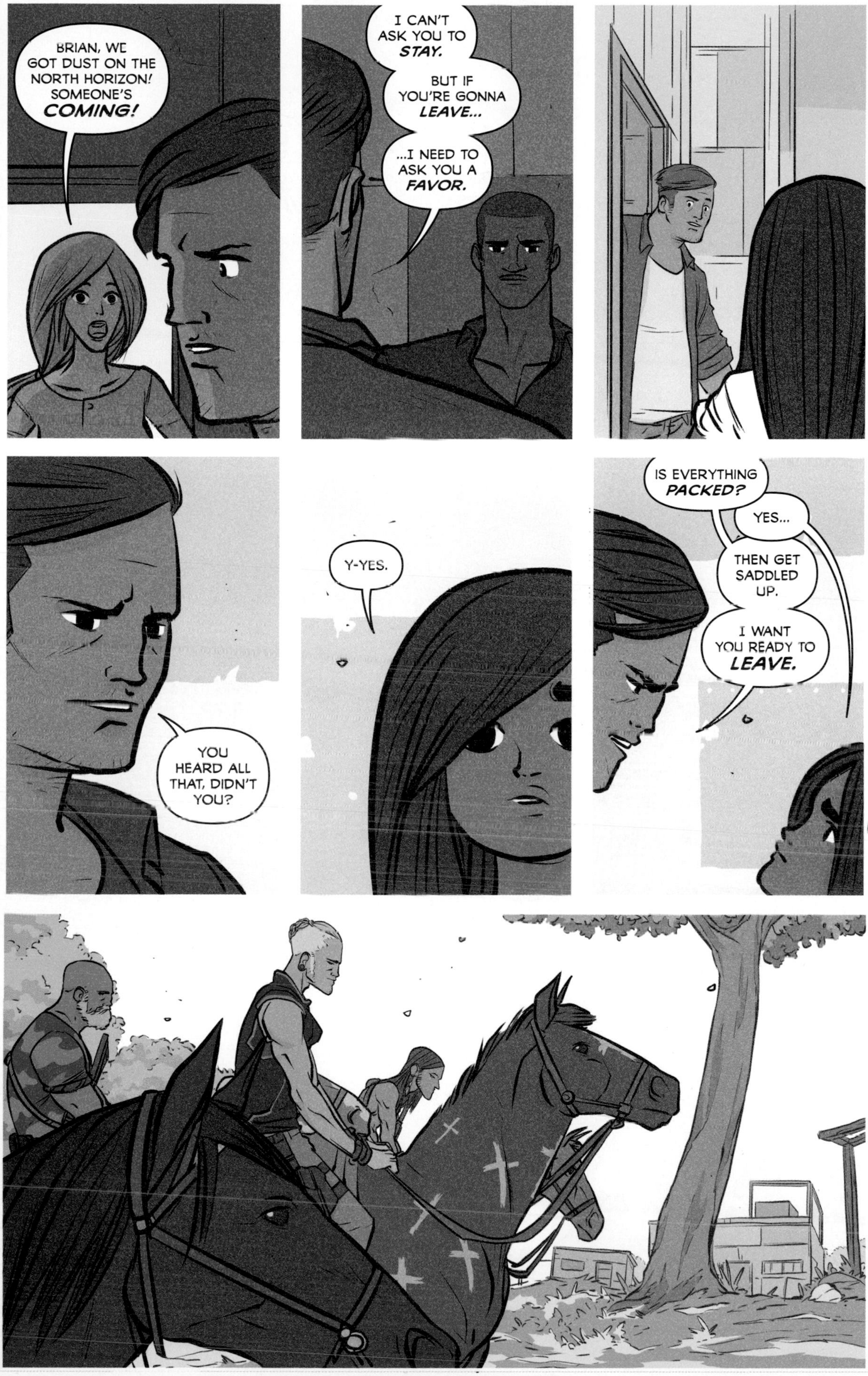
BRIAN, WE GOT DUST ON THE NORTH HORIZON! SOMEONE'S COMING!
I CAN'T ASK YOU TO STAY.
BUT IF YOU'RE GONNA LEAVE...
...I NEED TO ASK YOU A FAVOR.
YOU HEARD ALL THAT, DIDN'T YOU?
Y-YES.
IS EVERYTHING PACKED?
YES...
THEN GET SADDLED UP.
I WANT YOU READY TO LEAVE.

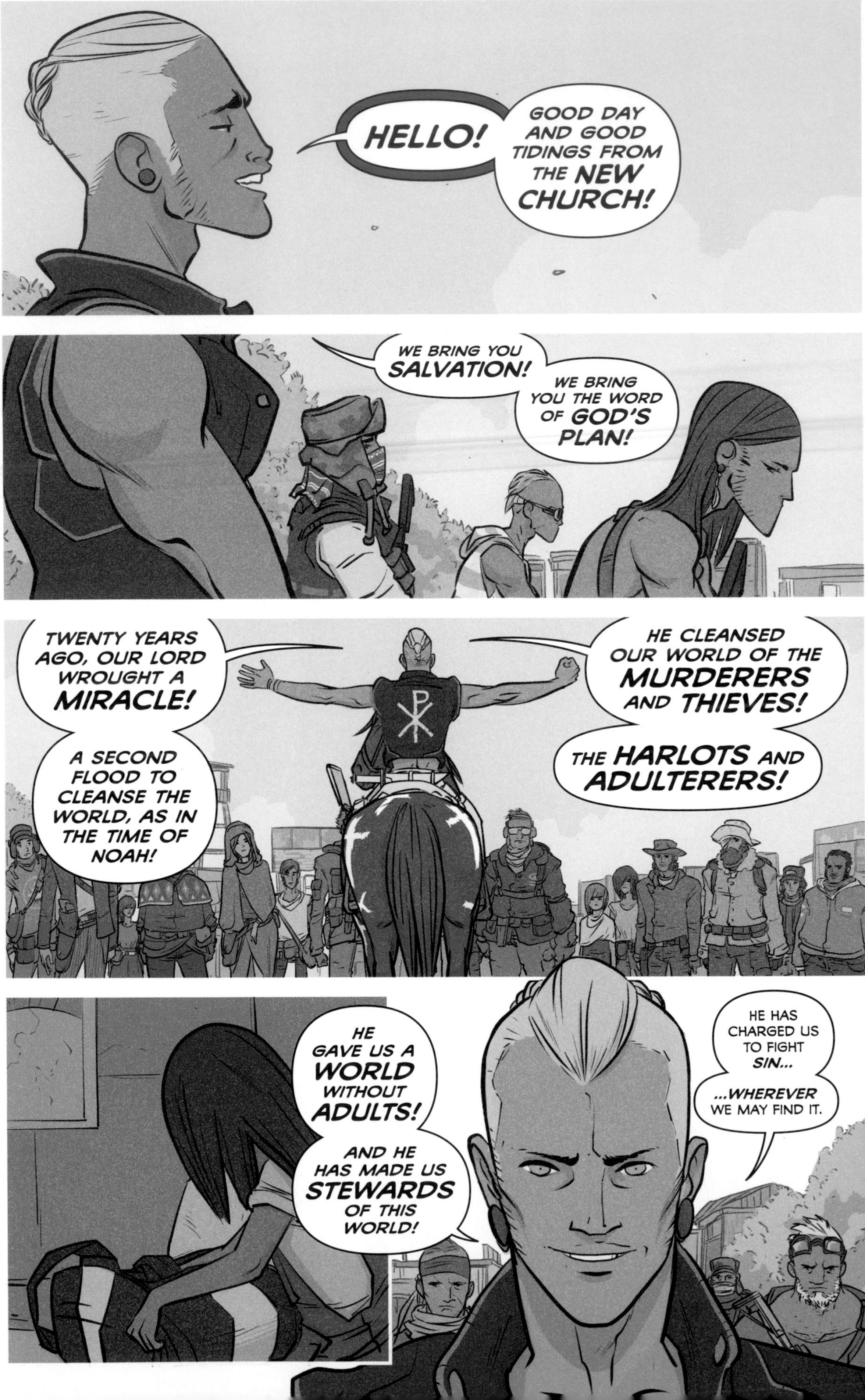
HELLO!
GOOD DAY AND GOOD TIDINGS FROM THE NEW CHURCH!
WE BRING YOU SALVATION!
WE BRING YOU THE WORD OF GOD'S PLAN!
TWENTY YEARS AGO, OUR LORD WROUGHT A MIRACLE!
A SECOND FLOOD TO CLEANSE THE WORLD, AS IN THE TIME OF NOAH!
HE CLEANSED OUR WORLD OF THE MURDERERS AND THIEVES!
THE HARLOTS AND ADULTERERS!
HE GAVE US A WORLD WITHOUT ADULTS!
AND HE HAS MADE US STEWARDS OF THIS WORLD!
HE HAS CHARGED US TO FIGHT SIN...
...WHEREVER WE MAY FIND IT.

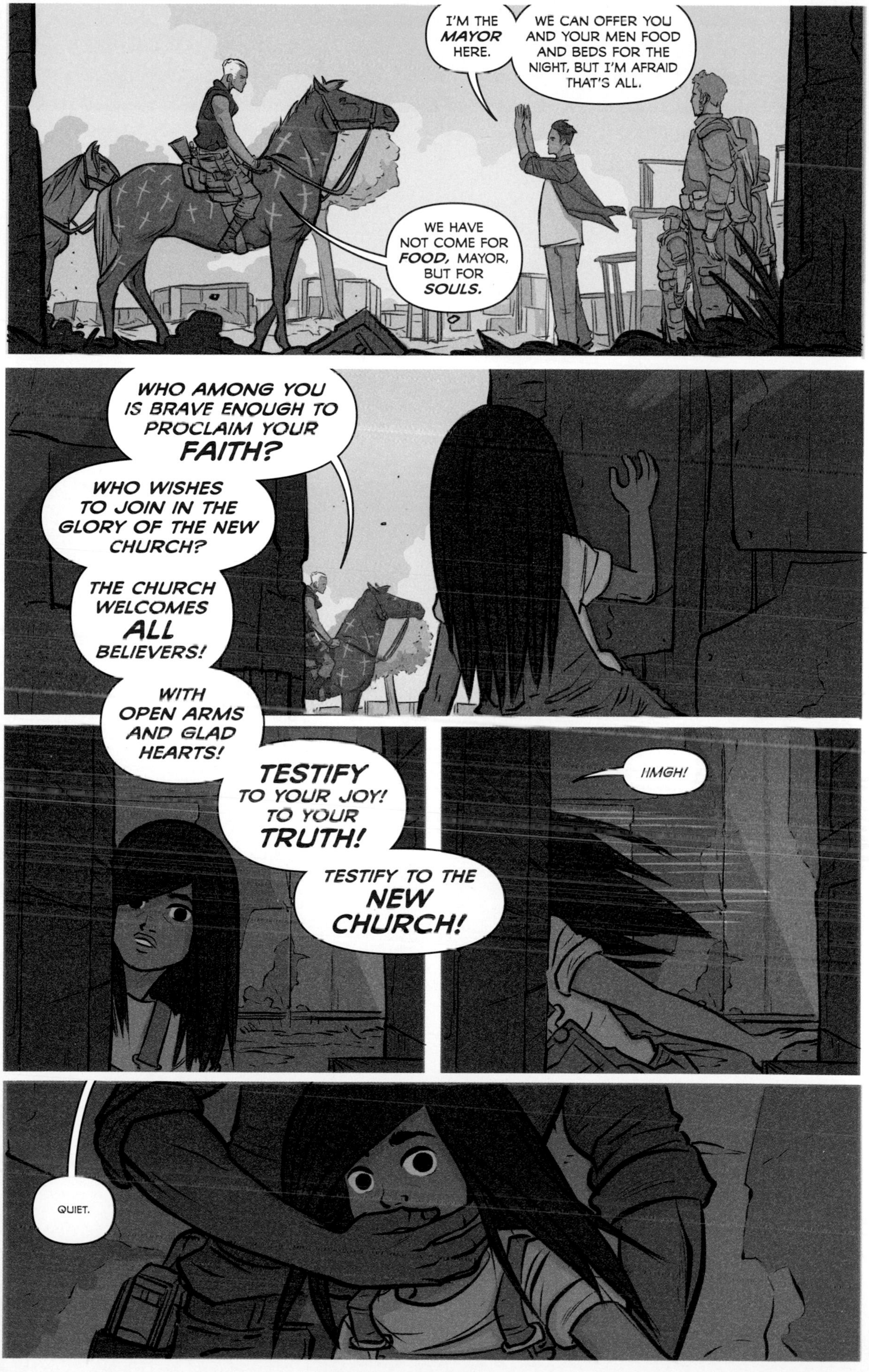
I'M THE MAYOR HERE.
WE CAN OFFER YOU AND YOUR MEN FOOD AND BEDS FOR THE NIGHT, BUT I'M AFRAID THAT'S ALL.
WE HAVE NOT COME FOR FOOD, MAYOR, BUT FOR SOULS.
WHO AMONG YOU IS BRAVE ENOUGH TO PROCLAIM YOUR FAITH?
WHO WISHES TO JOIN IN THE GLORY OF THE NEW CHURCH?
THE CHURCH WELCOMES ALL BELIEVERS!
WITH OPEN ARMS AND GLAD HEARTS!
TESTIFY TO YOUR JOY! TO YOUR TRUTH!
TESTIFY TO THE NEW CHURCH!
IIMGH!
QUIET.

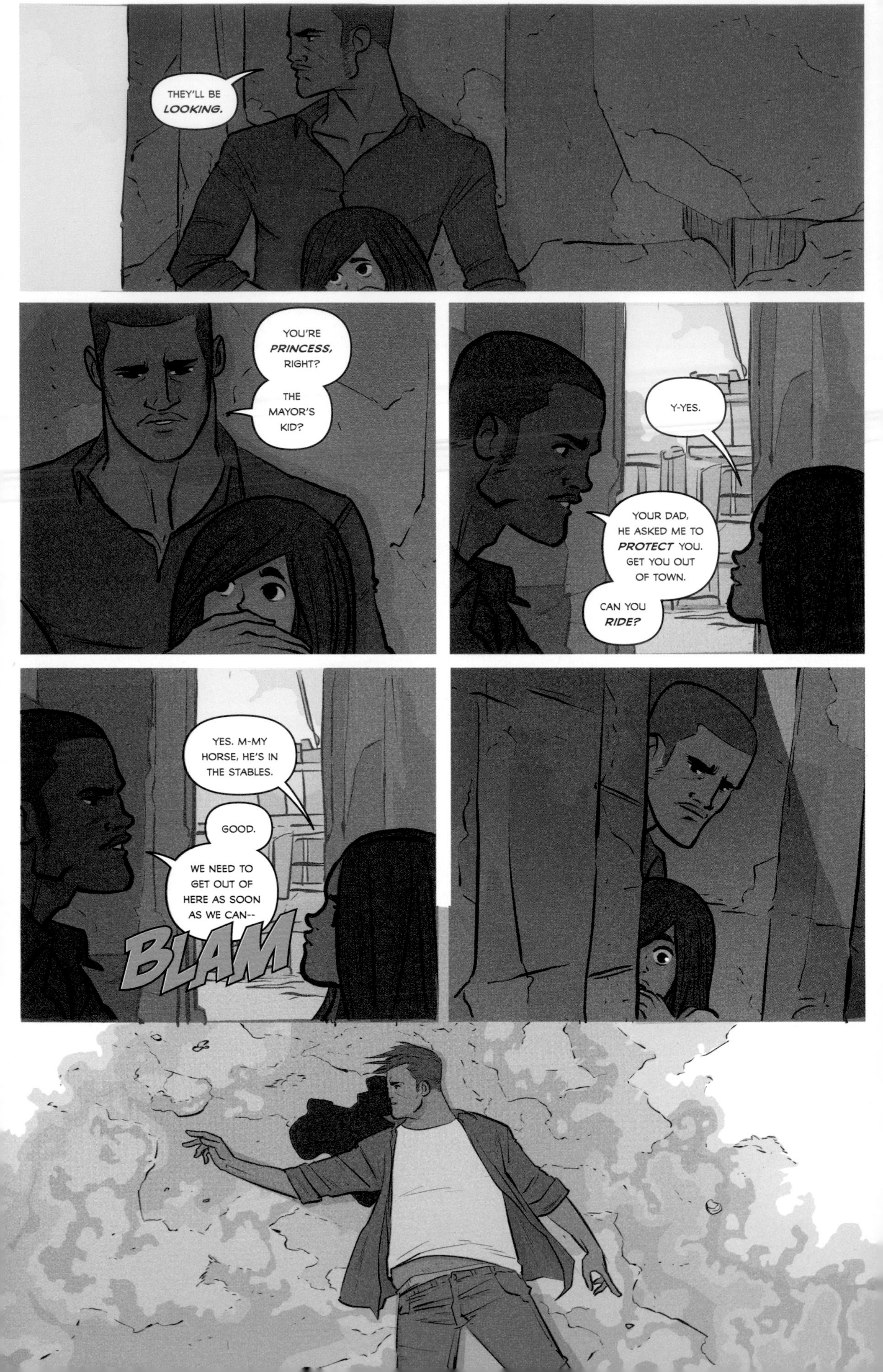
THEY'LL BE *LOOKING.*
YOU'RE *PRINCESS,* RIGHT?
THE MAYOR'S KID?
Y-YES.
YOUR DAD, HE ASKED ME TO *PROTECT* YOU. GET YOU OUT OF TOWN.
CAN YOU *RIDE?*
YES. M-MY HORSE, HE'S IN THE STABLES.
GOOD.
WE NEED TO GET OUT OF HERE AS SOON AS WE CAN--
BLAM

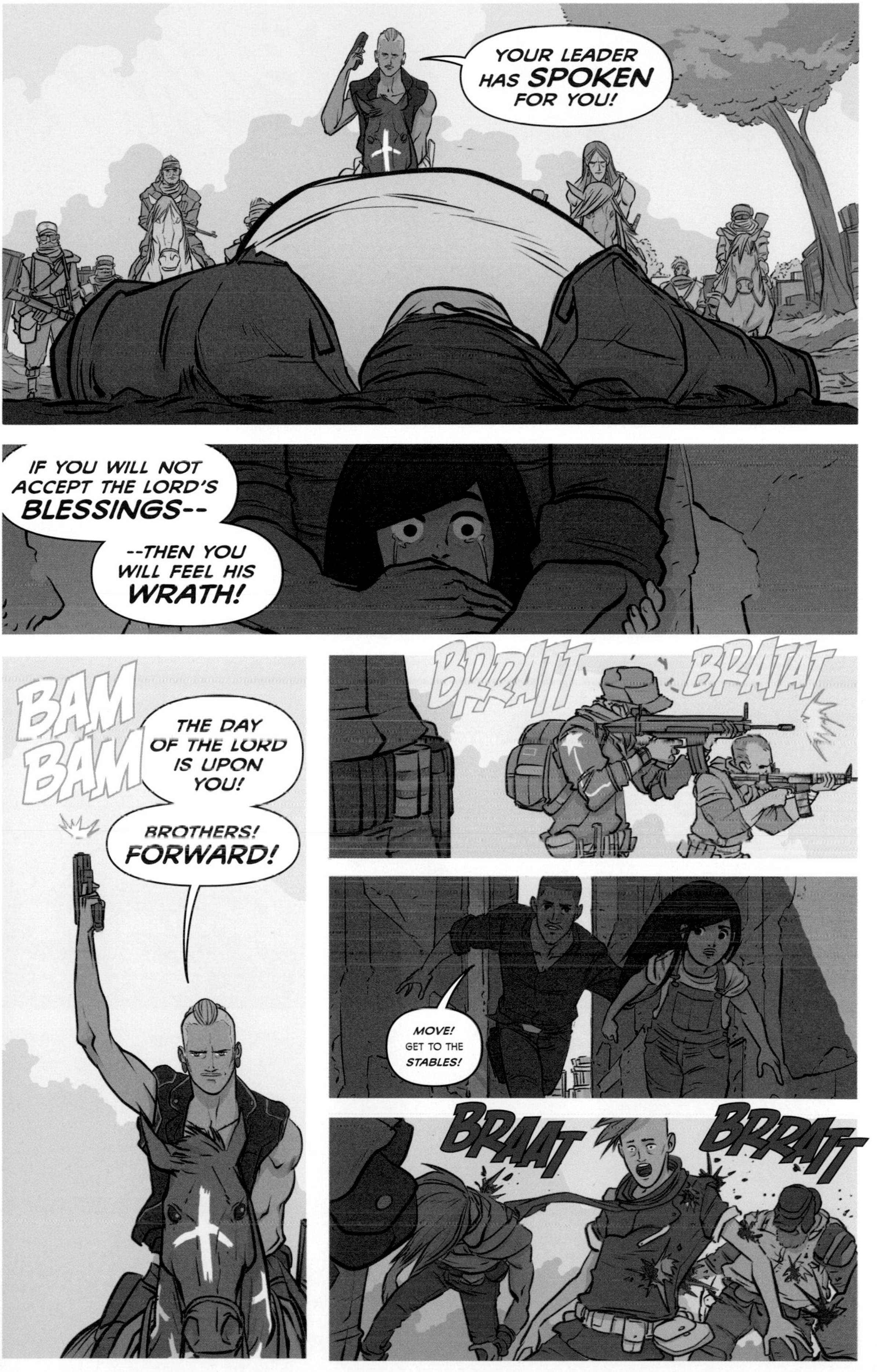
YOUR LEADER HAS SPOKEN FOR YOU!
IF YOU WILL NOT ACCEPT THE LORD'S BLESSINGS--
--THEN YOU WILL FEEL HIS WRATH!
BAM BAM
THE DAY OF THE LORD IS UPON YOU!
BROTHERS! FORWARD!
BRRATT BRATAT
MOVE! GET TO THE STABLES!
BRAAT BRRATT

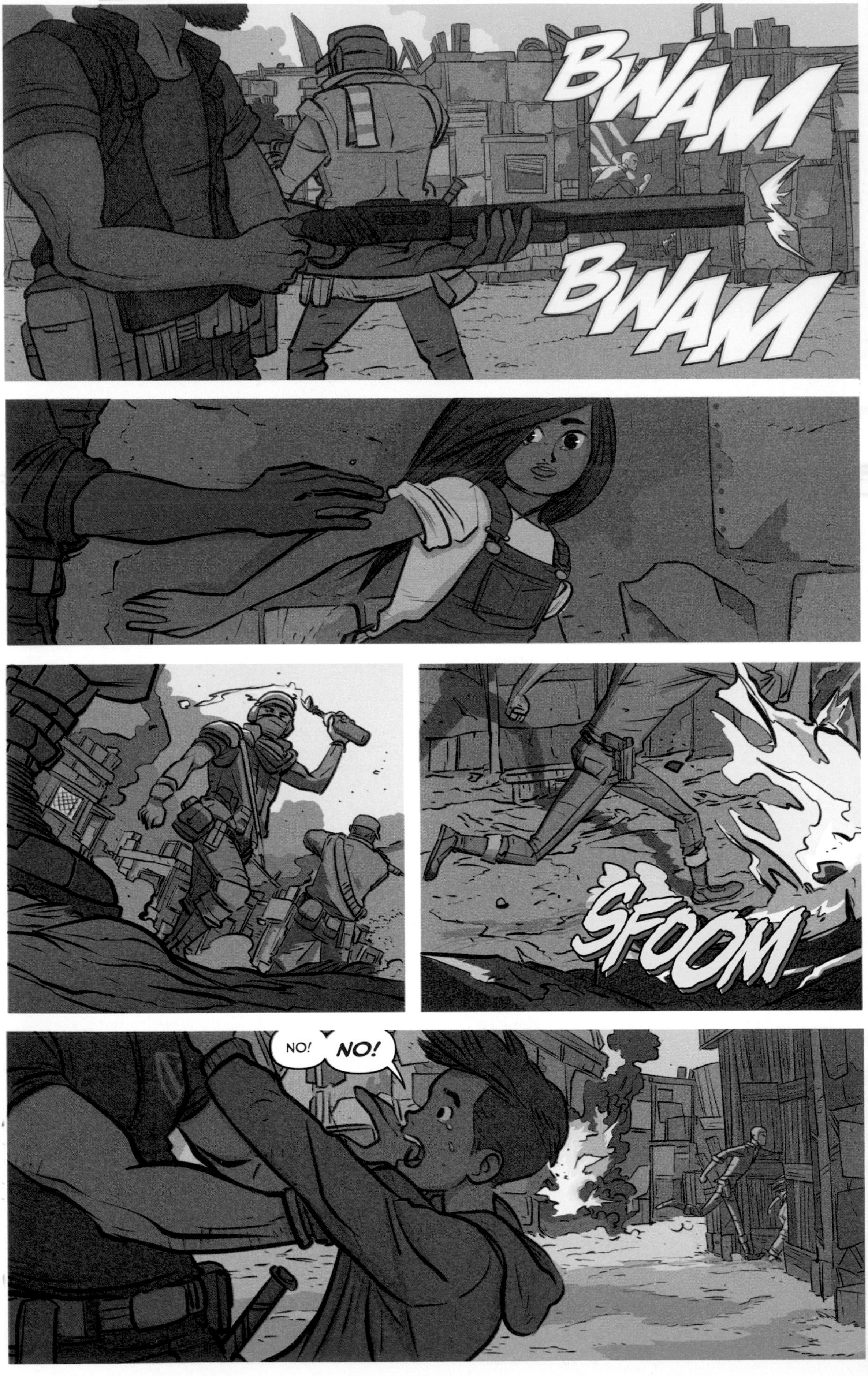
BWAM
BWAM
SFOOM
NO!
NO!

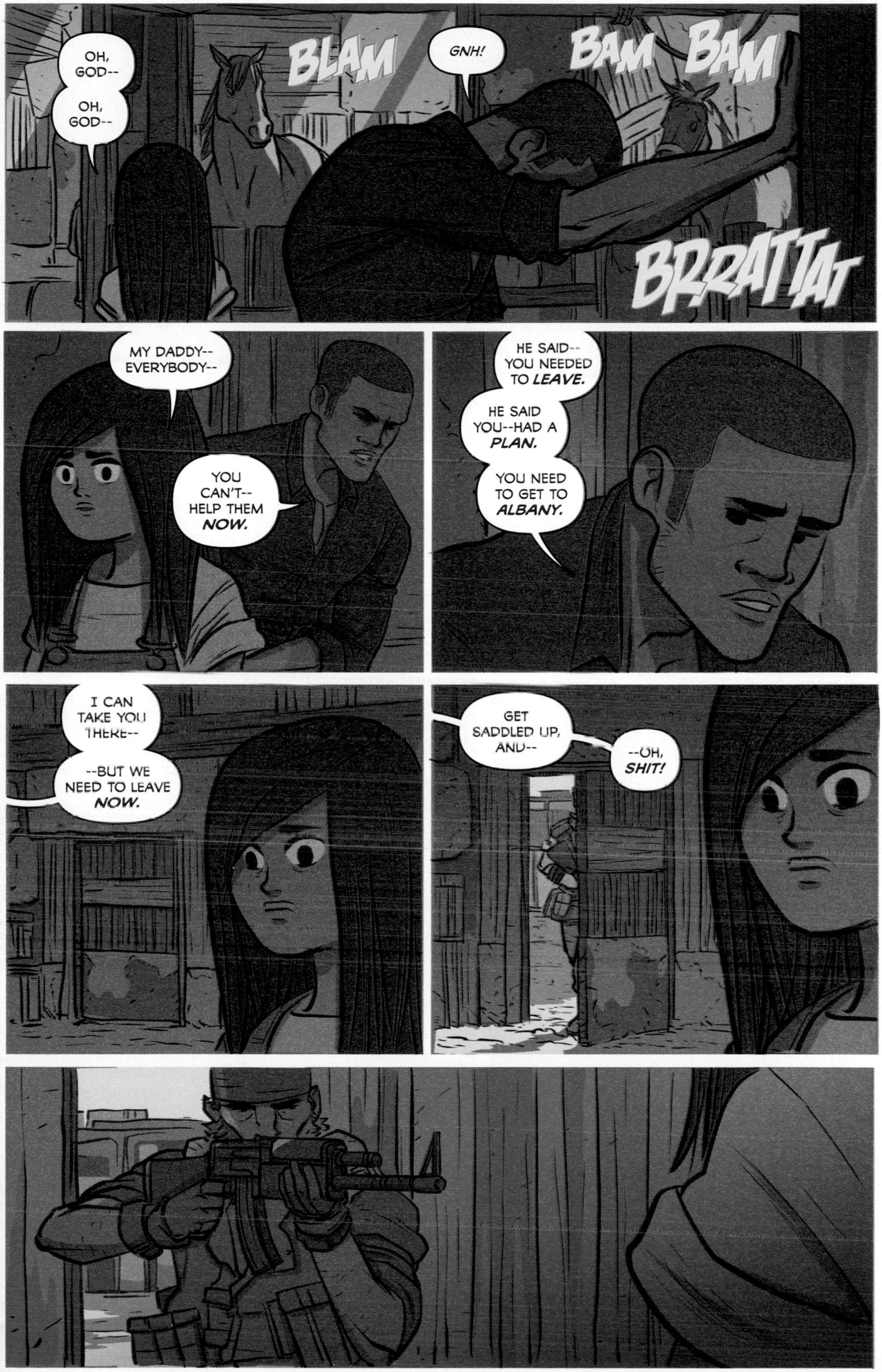

OH, GOD--
OH, GOD--
BLAM
GNH!
BAM BAM
BRRATTAT
MY DADDY-- EVERYBODY--
YOU CAN'T-- HELP THEM NOW.
HE SAID-- YOU NEEDED TO LEAVE.
HE SAID YOU--HAD A PLAN.
YOU NEED TO GET TO ALBANY.
I CAN TAKE YOU THERE--
--BUT WE NEED TO LEAVE NOW.
GET SADDLED UP, AND--
--OH, SHIT!

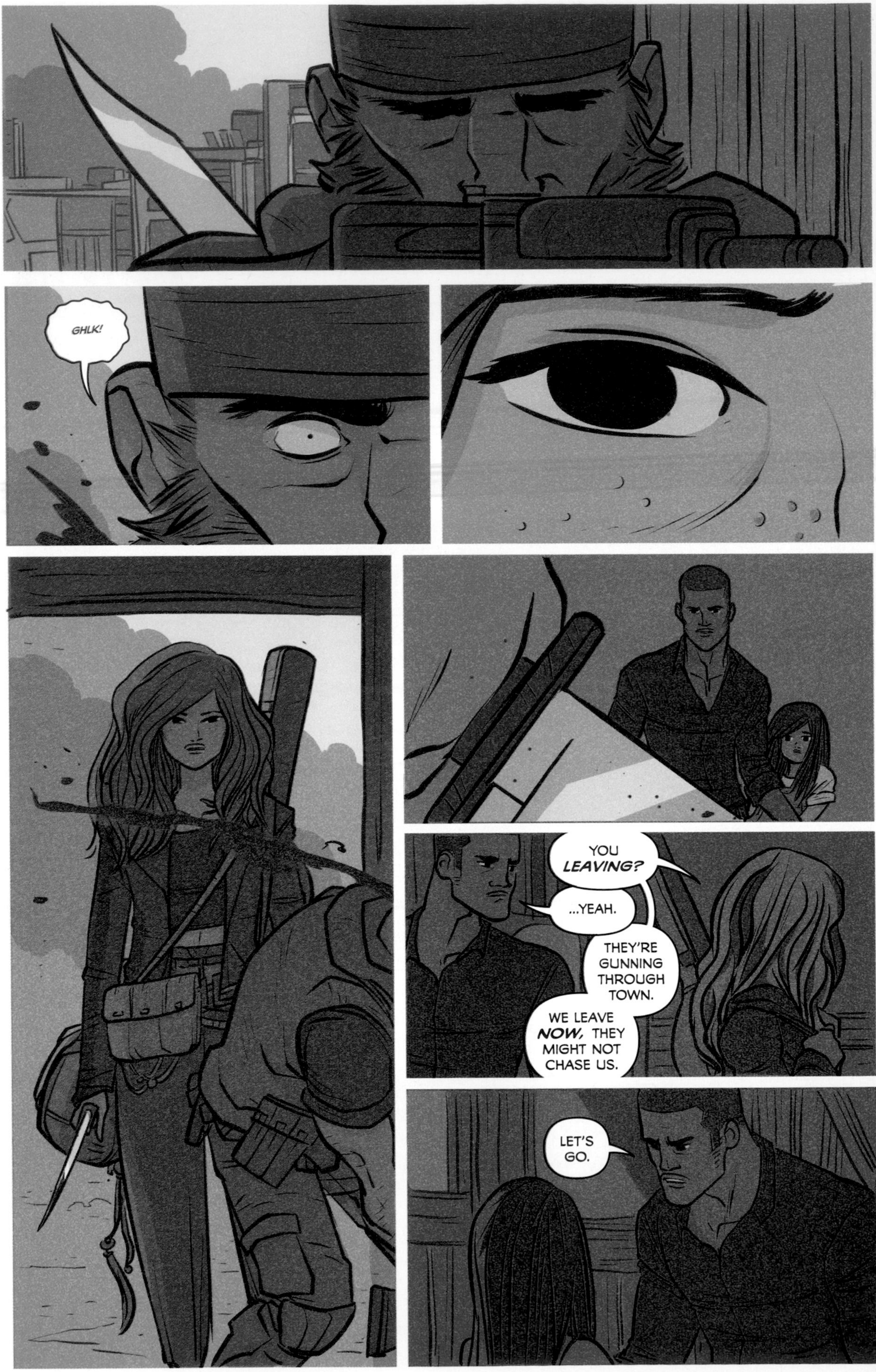
GHLK!
YOU LEAVING?
...YEAH.
THEY'RE GUNNING THROUGH TOWN.
WE LEAVE NOW, THEY MIGHT NOT CHASE US.
LET'S GO.

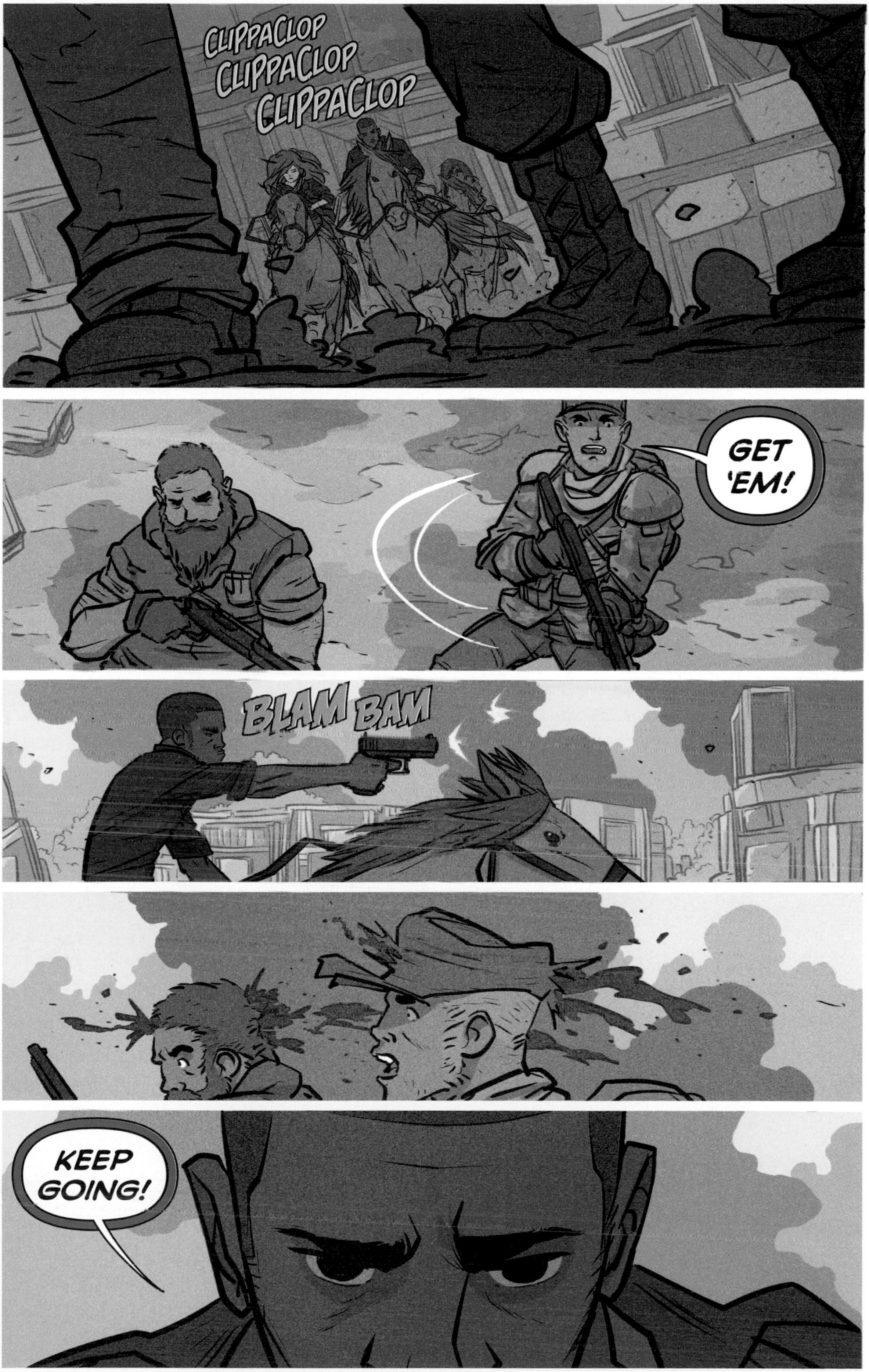
CLIPPACLOP
CLIPPACLOP
CLIPPACLOP
GET 'EM!
BLAM BAM
KEEP GOING!

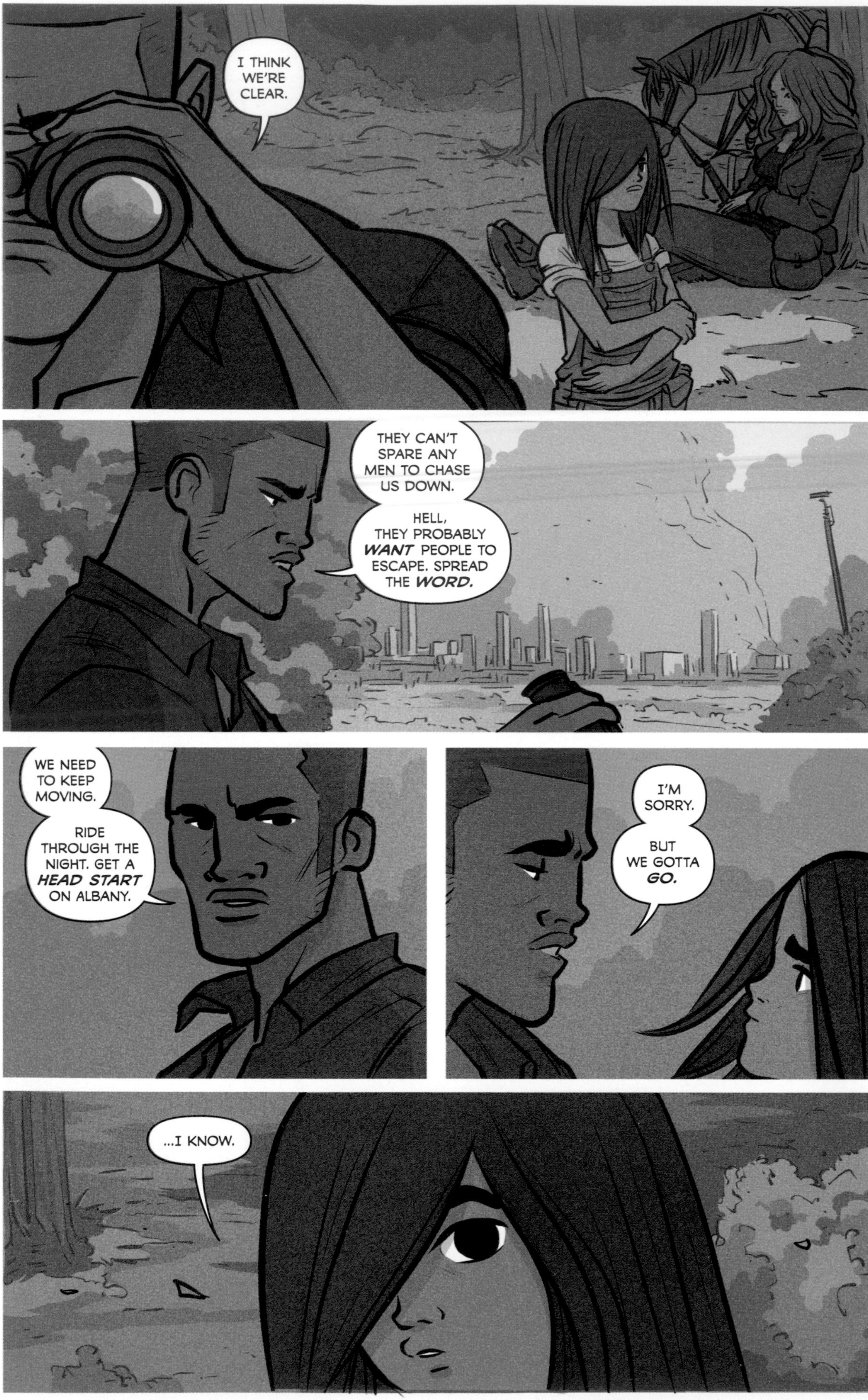
I THINK WE'RE CLEAR.
THEY CAN'T SPARE ANY MEN TO CHASE US DOWN.
HELL, THEY PROBABLY WANT PEOPLE TO ESCAPE. SPREAD THE WORD.
WE NEED TO KEEP MOVING.
RIDE THROUGH THE NIGHT. GET A HEAD START ON ALBANY.
I'M SORRY.
BUT WE GOTTA GO.
...I KNOW.

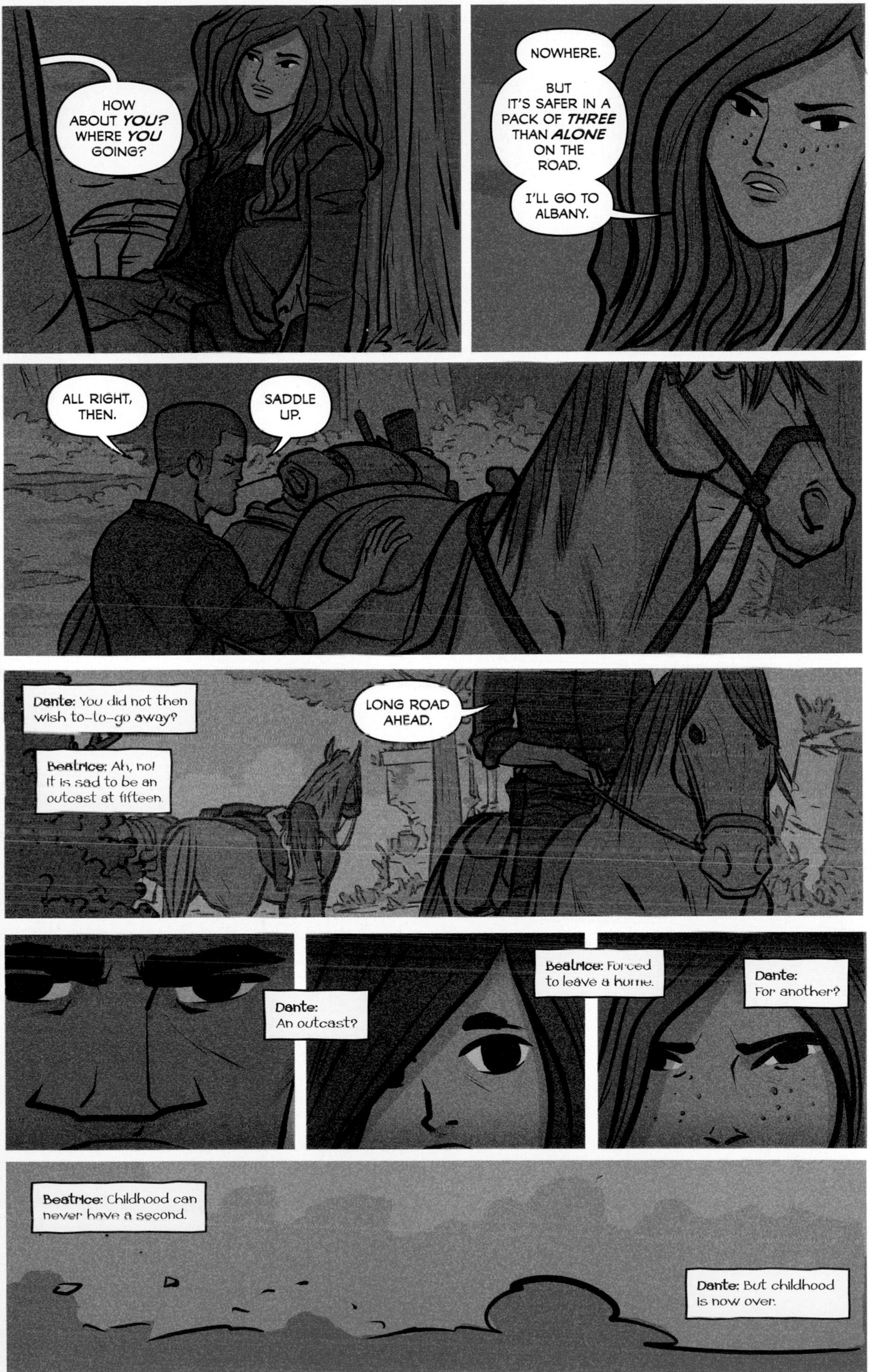
HOW ABOUT *YOU?* WHERE *YOU* GOING?
NOWHERE.
BUT IT'S SAFER IN A PACK OF *THREE* THAN *ALONE* ON THE ROAD.
I'LL GO TO ALBANY.
ALL RIGHT, THEN.
SADDLE UP.
Dante: You did not then wish to—to—go away?
Beatrice: Ah, no! It is sad to be an outcast at fifteen.
LONG ROAD AHEAD.
Dante: An outcast?
Beatrice: Forced to leave a home.
Dante: For another?
Beatrice: Childhood can never have a second.
Dante: But childhood is now over.

—from 'Dante and Beatrice', in *Imaginary Conversations*, Walter Savage Landor

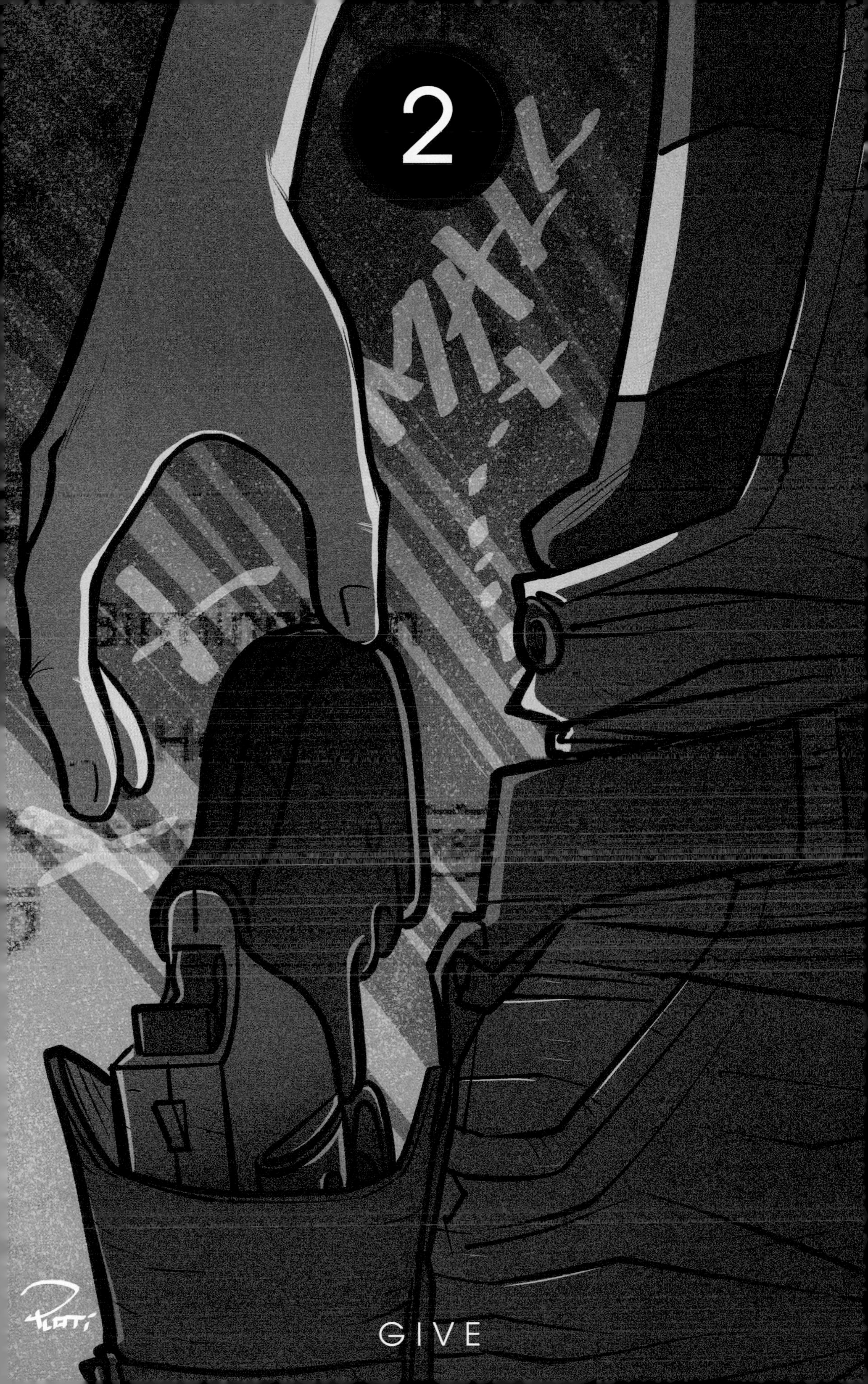
2
GIVE

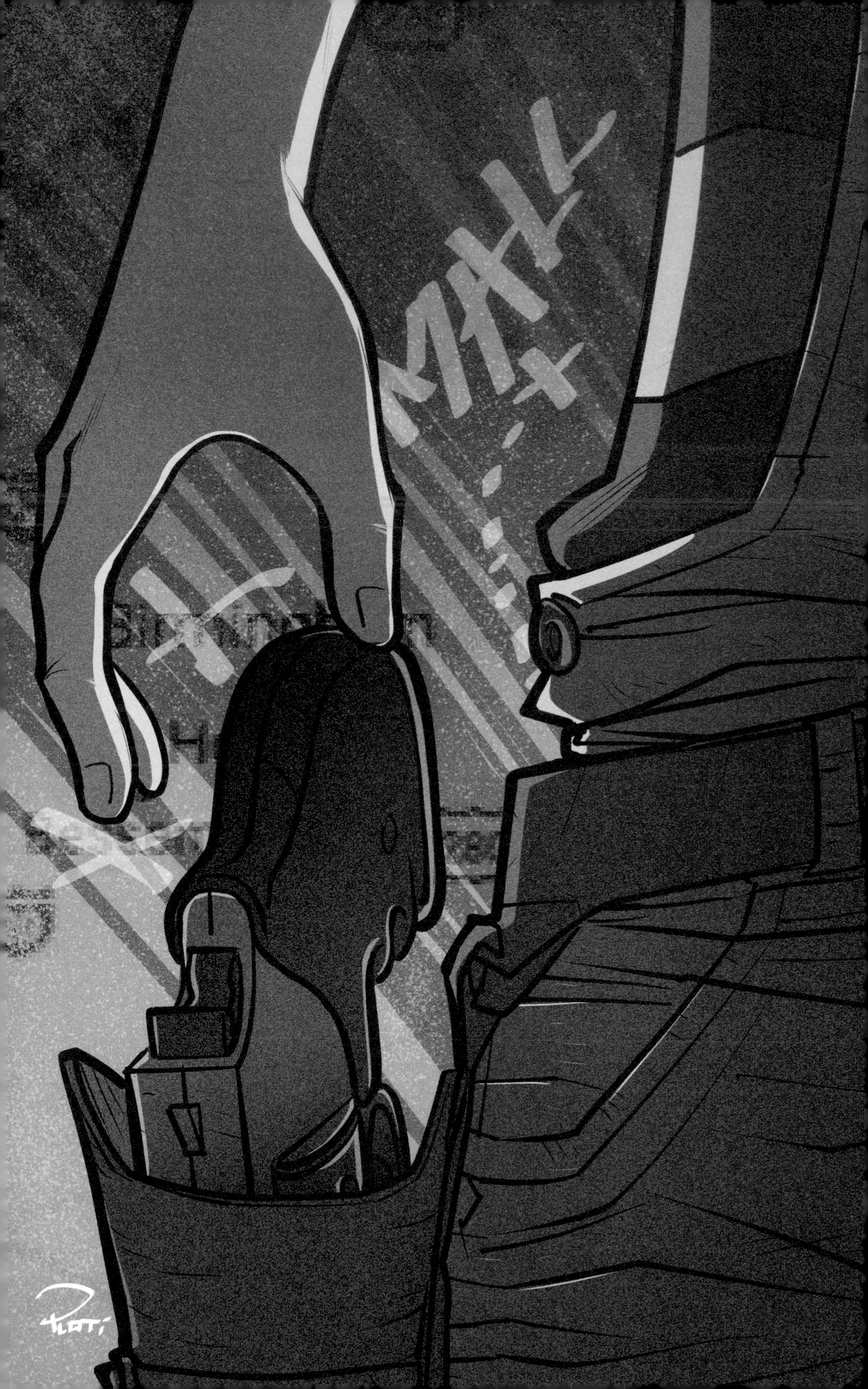

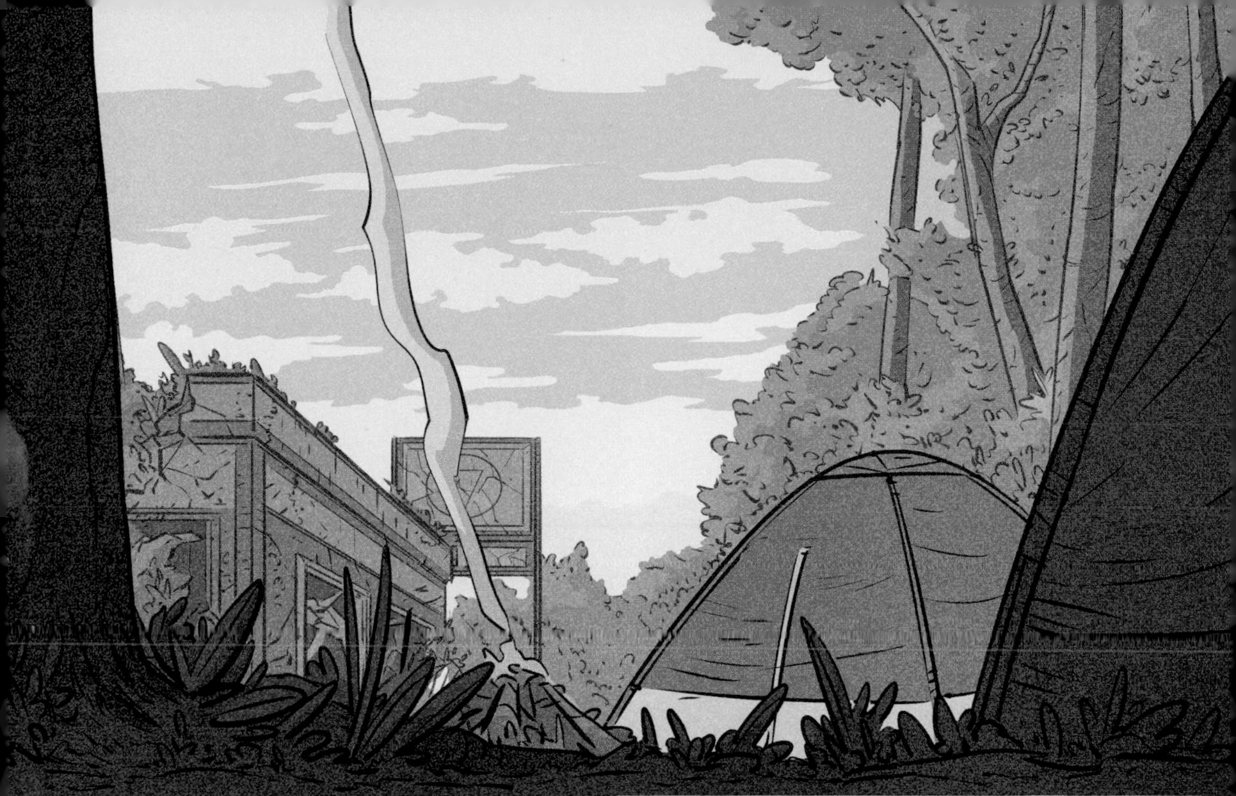

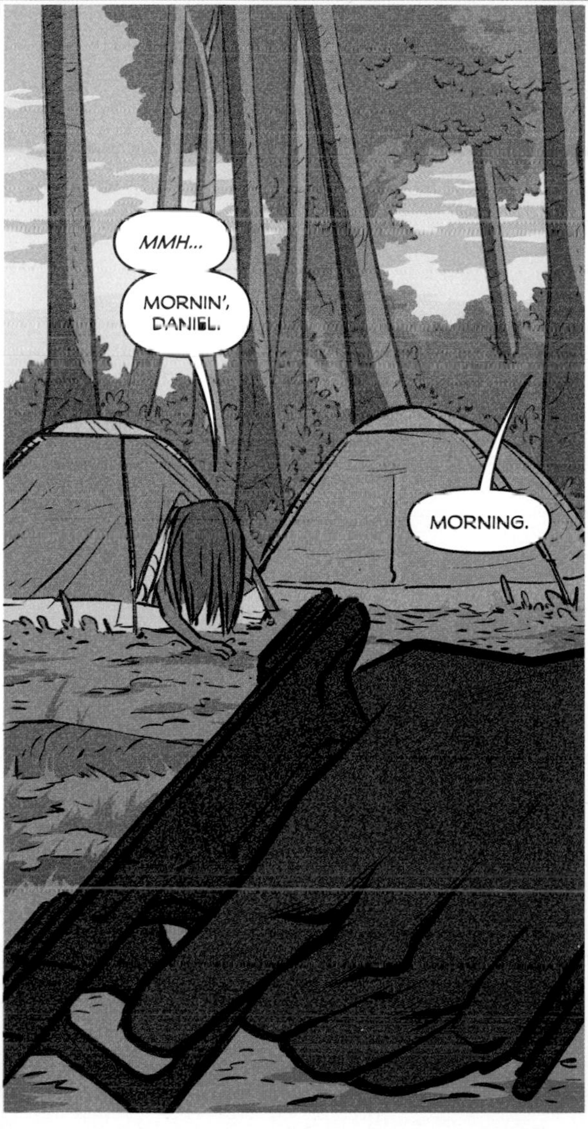
MMH...
MORNIN', DANIEL.
MORNING.

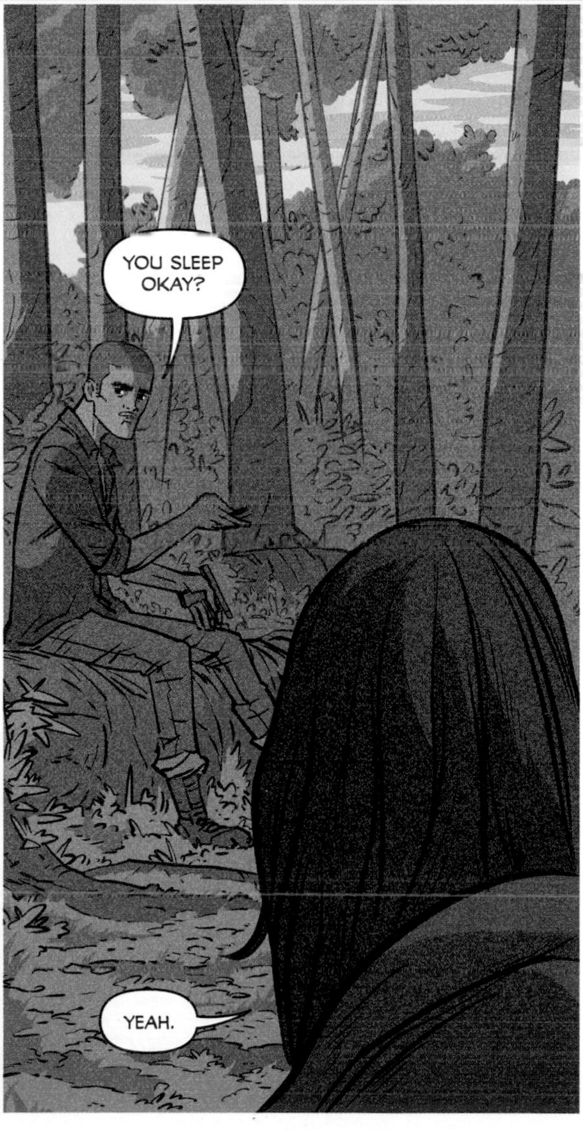
YOU SLEEP OKAY?
YEAH.

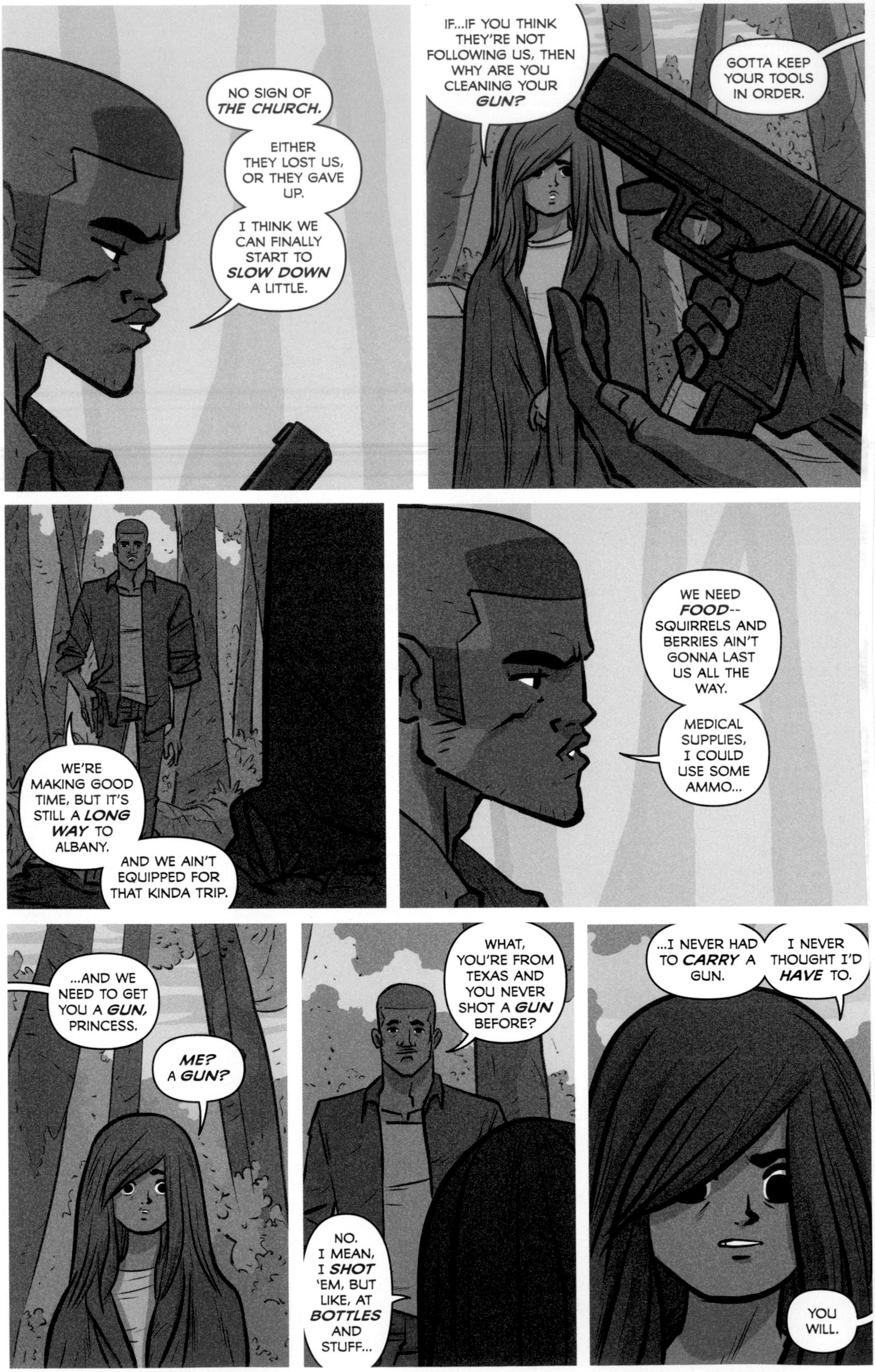

NO SIGN OF *THE CHURCH.*
EITHER THEY LOST US, OR THEY GAVE UP.
I THINK WE CAN FINALLY START TO *SLOW DOWN* A LITTLE.
IF...IF YOU THINK THEY'RE NOT FOLLOWING US, THEN WHY ARE YOU CLEANING YOUR *GUN?*
GOTTA KEEP YOUR TOOLS IN ORDER.
WE'RE MAKING GOOD TIME, BUT IT'S STILL A *LONG WAY* TO ALBANY.
AND WE AIN'T EQUIPPED FOR THAT KINDA TRIP.
WE NEED *FOOD*-- SQUIRRELS AND BERRIES AIN'T GONNA LAST US ALL THE WAY.
MEDICAL SUPPLIES, I COULD USE SOME AMMO...
...AND WE NEED TO GET YOU A *GUN,* PRINCESS.
ME? A *GUN?*
WHAT, YOU'RE FROM TEXAS AND YOU NEVER SHOT A *GUN* BEFORE?
NO. I MEAN, I *SHOT* 'EM, BUT LIKE, AT *BOTTLES* AND STUFF...
...I NEVER HAD TO *CARRY* A GUN.
I NEVER THOUGHT I'D *HAVE* TO.
YOU WILL.

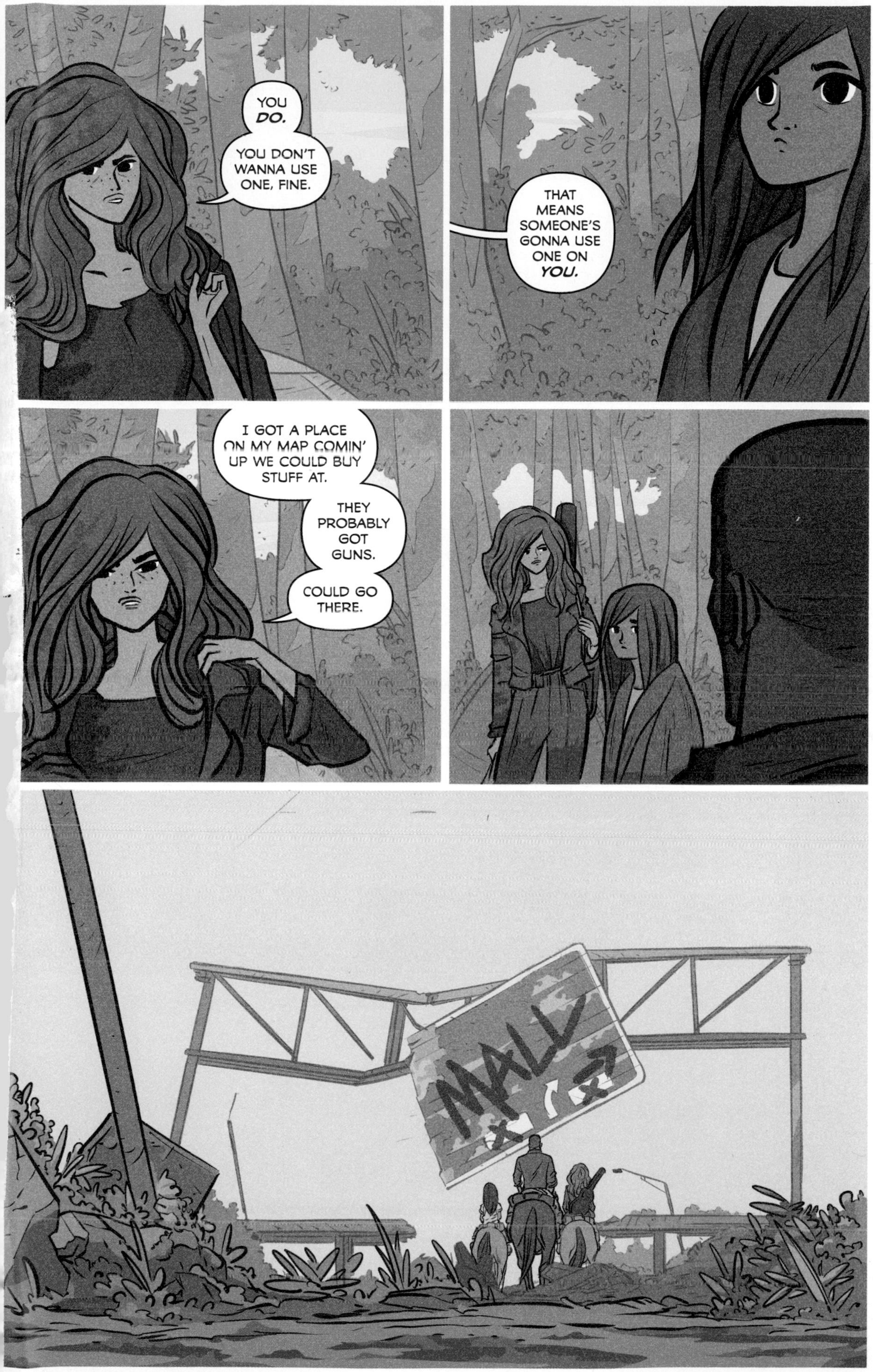
YOU DO.
YOU DON'T WANNA USE ONE, FINE.
THAT MEANS SOMEONE'S GONNA USE ONE ON YOU.
I GOT A PLACE ON MY MAP COMIN' UP WE COULD BUY STUFF AT.
THEY PROBABLY GOT GUNS.
COULD GO THERE.
MALL

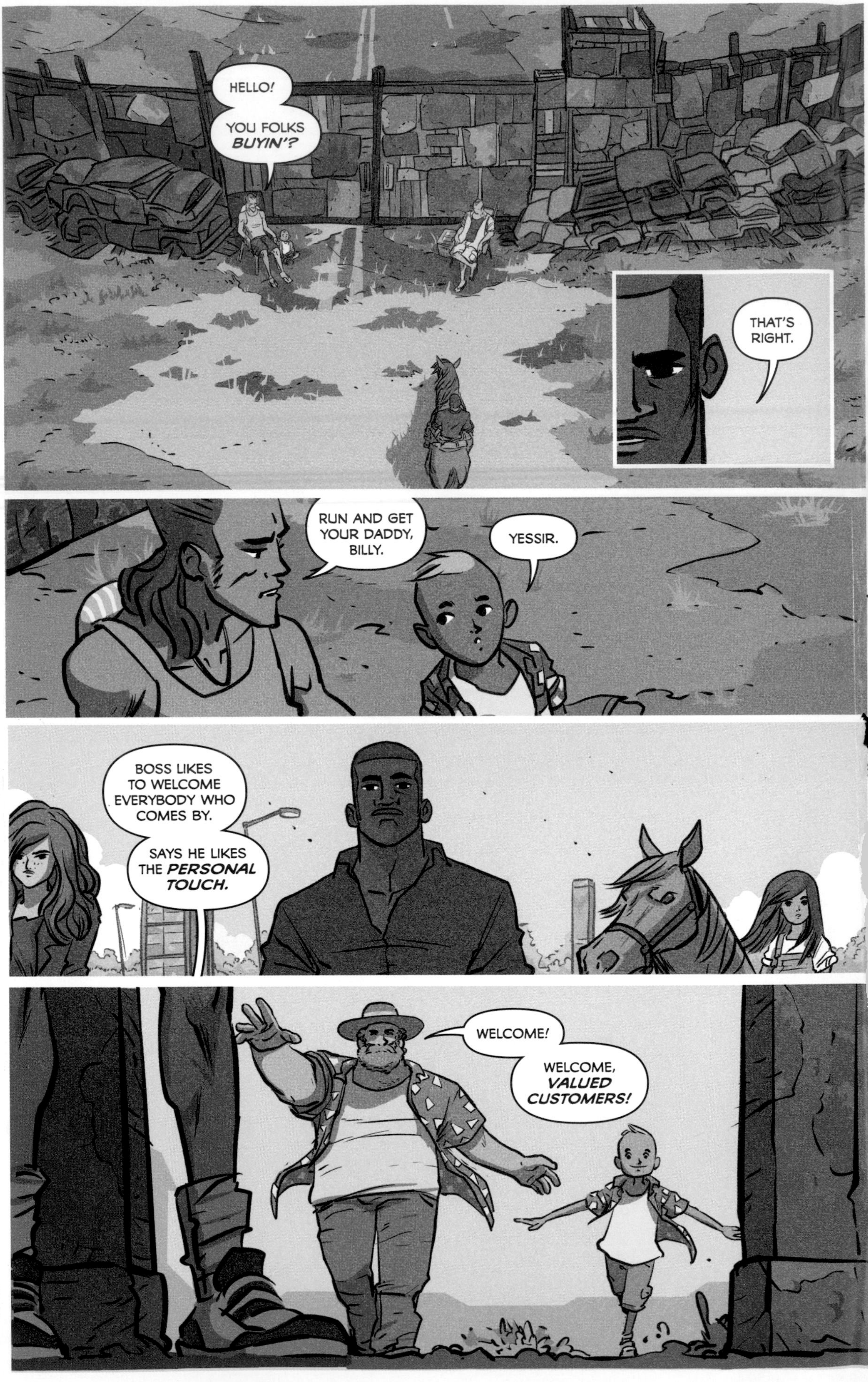
HELLO!
YOU FOLKS *BUYIN'?*
THAT'S RIGHT.
RUN AND GET YOUR DADDY, BILLY.
YESSIR.
BOSS LIKES TO WELCOME EVERYBODY WHO COMES BY.
SAYS HE LIKES THE *PERSONAL TOUCH.*
WELCOME!
WELCOME, *VALUED CUSTOMERS!*

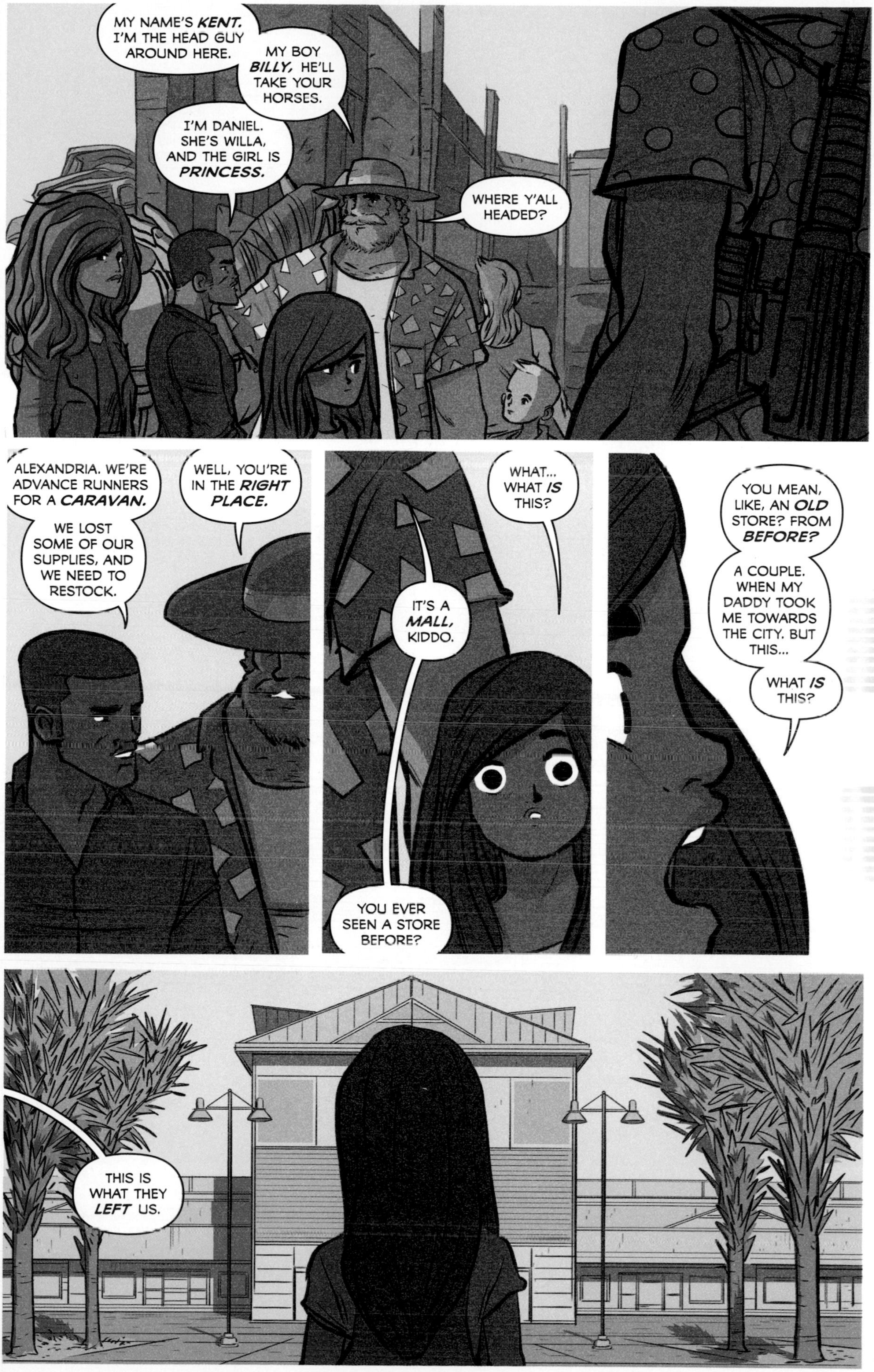
MY NAME'S KENT. I'M THE HEAD GUY AROUND HERE.
MY BOY BILLY, HE'LL TAKE YOUR HORSES.
I'M DANIEL. SHE'S WILLA, AND THE GIRL IS PRINCESS.
WHERE Y'ALL HEADED?
ALEXANDRIA. WE'RE ADVANCE RUNNERS FOR A CARAVAN.
WE LOST SOME OF OUR SUPPLIES, AND WE NEED TO RESTOCK.
WELL, YOU'RE IN THE RIGHT PLACE.
WHAT... WHAT IS THIS?
IT'S A MALL, KIDDO.
YOU EVER SEEN A STORE BEFORE?
YOU MEAN, LIKE, AN OLD STORE? FROM BEFORE?
A COUPLE. WHEN MY DADDY TOOK ME TOWARDS THE CITY. BUT THIS...
WHAT IS THIS?
THIS IS WHAT THEY LEFT US.

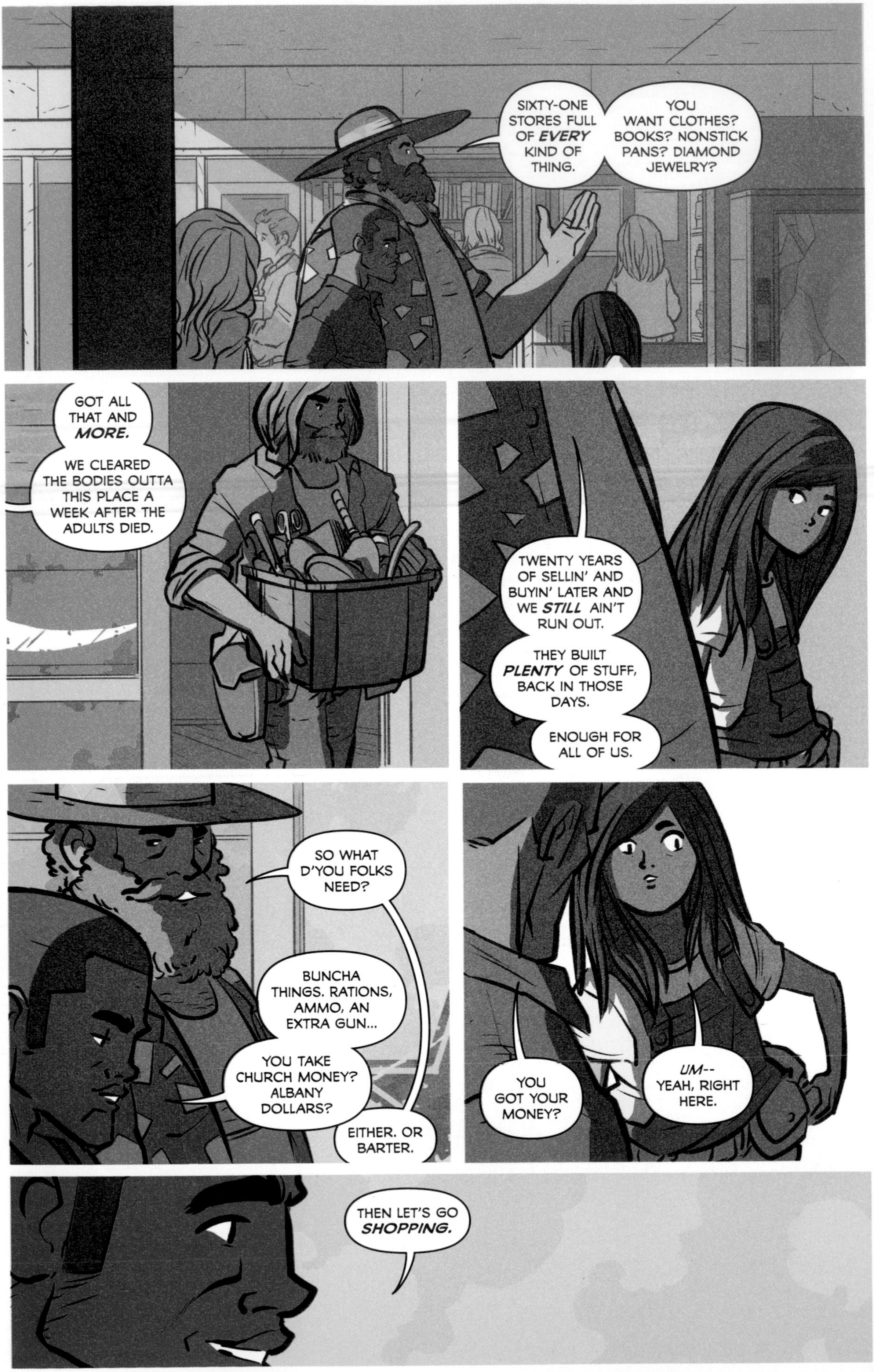
SIXTY-ONE STORES FULL OF *EVERY* KIND OF THING.
YOU WANT CLOTHES? BOOKS? NONSTICK PANS? DIAMOND JEWELRY?
GOT ALL THAT AND *MORE.*
WE CLEARED THE BODIES OUTTA THIS PLACE A WEEK AFTER THE ADULTS DIED.
TWENTY YEARS OF SELLIN' AND BUYIN' LATER AND WE *STILL* AIN'T RUN OUT.
THEY BUILT *PLENTY* OF STUFF, BACK IN THOSE DAYS.
ENOUGH FOR ALL OF US.
SO WHAT D'YOU FOLKS NEED?
BUNCHA THINGS. RATIONS, AMMO, AN EXTRA GUN...
YOU TAKE CHURCH MONEY? ALBANY DOLLARS?
EITHER. OR BARTER.
YOU GOT YOUR MONEY?
UM-- YEAH, RIGHT HERE.
THEN LET'S GO *SHOPPING.*

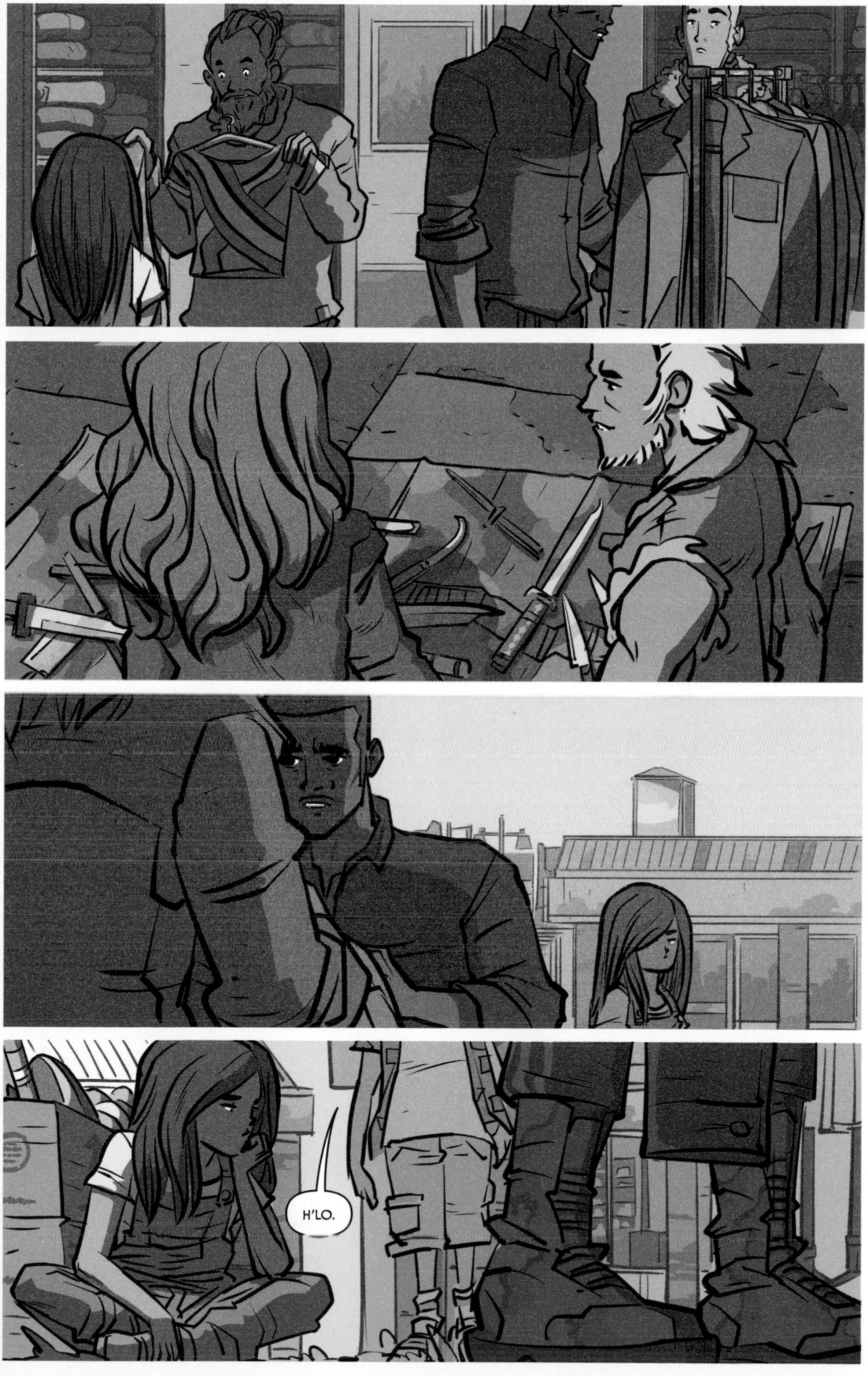
H'LO.

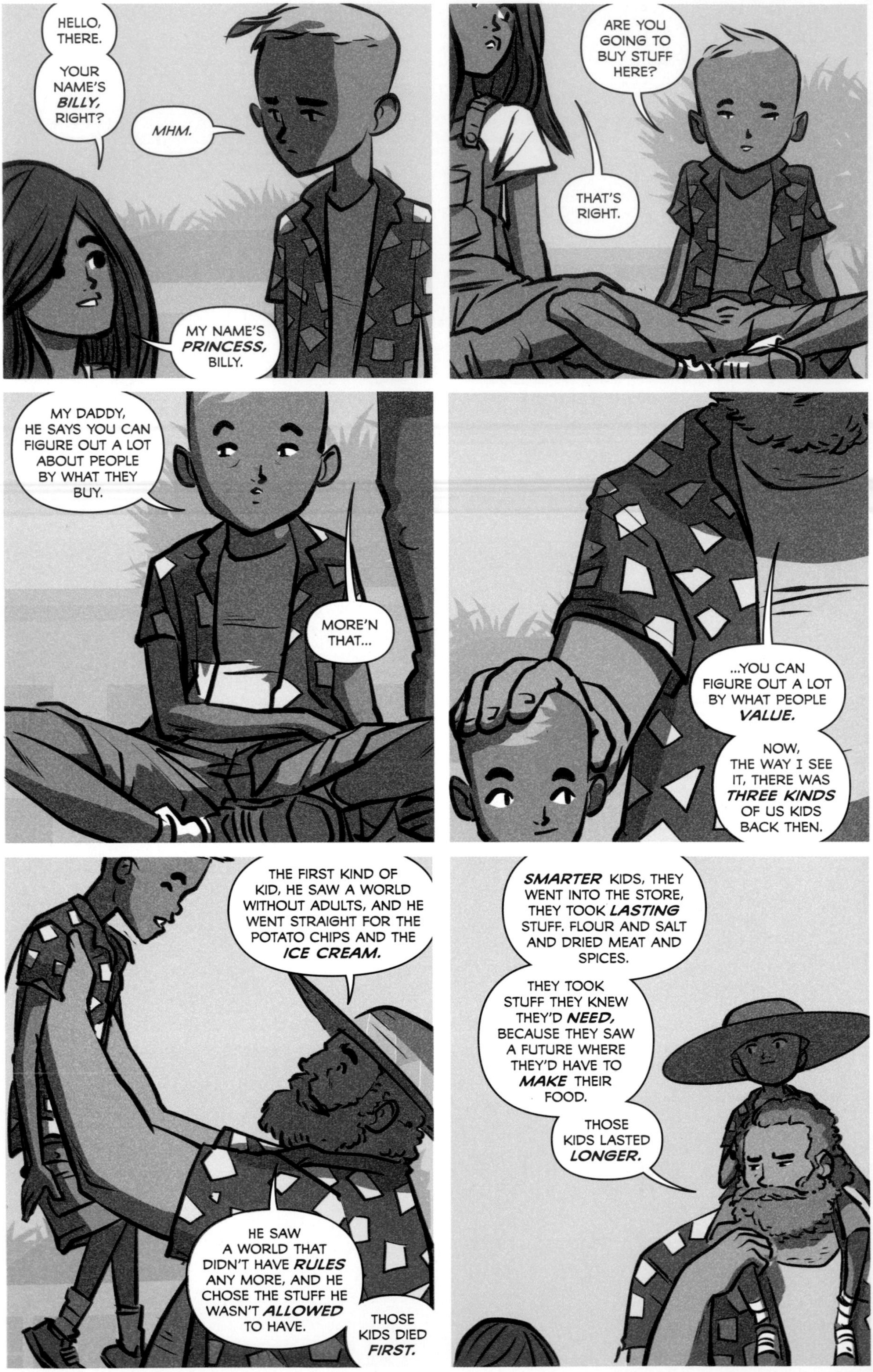
HELLO, THERE.
YOUR NAME'S BILLY, RIGHT?
MHM.
MY NAME'S PRINCESS, BILLY.
ARE YOU GOING TO BUY STUFF HERE?
THAT'S RIGHT.
MY DADDY, HE SAYS YOU CAN FIGURE OUT A LOT ABOUT PEOPLE BY WHAT THEY BUY.
MORE'N THAT...
...YOU CAN FIGURE OUT A LOT BY WHAT PEOPLE VALUE.
NOW, THE WAY I SEE IT, THERE WAS THREE KINDS OF US KIDS BACK THEN.
THE FIRST KIND OF KID, HE SAW A WORLD WITHOUT ADULTS, AND HE WENT STRAIGHT FOR THE POTATO CHIPS AND THE ICE CREAM.
HE SAW A WORLD THAT DIDN'T HAVE RULES ANY MORE, AND HE CHOSE THE STUFF HE WASN'T ALLOWED TO HAVE.
THOSE KIDS DIED FIRST.
SMARTER KIDS, THEY WENT INTO THE STORE, THEY TOOK LASTING STUFF. FLOUR AND SALT AND DRIED MEAT AND SPICES.
THEY TOOK STUFF THEY KNEW THEY'D NEED, BECAUSE THEY SAW A FUTURE WHERE THEY'D HAVE TO MAKE THEIR FOOD.
THOSE KIDS LASTED LONGER.

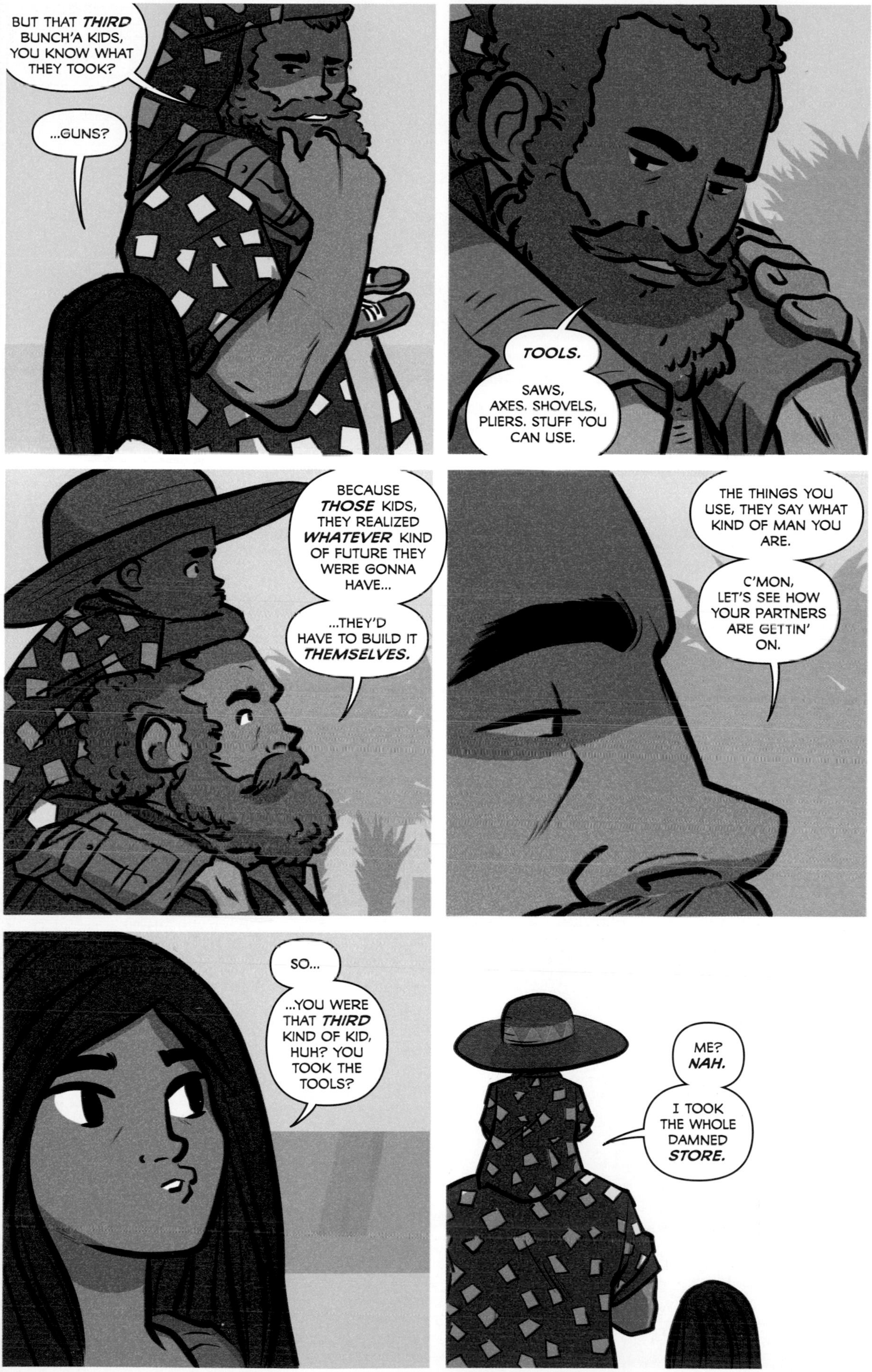

BUT THAT *THIRD* BUNCH'A KIDS, YOU KNOW WHAT THEY TOOK?
...GUNS?
TOOLS.
SAWS, AXES, SHOVELS, PLIERS. STUFF YOU CAN USE.
BECAUSE *THOSE* KIDS, THEY REALIZED *WHATEVER* KIND OF FUTURE THEY WERE GONNA HAVE...
...THEY'D HAVE TO BUILD IT *THEMSELVES.*
THE THINGS YOU USE, THEY SAY WHAT KIND OF MAN YOU ARE.
C'MON, LET'S SEE HOW YOUR PARTNERS ARE GETTIN' ON.
SO...
...YOU WERE THAT *THIRD* KIND OF KID, HUH? YOU TOOK THE TOOLS?
ME? *NAH.*
I TOOK THE WHOLE DAMNED *STORE.*

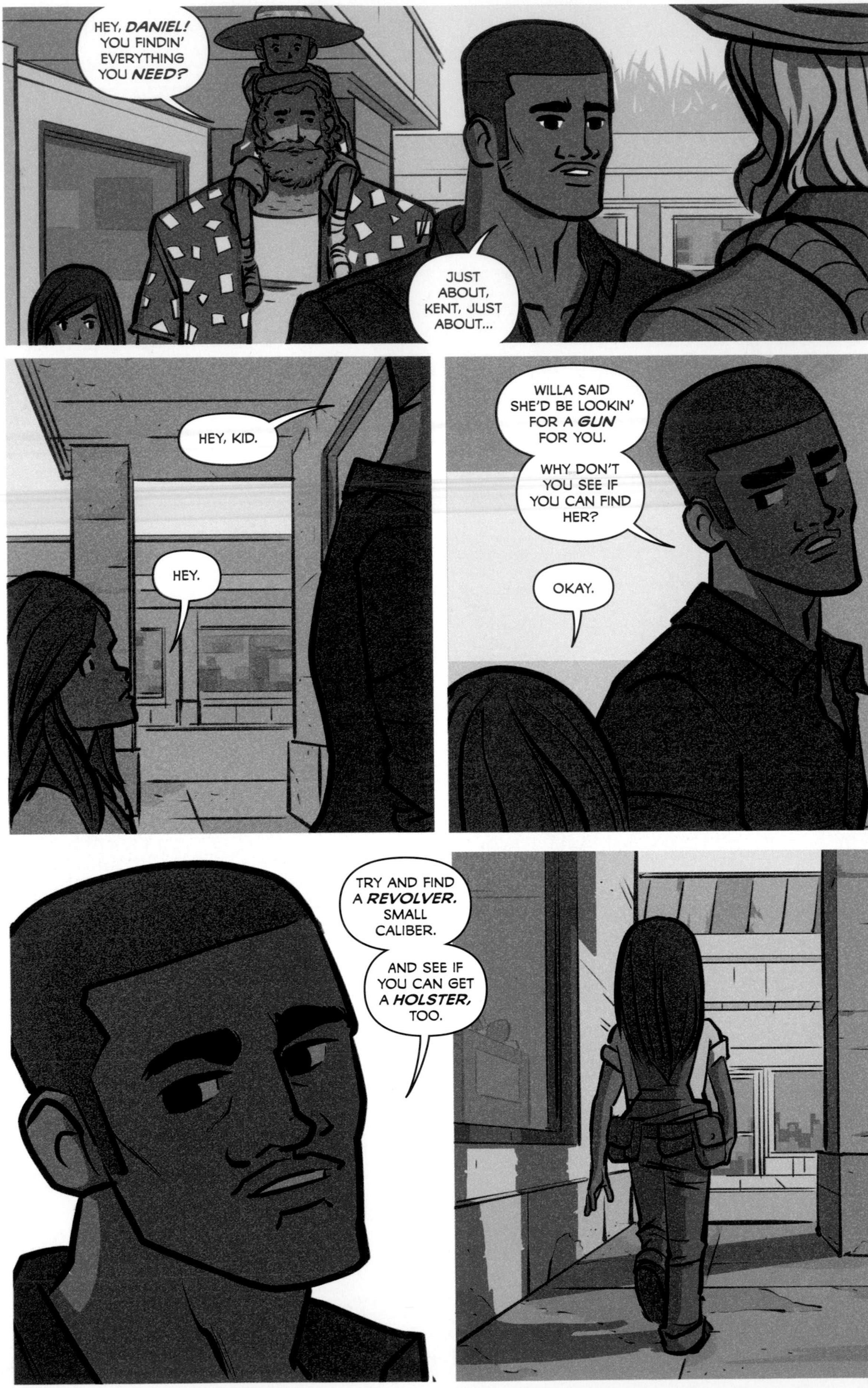
HEY, DANIEL! YOU FINDIN' EVERYTHING YOU NEED?
JUST ABOUT, KENT, JUST ABOUT...
HEY, KID.
HEY.
WILLA SAID SHE'D BE LOOKIN' FOR A GUN FOR YOU.
WHY DON'T YOU SEE IF YOU CAN FIND HER?
OKAY.
TRY AND FIND A REVOLVER. SMALL CALIBER.
AND SEE IF YOU CAN GET A HOLSTER, TOO.

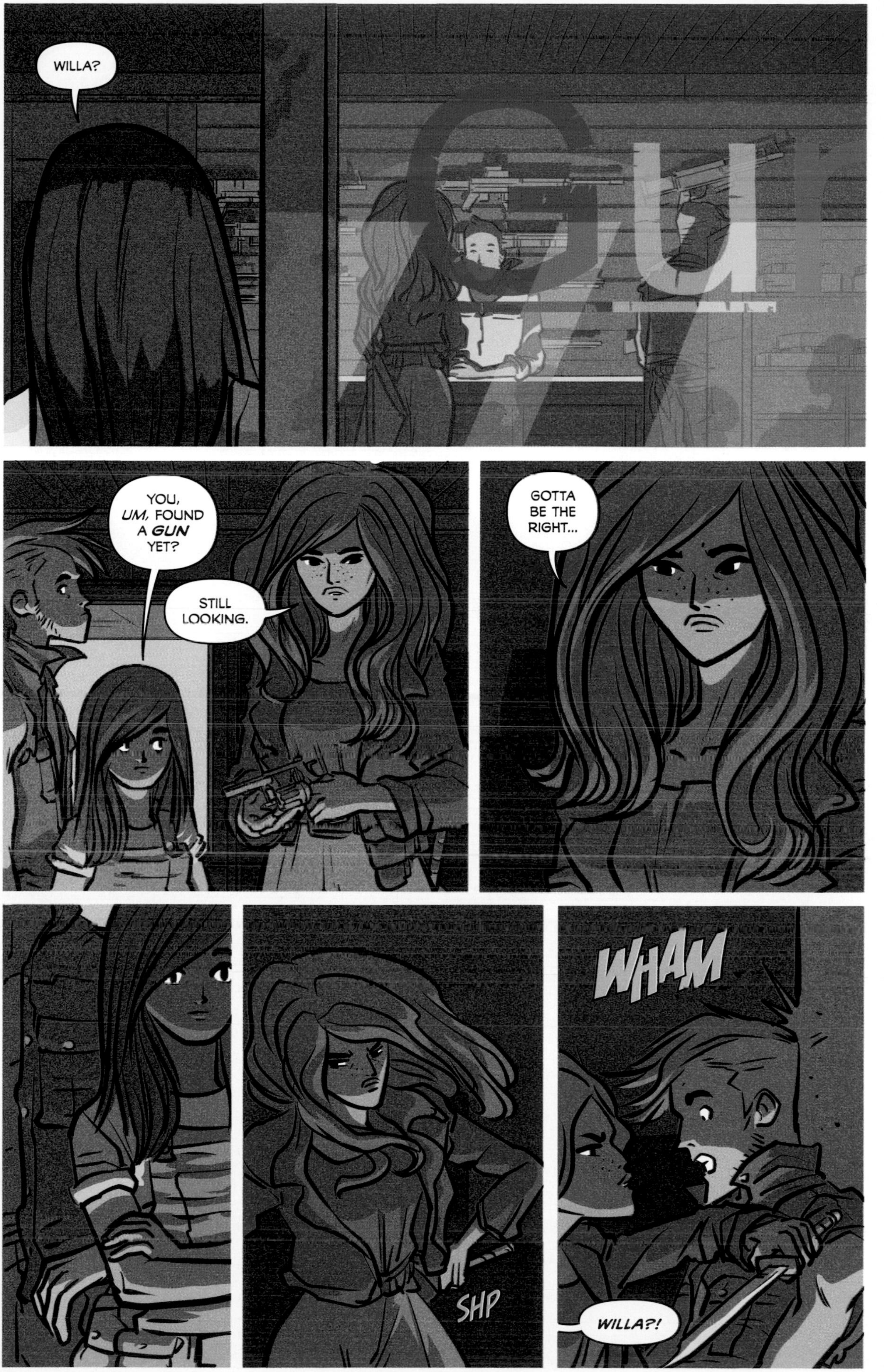
WILLA?
YOU, *UM,* FOUND A ***GUN*** YET?
STILL LOOKING.
GOTTA BE THE RIGHT...
SHP
WHAM
WILLA?!

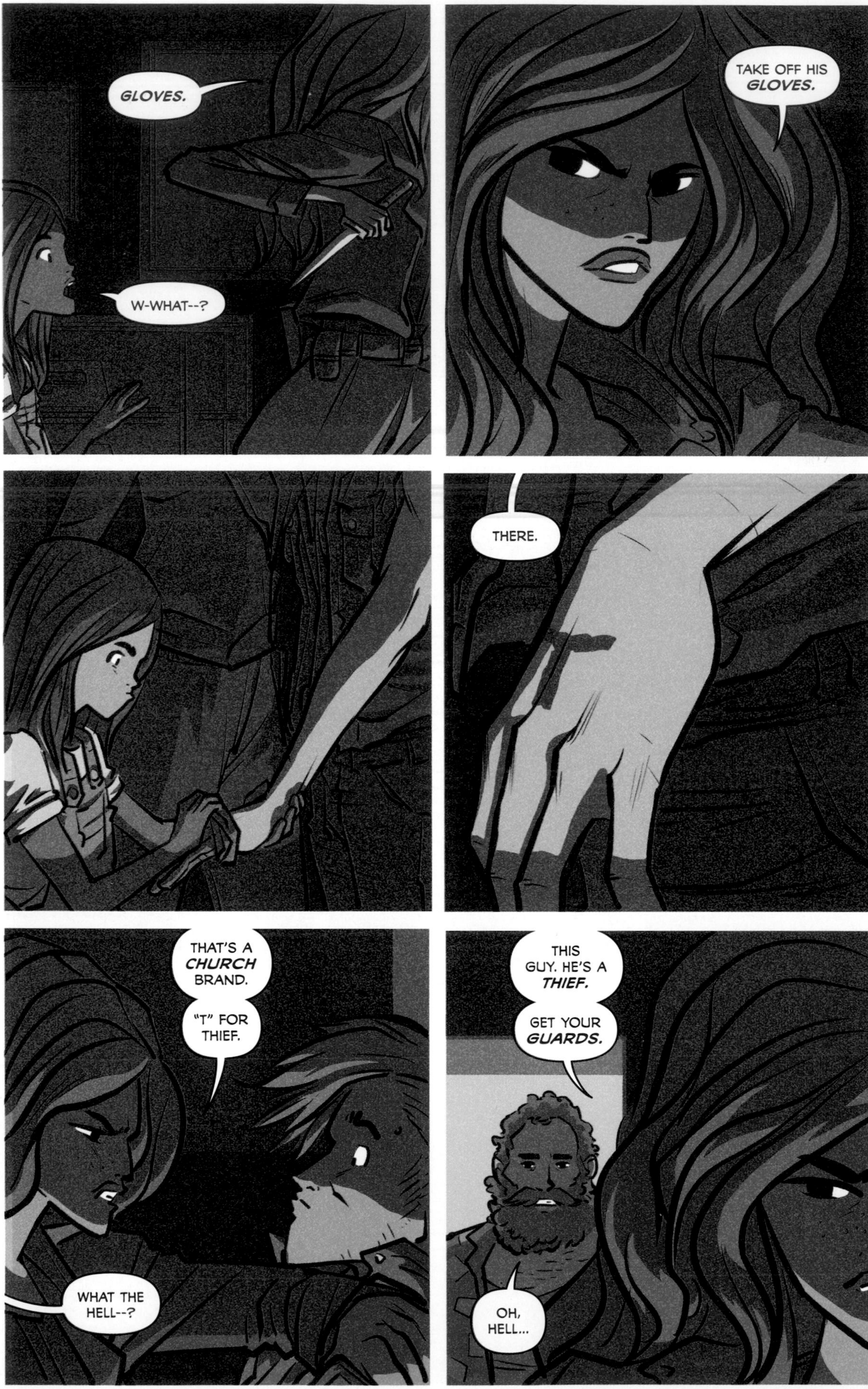
GLOVES.
W-WHAT--?
TAKE OFF HIS GLOVES.
THERE.
THAT'S A CHURCH BRAND.
"T" FOR THIEF.
WHAT THE HELL--?
THIS GUY. HE'S A THIEF.
GET YOUR GUARDS.
OH, HELL...

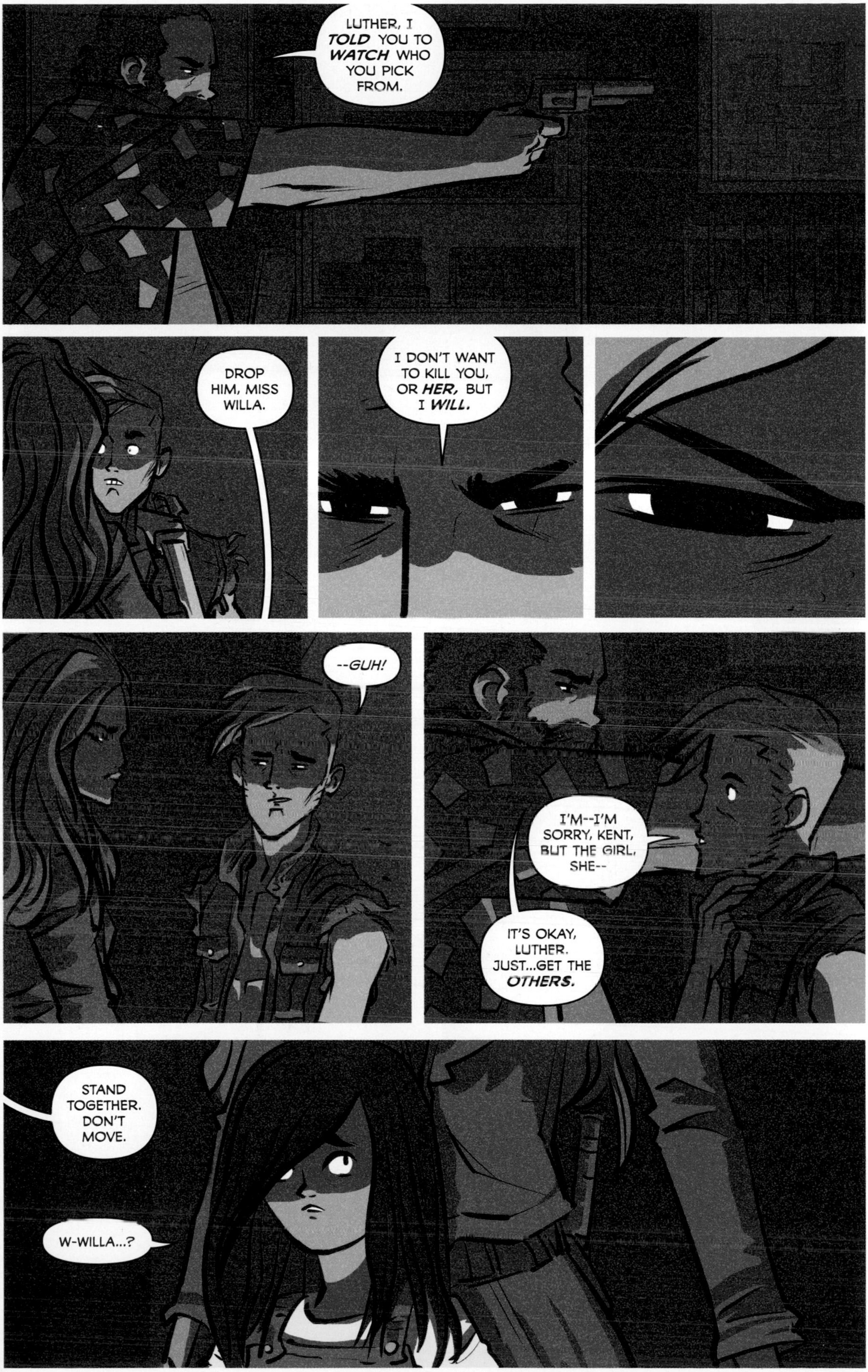
LUTHER, I TOLD YOU TO WATCH WHO YOU PICK FROM.
DROP HIM, MISS WILLA.
I DON'T WANT TO KILL YOU, OR HER, BUT I WILL.
--GUH!
I'M--I'M SORRY, KENT, BUT THE GIRL, SHE--
IT'S OKAY, LUTHER. JUST...GET THE OTHERS.
STAND TOGETHER. DON'T MOVE.
W-WILLA...?

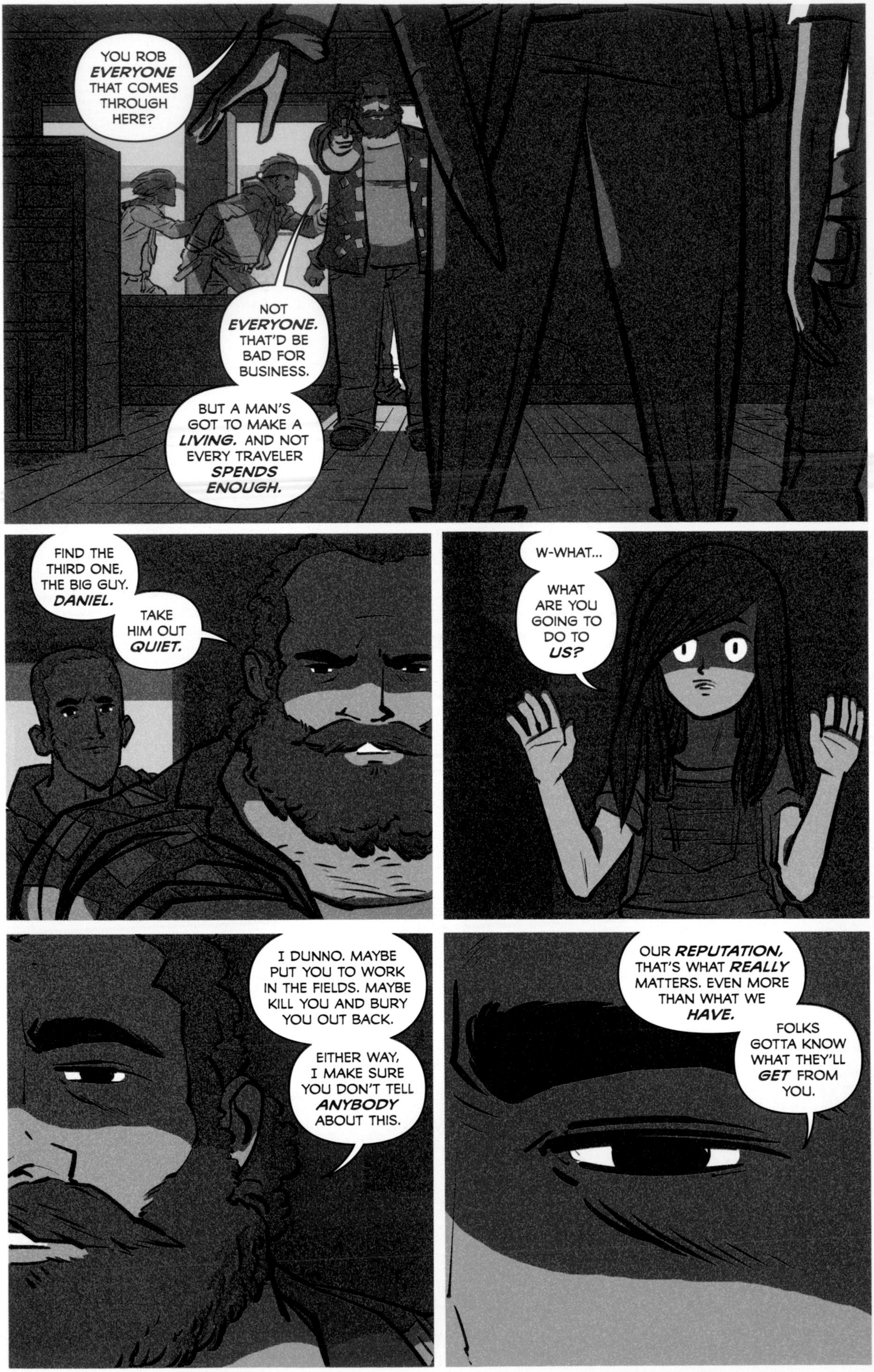

YOU ROB EVERYONE THAT COMES THROUGH HERE?
NOT EVERYONE. THAT'D BE BAD FOR BUSINESS.
BUT A MAN'S GOT TO MAKE A LIVING. AND NOT EVERY TRAVELER SPENDS ENOUGH.
FIND THE THIRD ONE, THE BIG GUY. DANIEL.
TAKE HIM OUT QUIET.
W-WHAT...
WHAT ARE YOU GOING TO DO TO US?
I DUNNO. MAYBE PUT YOU TO WORK IN THE FIELDS. MAYBE KILL YOU AND BURY YOU OUT BACK.
EITHER WAY, I MAKE SURE YOU DON'T TELL ANYBODY ABOUT THIS.
OUR REPUTATION, THAT'S WHAT REALLY MATTERS. EVEN MORE THAN WHAT WE HAVE.
FOLKS GOTTA KNOW WHAT THEY'LL GET FROM YOU.

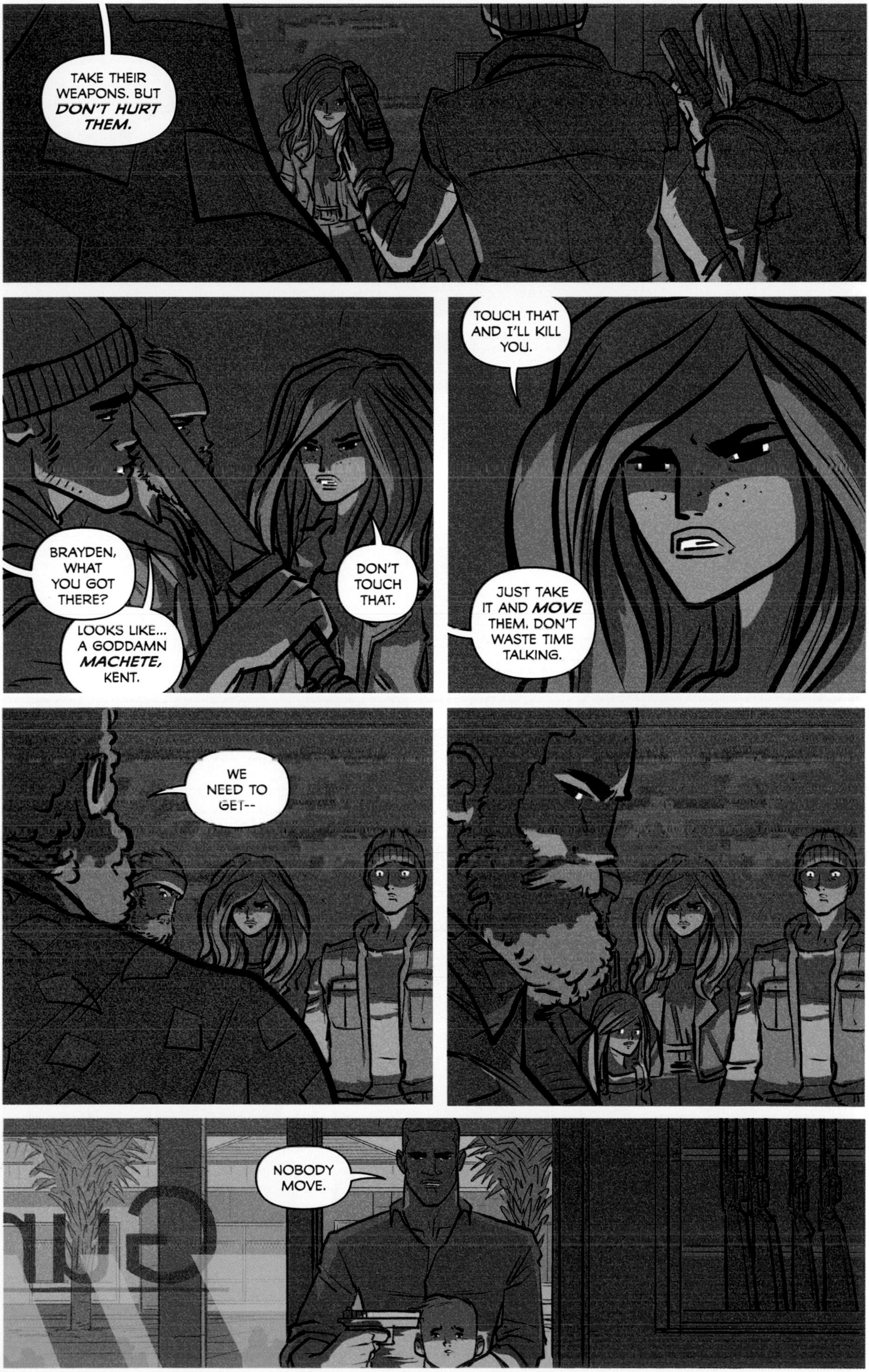
TAKE THEIR WEAPONS. BUT DON'T HURT THEM.
BRAYDEN, WHAT YOU GOT THERE?
LOOKS LIKE... A GODDAMN MACHETE, KENT.
DON'T TOUCH THAT.
TOUCH THAT AND I'LL KILL YOU.
JUST TAKE IT AND MOVE THEM. DON'T WASTE TIME TALKING.
WE NEED TO GET--
NOBODY MOVE.

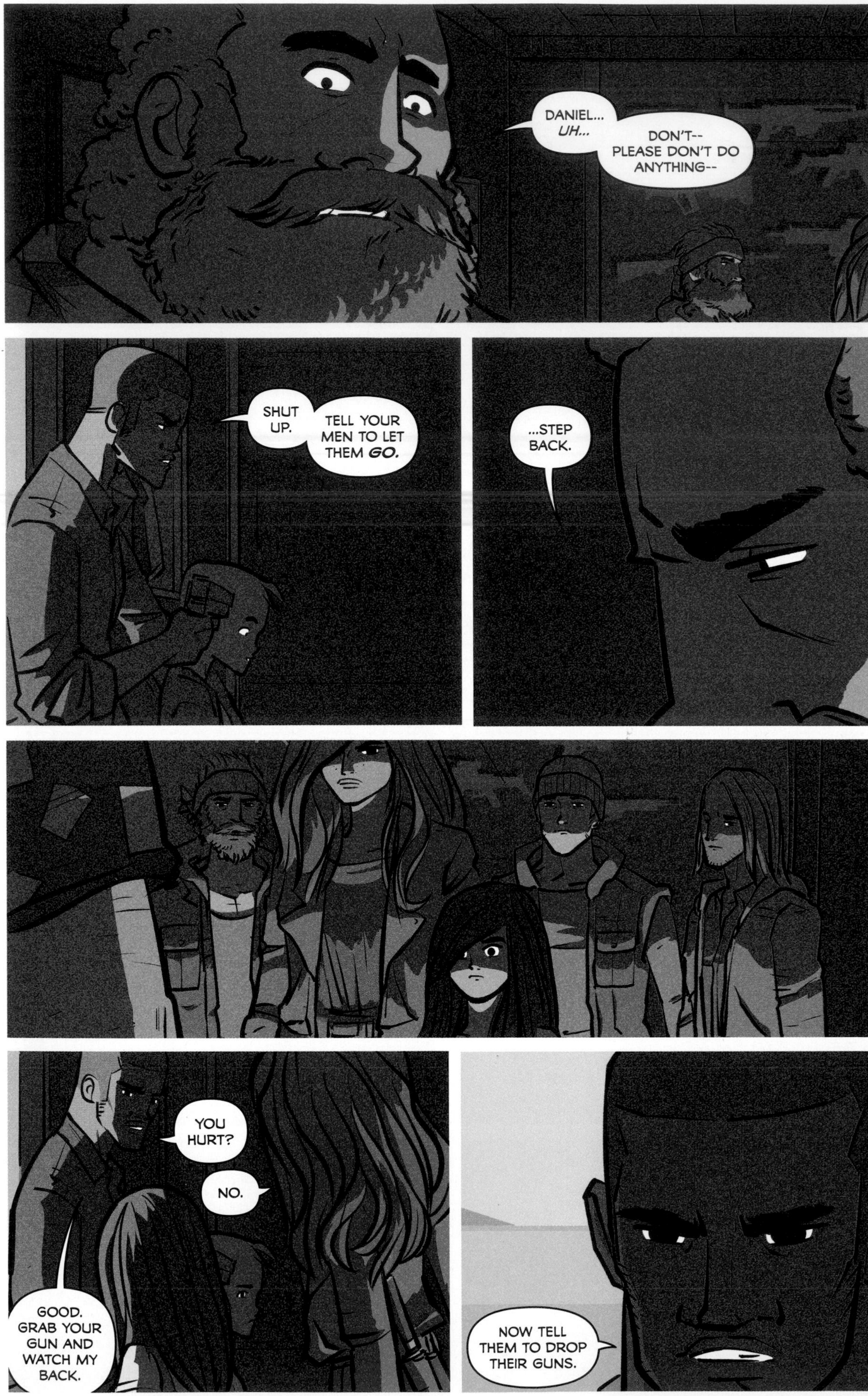
DANIEL... UH...
DON'T-- PLEASE DON'T DO ANYTHING--
SHUT UP.
TELL YOUR MEN TO LET THEM GO.
...STEP BACK.
YOU HURT?
NO.
GOOD. GRAB YOUR GUN AND WATCH MY BACK.
NOW TELL THEM TO DROP THEIR GUNS.

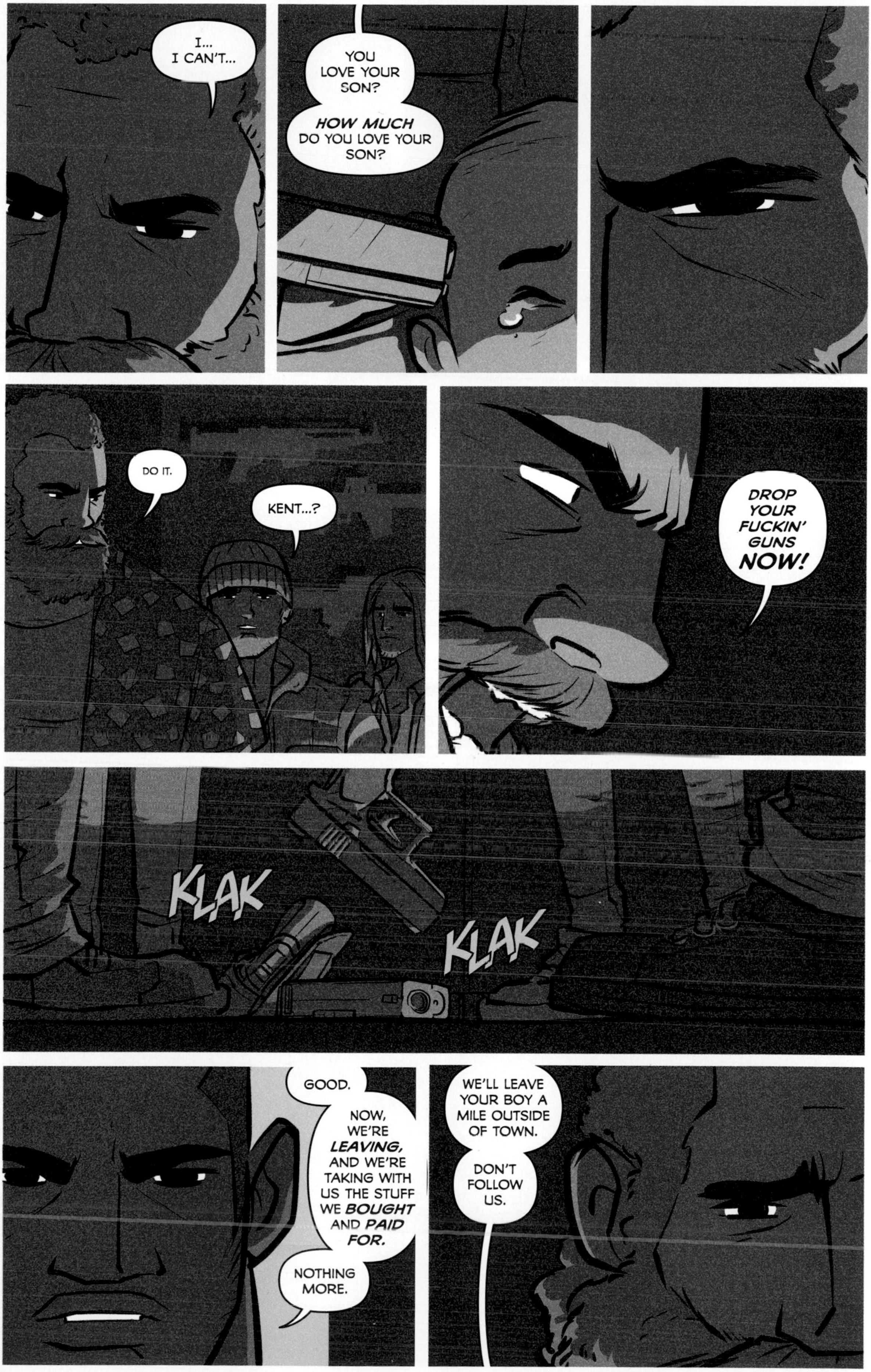
I...
I CAN'T...
YOU LOVE YOUR SON?
HOW MUCH DO YOU LOVE YOUR SON?
DO IT.
KENT...?
DROP YOUR FUCKIN' GUNS NOW!
KLAK
KLAK
GOOD.
NOW, WE'RE LEAVING, AND WE'RE TAKING WITH US THE STUFF WE BOUGHT AND PAID FOR.
NOTHING MORE.
WE'LL LEAVE YOUR BOY A MILE OUTSIDE OF TOWN.
DON'T FOLLOW US.

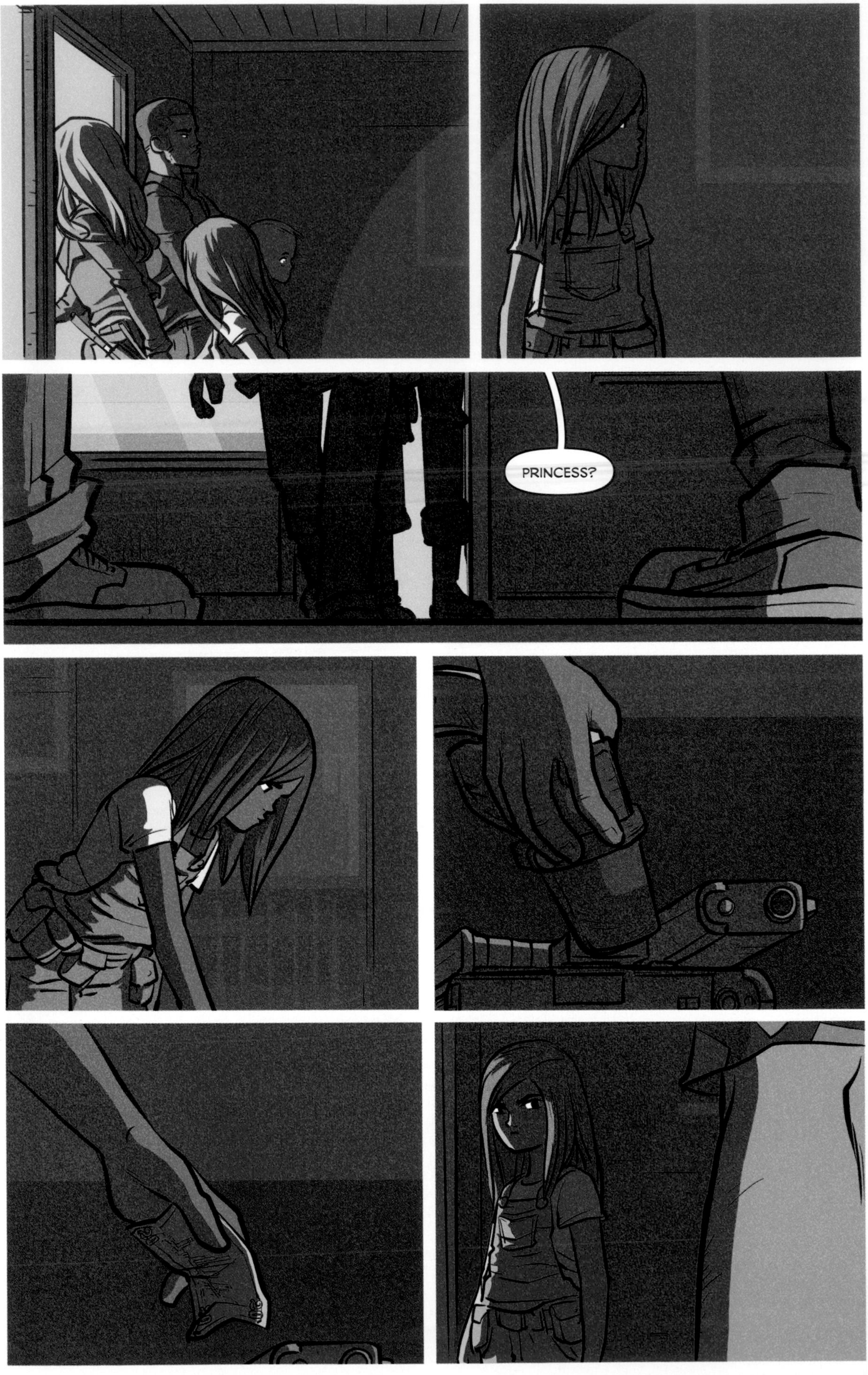
PRINCESS?

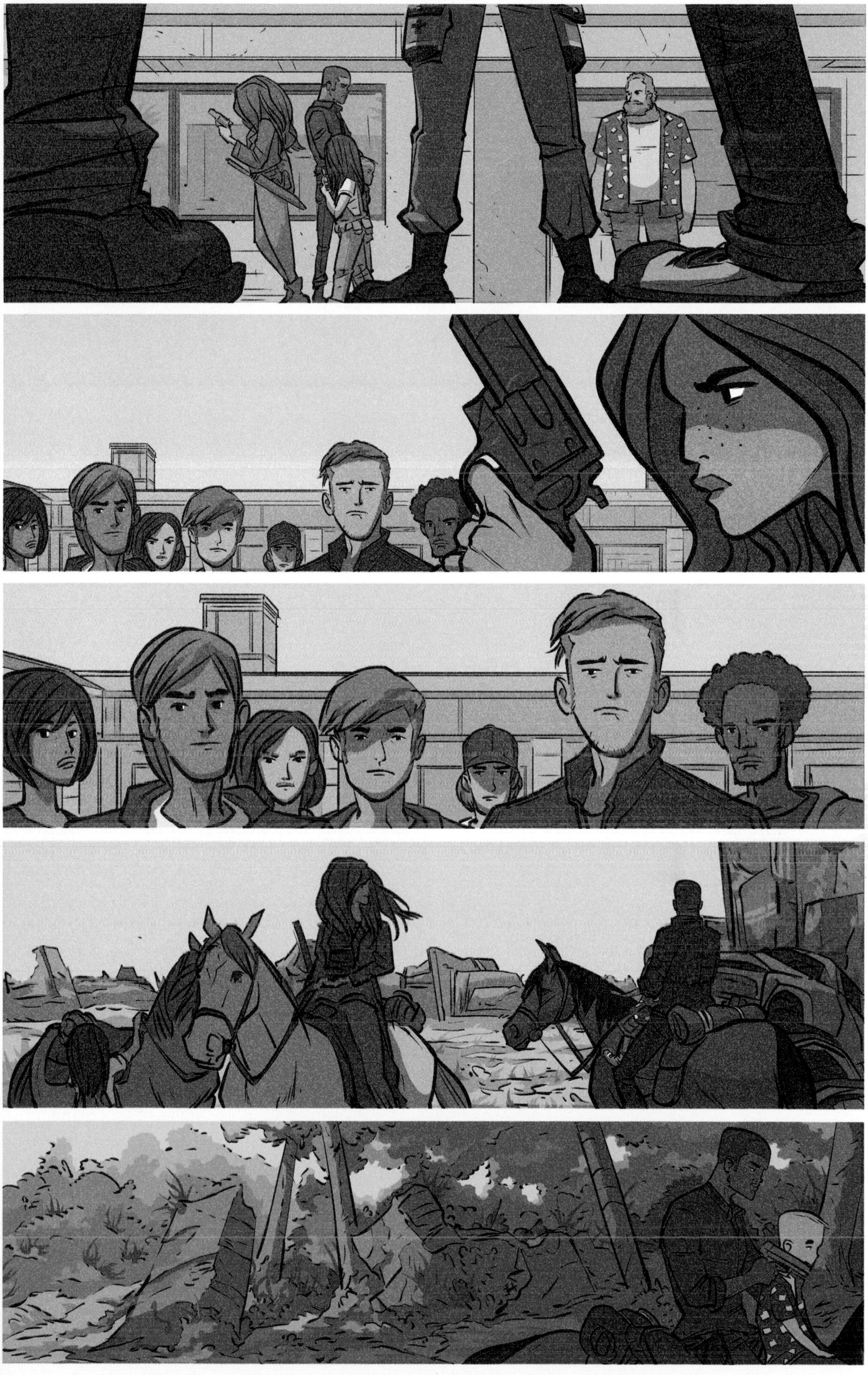

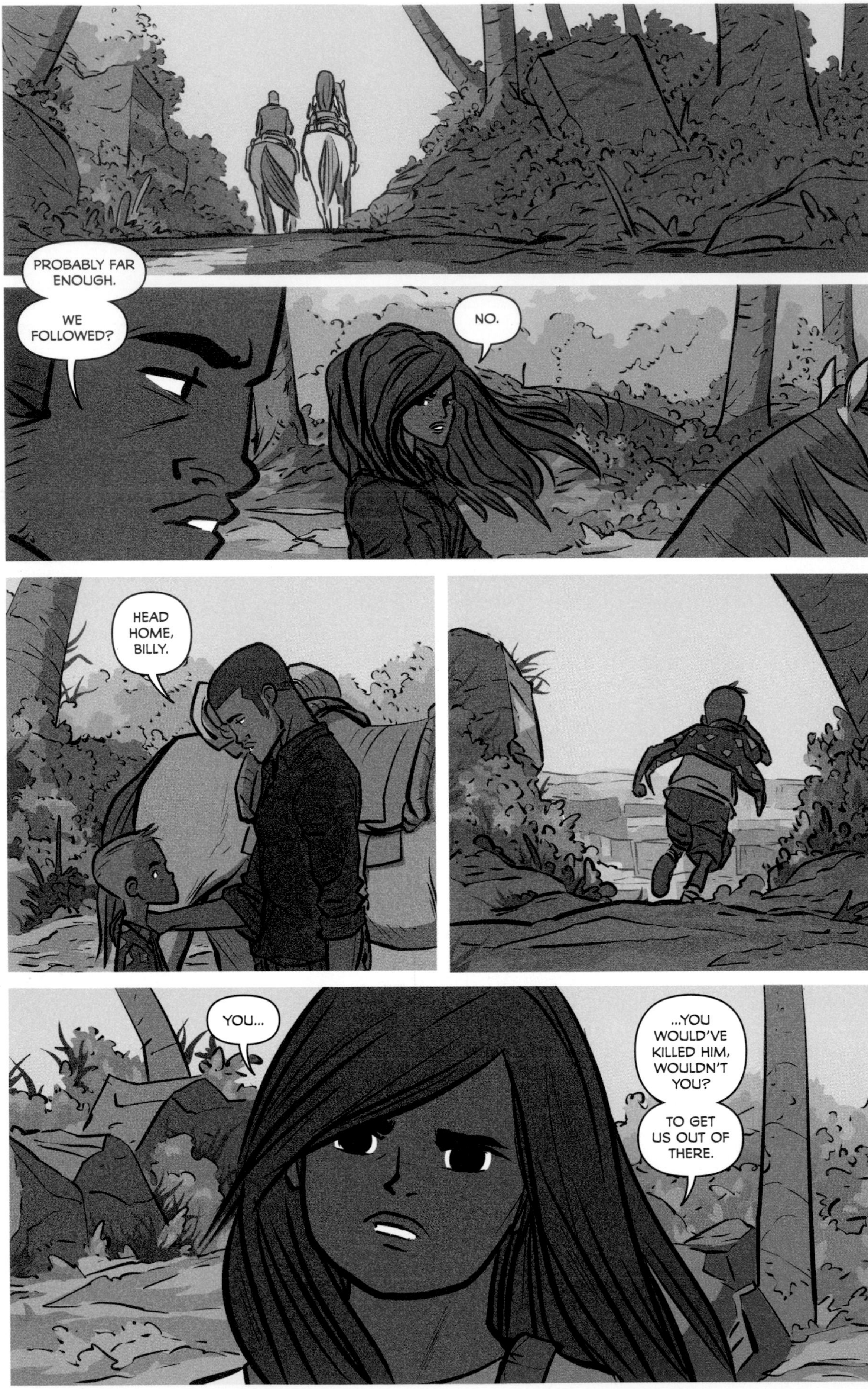
PROBABLY FAR ENOUGH.
WE FOLLOWED?
NO.
HEAD HOME, BILLY.
YOU...
...YOU WOULD'VE KILLED HIM, WOULDN'T YOU?
TO GET US OUT OF THERE.

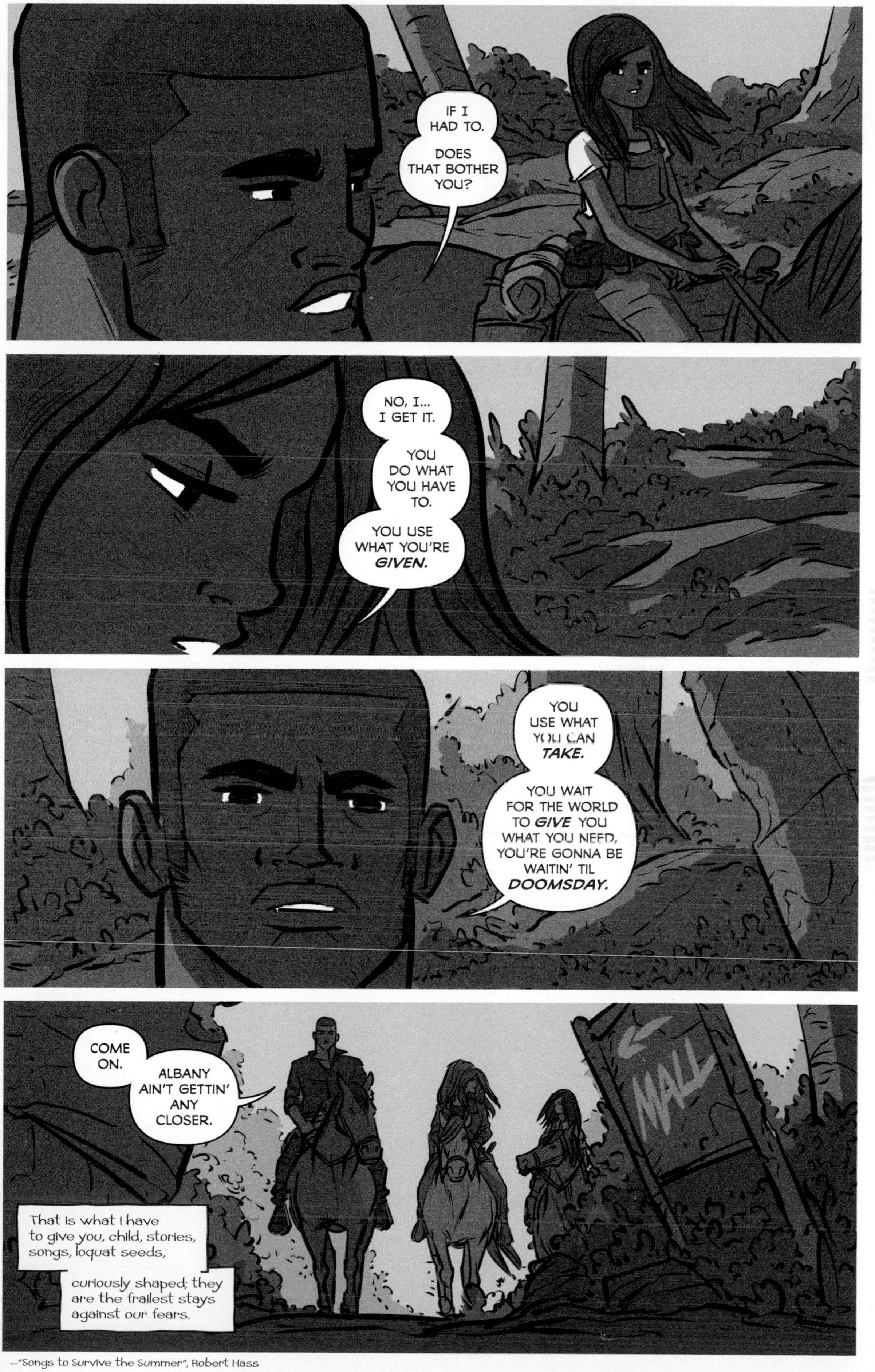
IF I HAD TO.
DOES THAT BOTHER YOU?
NO, I... I GET IT.
YOU DO WHAT YOU HAVE TO.
YOU USE WHAT YOU'RE *GIVEN.*
YOU USE WHAT YOU CAN *TAKE.*
YOU WAIT FOR THE WORLD TO *GIVE* YOU WHAT YOU NEED, YOU'RE GONNA BE WAITIN' TIL *DOOMSDAY.*
COME ON.
ALBANY AIN'T GETTIN' ANY CLOSER.
MALL
That is what I have to give you, child, stories, songs, loquat seeds,
curiously shaped; they are the frailest stays against our fears.

--"Songs to Survive the Summer", Robert Hass

3

WILD

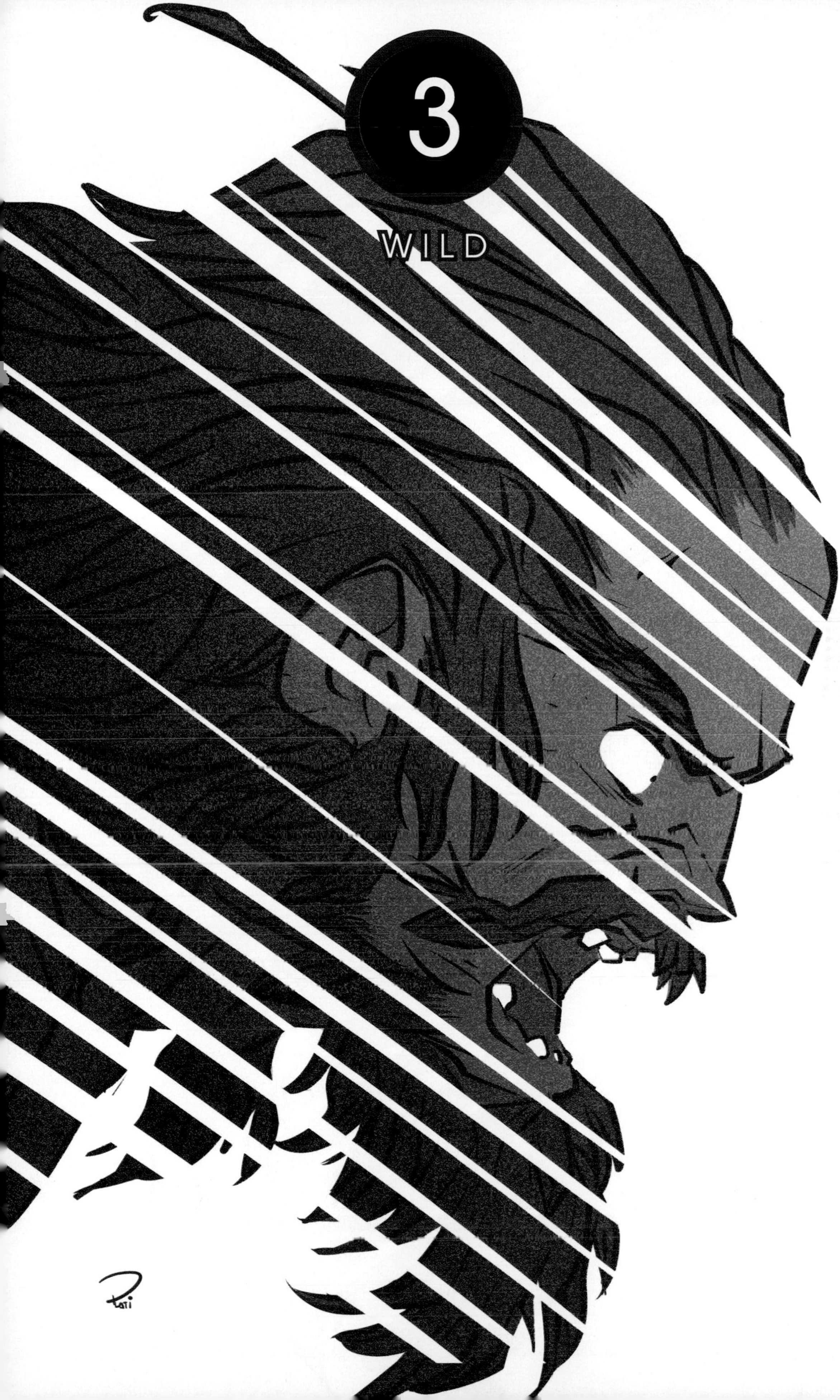

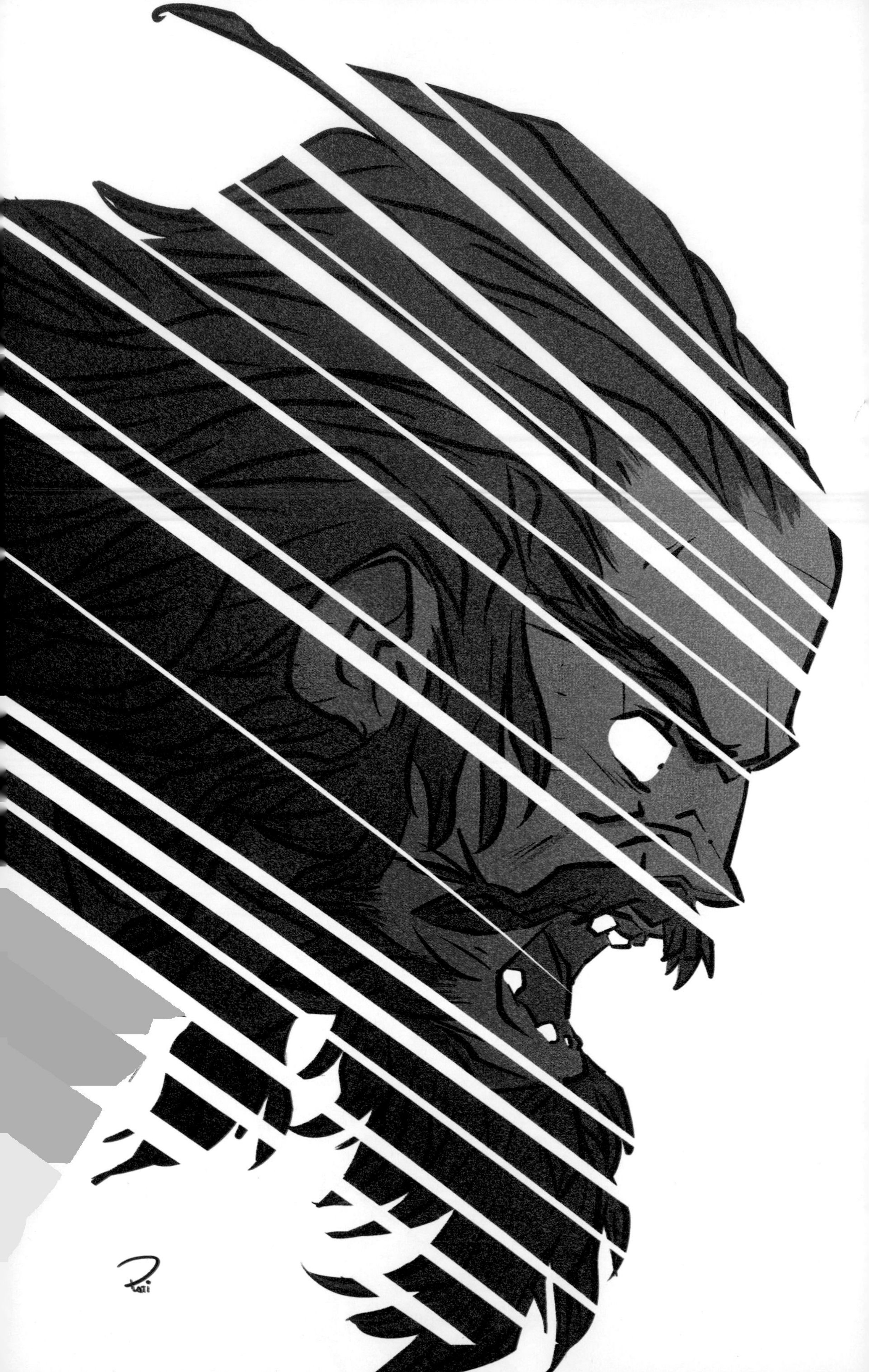

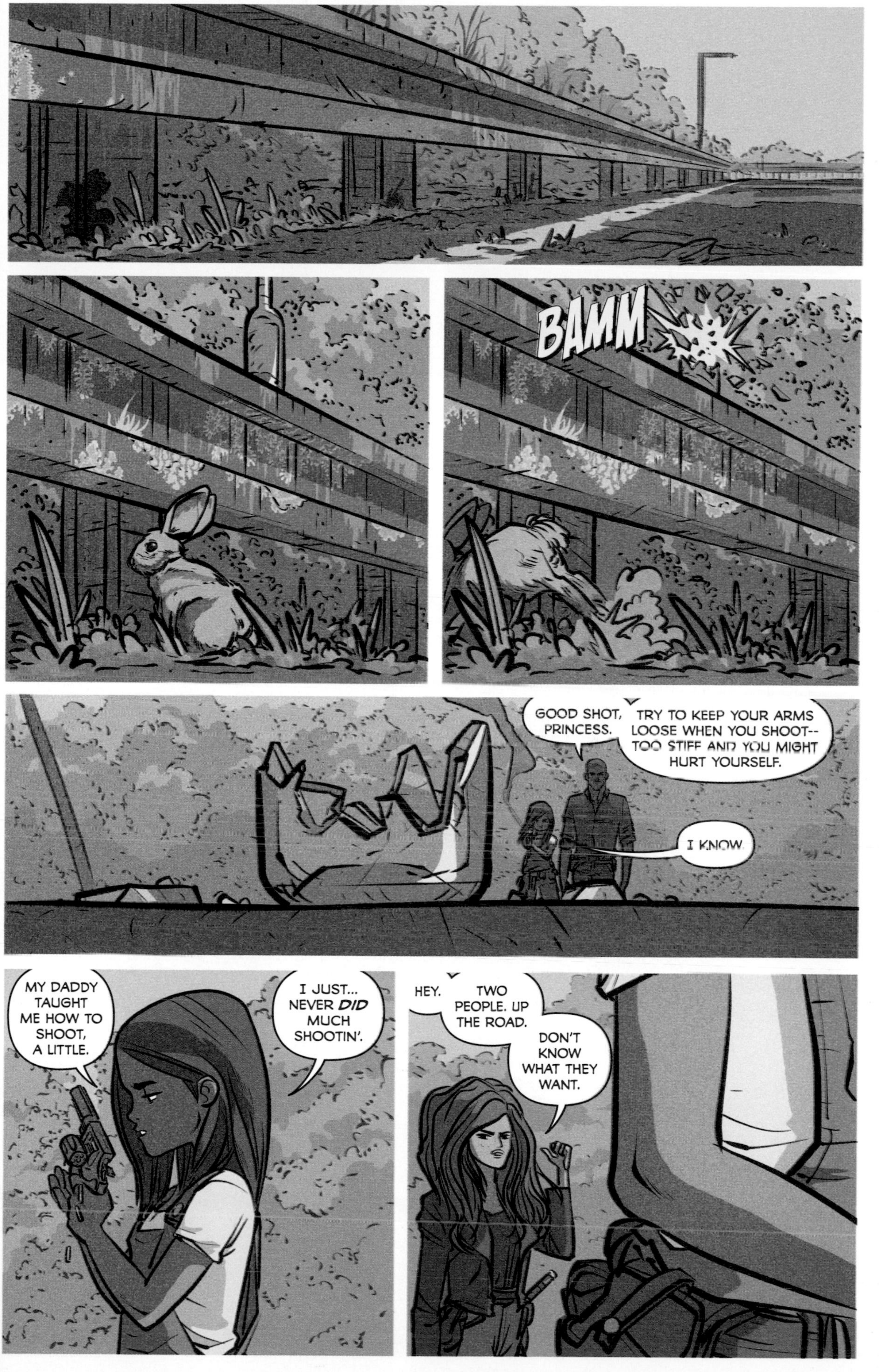
BAMM
GOOD SHOT, PRINCESS.
TRY TO KEEP YOUR ARMS LOOSE WHEN YOU SHOOT-- TOO STIFF AND YOU MIGHT HURT YOURSELF.
I KNOW.
MY DADDY TAUGHT ME HOW TO SHOOT, A LITTLE.
I JUST... NEVER *DID* MUCH SHOOTIN'.
HEY.
TWO PEOPLE. UP THE ROAD.
DON'T KNOW WHAT THEY WANT.

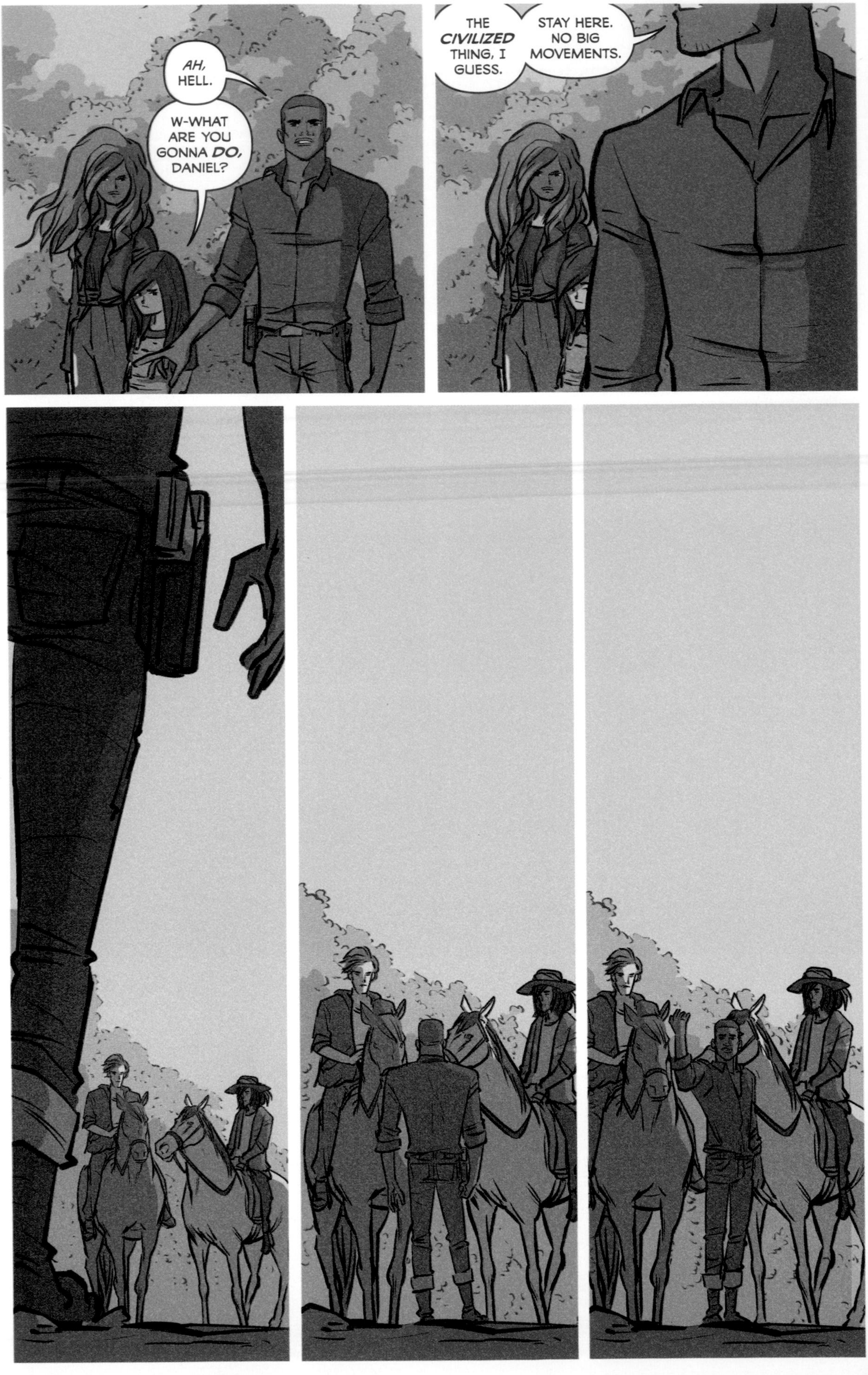
AH, HELL.
W-WHAT ARE YOU GONNA DO, DANIEL?
THE CIVILIZED THING, I GUESS.
STAY HERE. NO BIG MOVEMENTS.

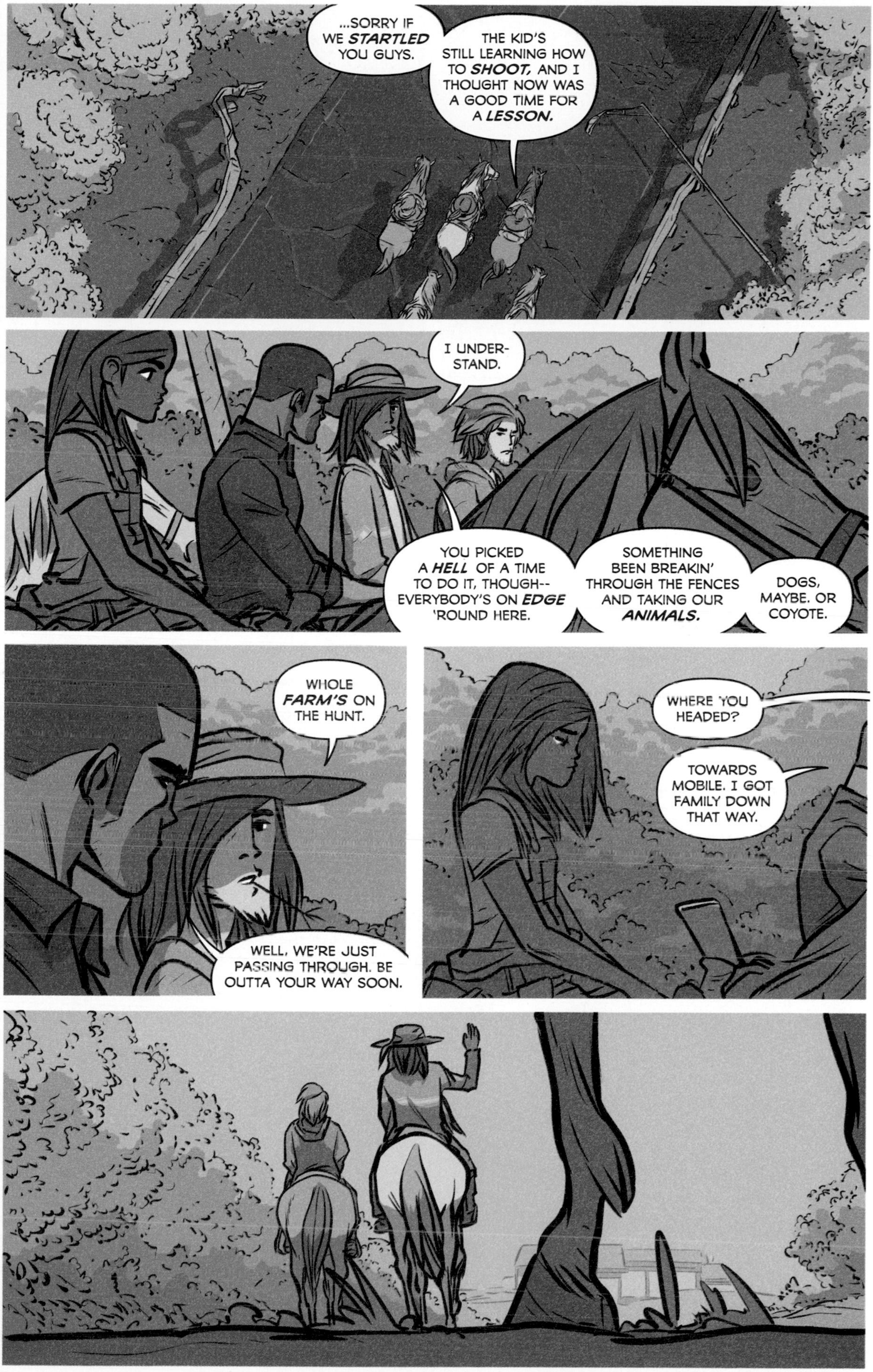
...SORRY IF WE STARTLED YOU GUYS.
THE KID'S STILL LEARNING HOW TO SHOOT, AND I THOUGHT NOW WAS A GOOD TIME FOR A LESSON.
I UNDER-STAND.
YOU PICKED A HELL OF A TIME TO DO IT, THOUGH-- EVERYBODY'S ON EDGE 'ROUND HERE.
SOMETHING BEEN BREAKIN' THROUGH THE FENCES AND TAKING OUR ANIMALS.
DOGS, MAYBE. OR COYOTE.
WHOLE FARM'S ON THE HUNT.
WELL, WE'RE JUST PASSING THROUGH. BE OUTTA YOUR WAY SOON.
WHERE YOU HEADED?
TOWARDS MOBILE. I GOT FAMILY DOWN THAT WAY.

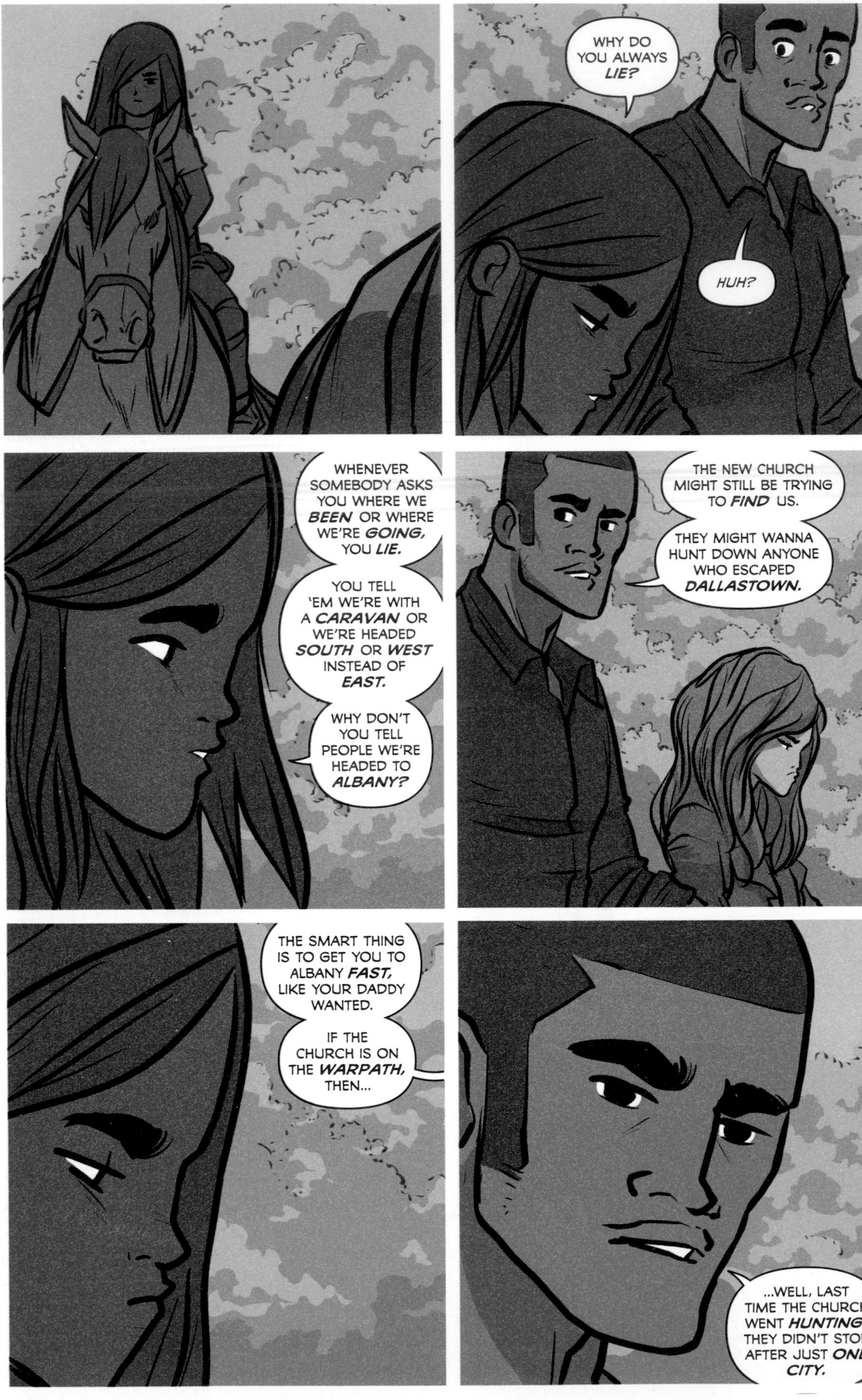
WHY DO YOU ALWAYS LIE?
HUH?
WHENEVER SOMEBODY ASKS YOU WHERE WE BEEN OR WHERE WE'RE GOING, YOU LIE.
YOU TELL 'EM WE'RE WITH A CARAVAN OR WE'RE HEADED SOUTH OR WEST INSTEAD OF EAST.
WHY DON'T YOU TELL PEOPLE WE'RE HEADED TO ALBANY?
THE NEW CHURCH MIGHT STILL BE TRYING TO FIND US.
THEY MIGHT WANNA HUNT DOWN ANYONE WHO ESCAPED DALLASTOWN.
THE SMART THING IS TO GET YOU TO ALBANY FAST, LIKE YOUR DADDY WANTED.
IF THE CHURCH IS ON THE WARPATH, THEN...
...WELL, LAST TIME THE CHURCH WENT HUNTING, THEY DIDN'T STOP AFTER JUST ONE CITY.

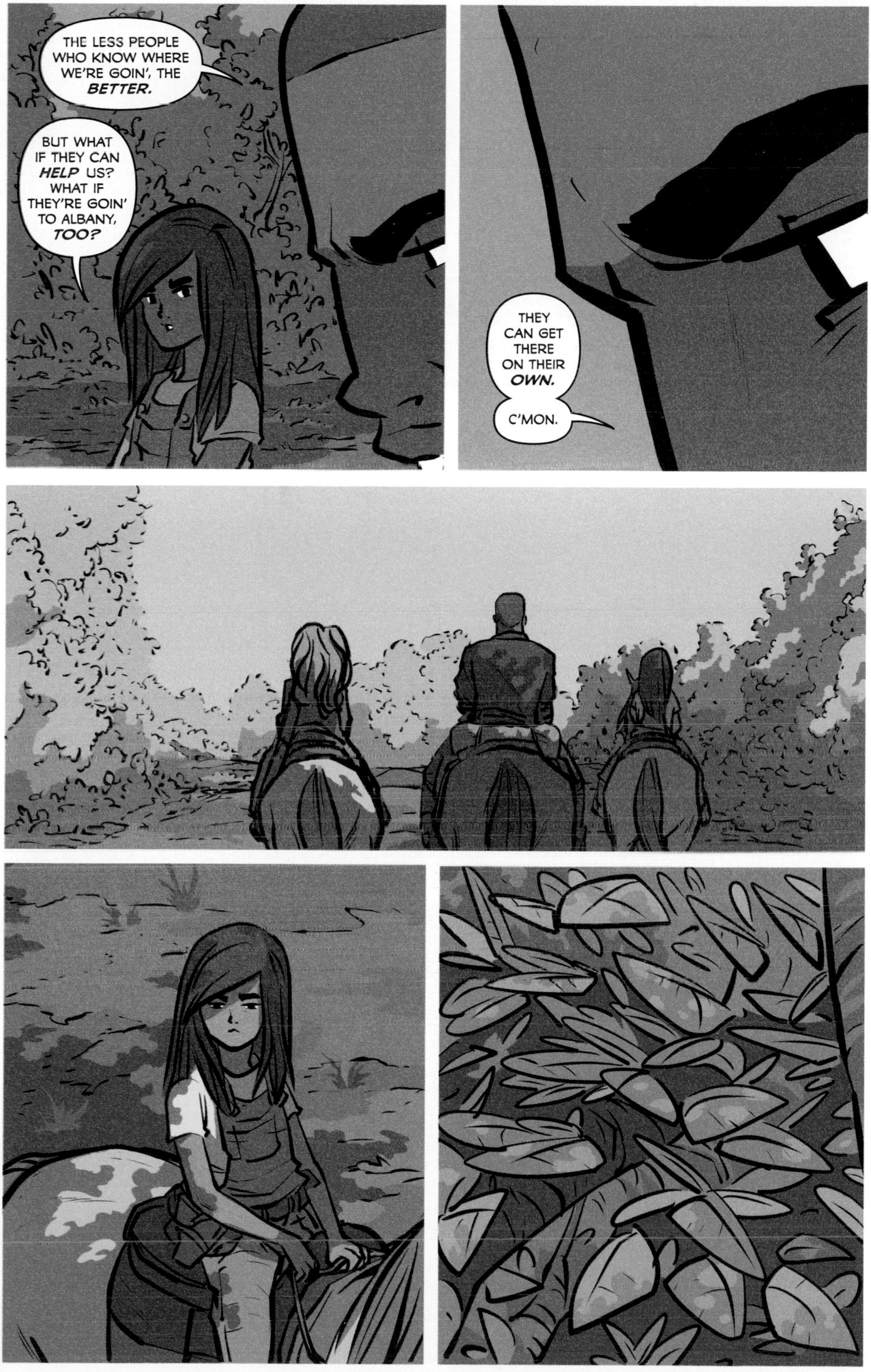
THE LESS PEOPLE WHO KNOW WHERE WE'RE GOIN', THE *BETTER.*
BUT WHAT IF THEY CAN *HELP* US? WHAT IF THEY'RE GOIN' TO ALBANY, *TOO?*
THEY CAN GET THERE ON THEIR *OWN.*
C'MON.

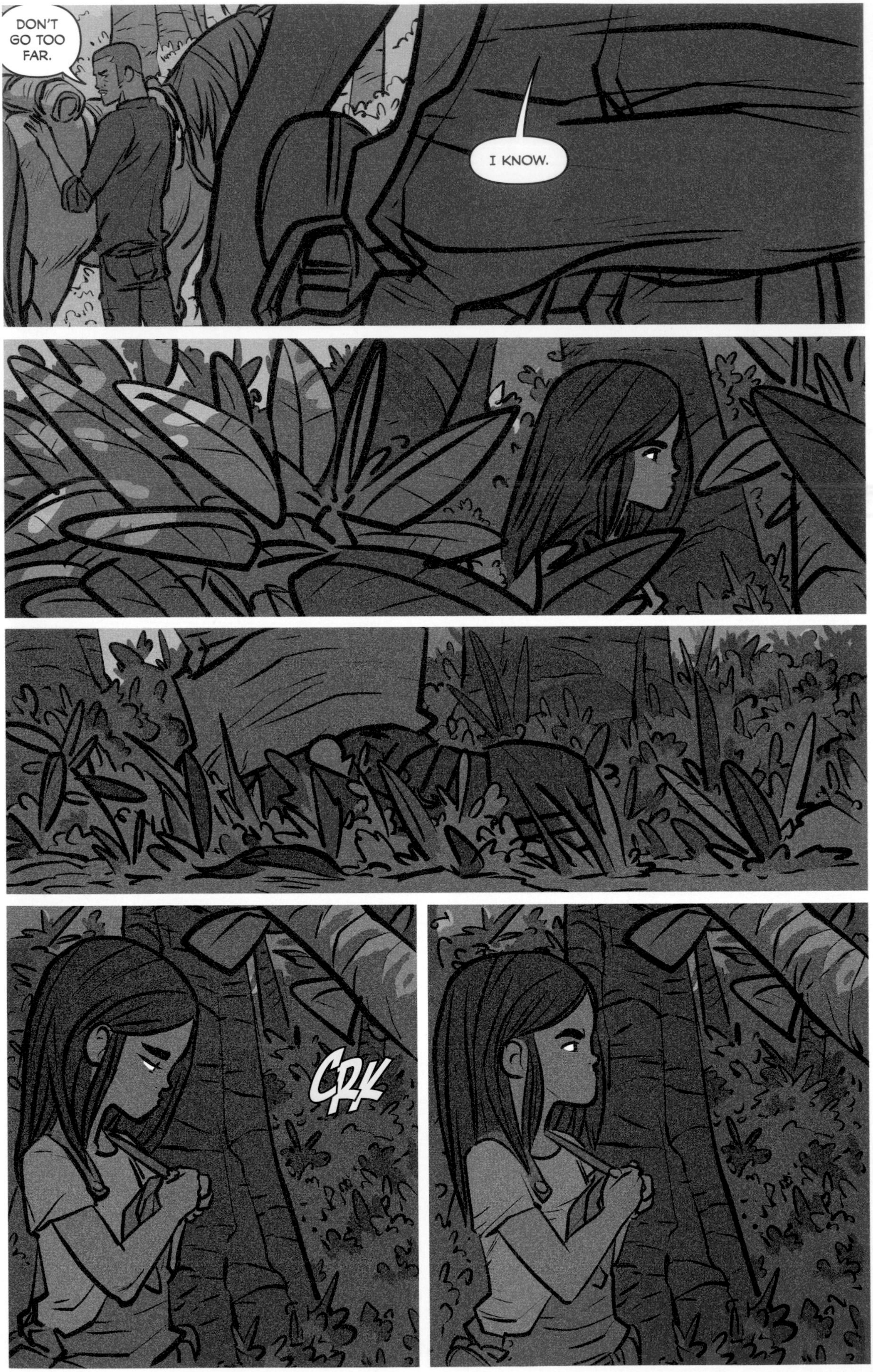
DON'T GO TOO FAR.
I KNOW.
CRK

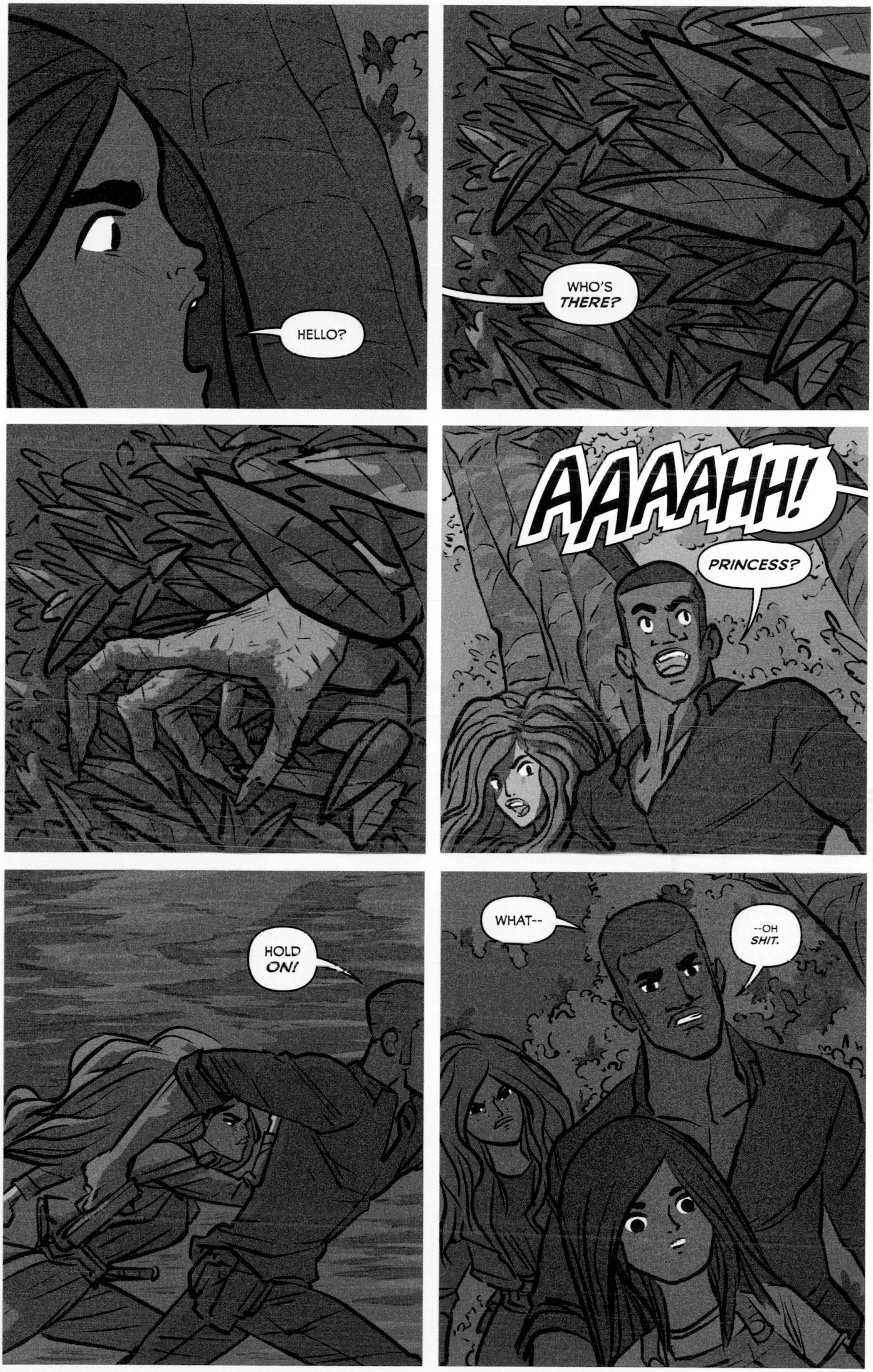
HELLO?
WHO'S *THERE?*
AAAAHH!
PRINCESS?
HOLD *ON!*
WHAT--
--OH *SHIT.*

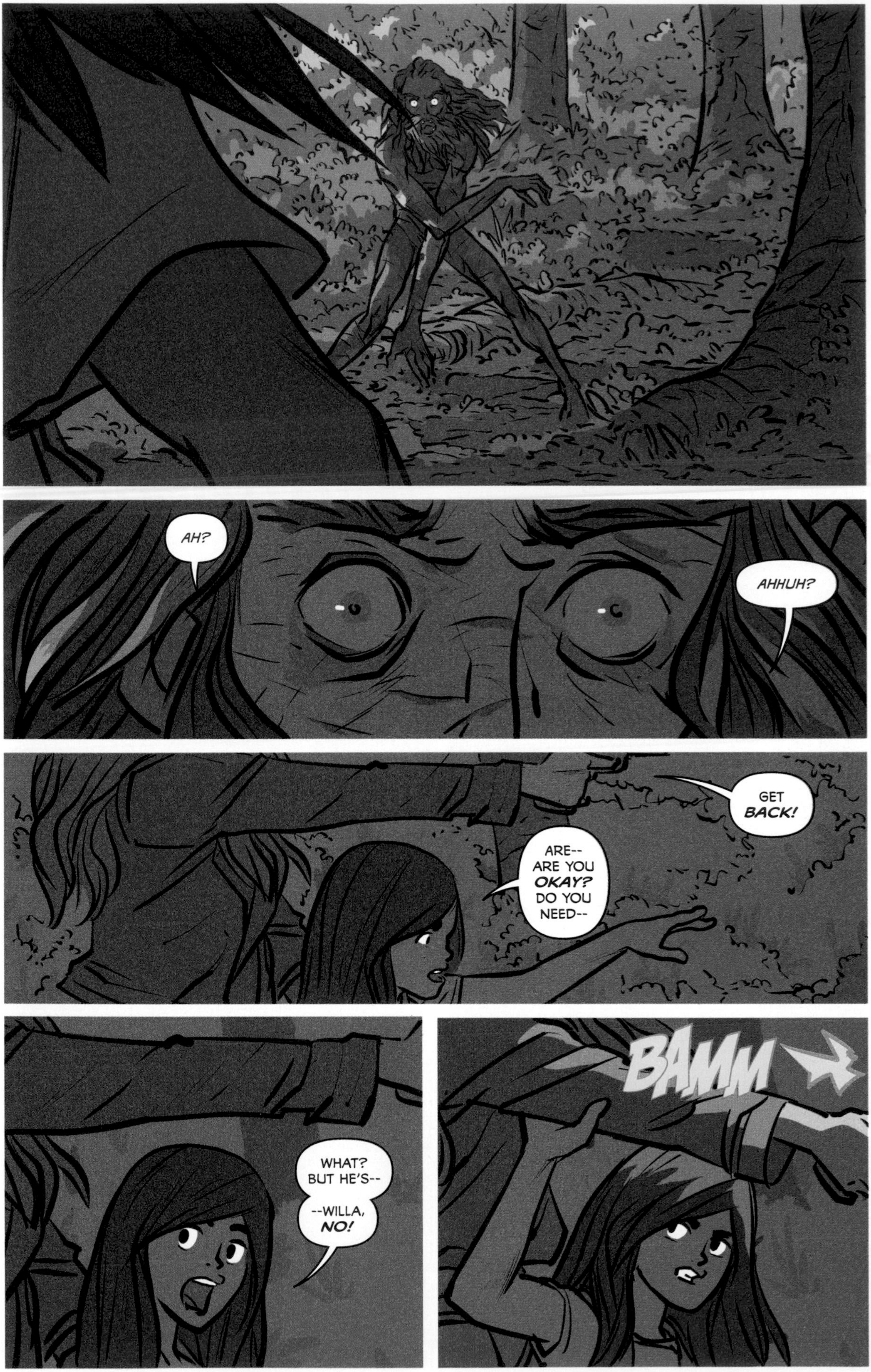
AH?
AHHUH?
GET BACK!
ARE-- ARE YOU OKAY? DO YOU NEED--
WHAT? BUT HE'S--
--WILLA, NO!
BAMM

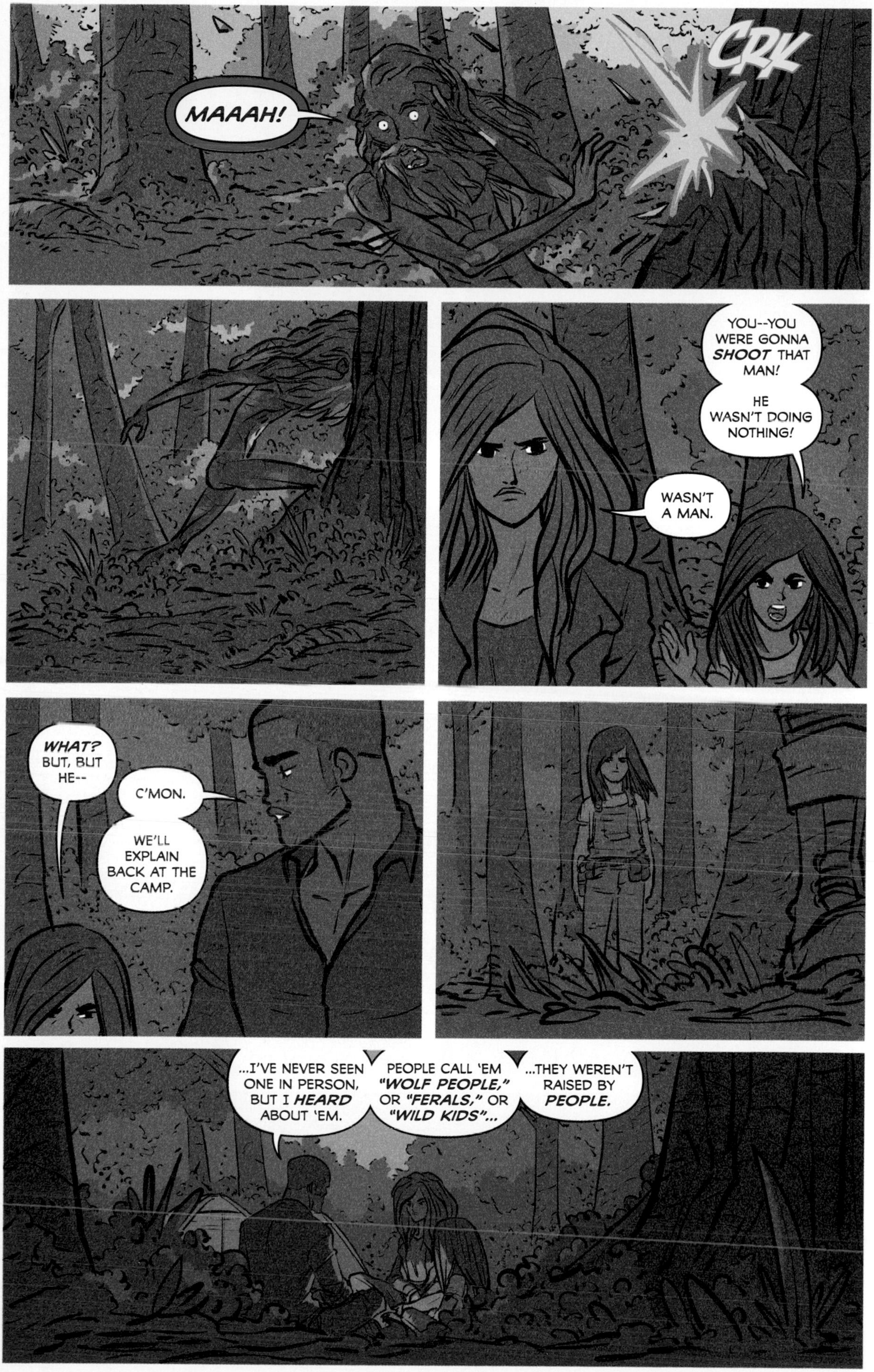

MAAAH!
CRK
YOU--YOU WERE GONNA SHOOT THAT MAN!
HE WASN'T DOING NOTHING!
WASN'T A MAN.
WHAT? BUT, BUT HE--
C'MON.
WE'LL EXPLAIN BACK AT THE CAMP.
...I'VE NEVER SEEN ONE IN PERSON, BUT I HEARD ABOUT 'EM.
PEOPLE CALL 'EM "WOLF PEOPLE," OR "FERALS," OR "WILD KIDS"...
...THEY WEREN'T RAISED BY PEOPLE.

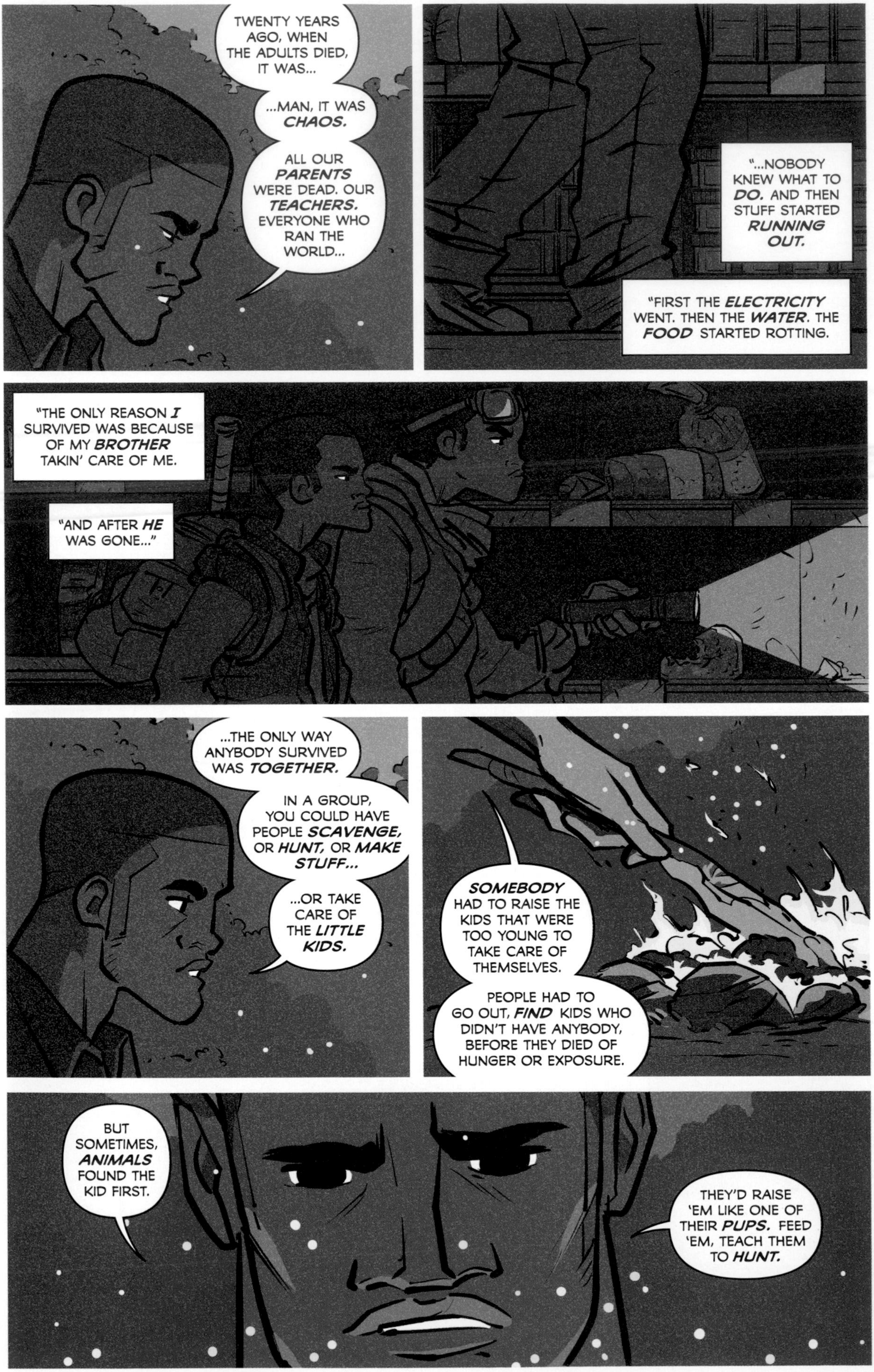
TWENTY YEARS AGO, WHEN THE ADULTS DIED, IT WAS...
...MAN, IT WAS CHAOS.
ALL OUR PARENTS WERE DEAD. OUR TEACHERS. EVERYONE WHO RAN THE WORLD...
"...NOBODY KNEW WHAT TO DO. AND THEN STUFF STARTED RUNNING OUT.
"FIRST THE ELECTRICITY WENT. THEN THE WATER. THE FOOD STARTED ROTTING.
"THE ONLY REASON I SURVIVED WAS BECAUSE OF MY BROTHER TAKIN' CARE OF ME.
"AND AFTER HE WAS GONE..."
...THE ONLY WAY ANYBODY SURVIVED WAS TOGETHER.
IN A GROUP, YOU COULD HAVE PEOPLE SCAVENGE, OR HUNT, OR MAKE STUFF...
...OR TAKE CARE OF THE LITTLE KIDS.
SOMEBODY HAD TO RAISE THE KIDS THAT WERE TOO YOUNG TO TAKE CARE OF THEMSELVES.
PEOPLE HAD TO GO OUT, FIND KIDS WHO DIDN'T HAVE ANYBODY, BEFORE THEY DIED OF HUNGER OR EXPOSURE.
BUT SOMETIMES, ANIMALS FOUND THE KID FIRST.
THEY'D RAISE 'EM LIKE ONE OF THEIR PUPS. FEED 'EM, TEACH THEM TO HUNT.

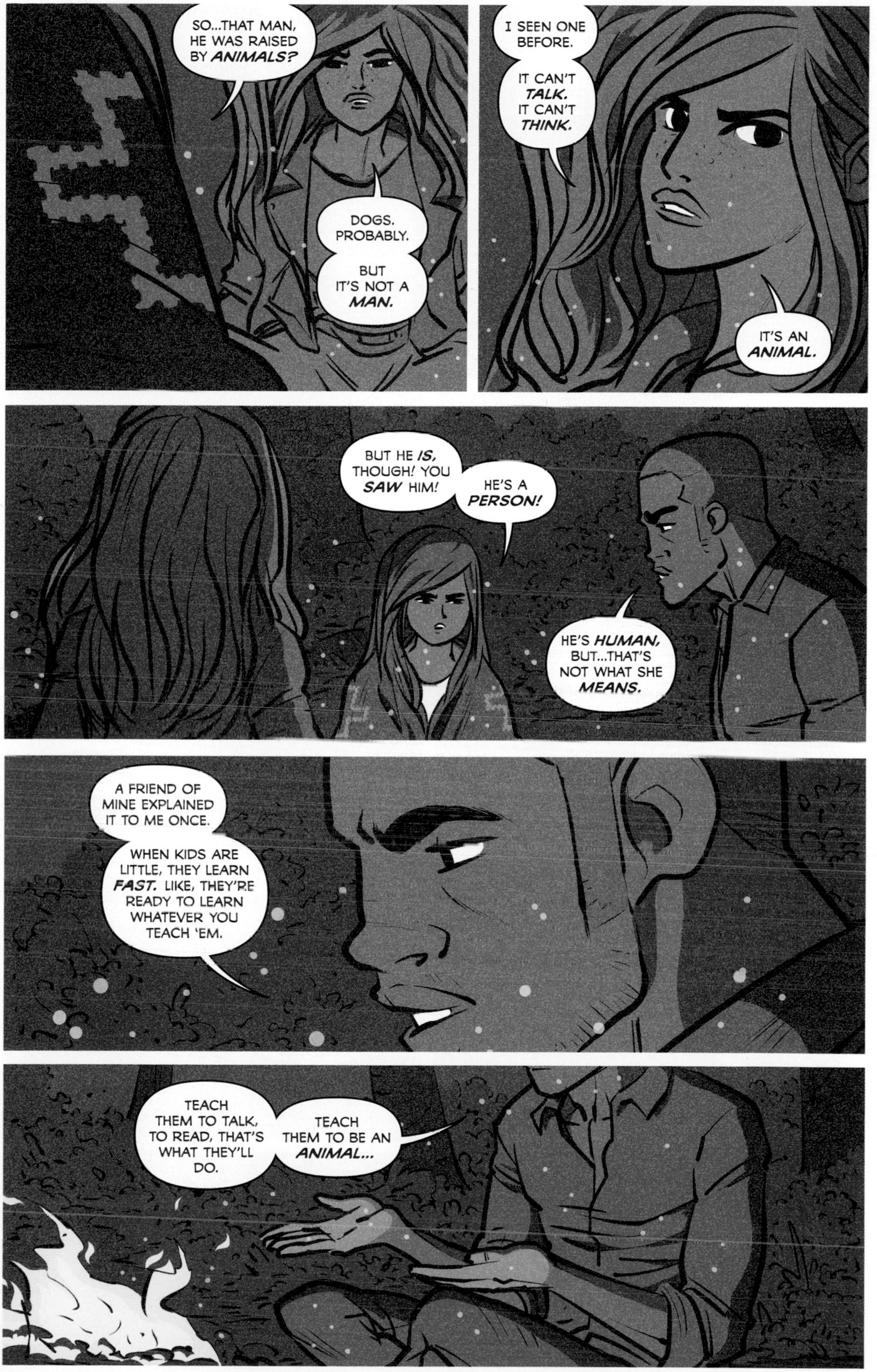
SO...THAT MAN, HE WAS RAISED BY ANIMALS?
DOGS. PROBABLY.
BUT IT'S NOT A MAN.
I SEEN ONE BEFORE.
IT CAN'T TALK. IT CAN'T THINK.
IT'S AN ANIMAL.
BUT HE IS, THOUGH! YOU SAW HIM!
HE'S A PERSON!
HE'S HUMAN, BUT...THAT'S NOT WHAT SHE MEANS.
A FRIEND OF MINE EXPLAINED IT TO ME ONCE.
WHEN KIDS ARE LITTLE, THEY LEARN FAST. LIKE, THEY'RE READY TO LEARN WHATEVER YOU TEACH 'EM.
TEACH THEM TO TALK, TO READ, THAT'S WHAT THEY'LL DO.
TEACH THEM TO BE AN ANIMAL...

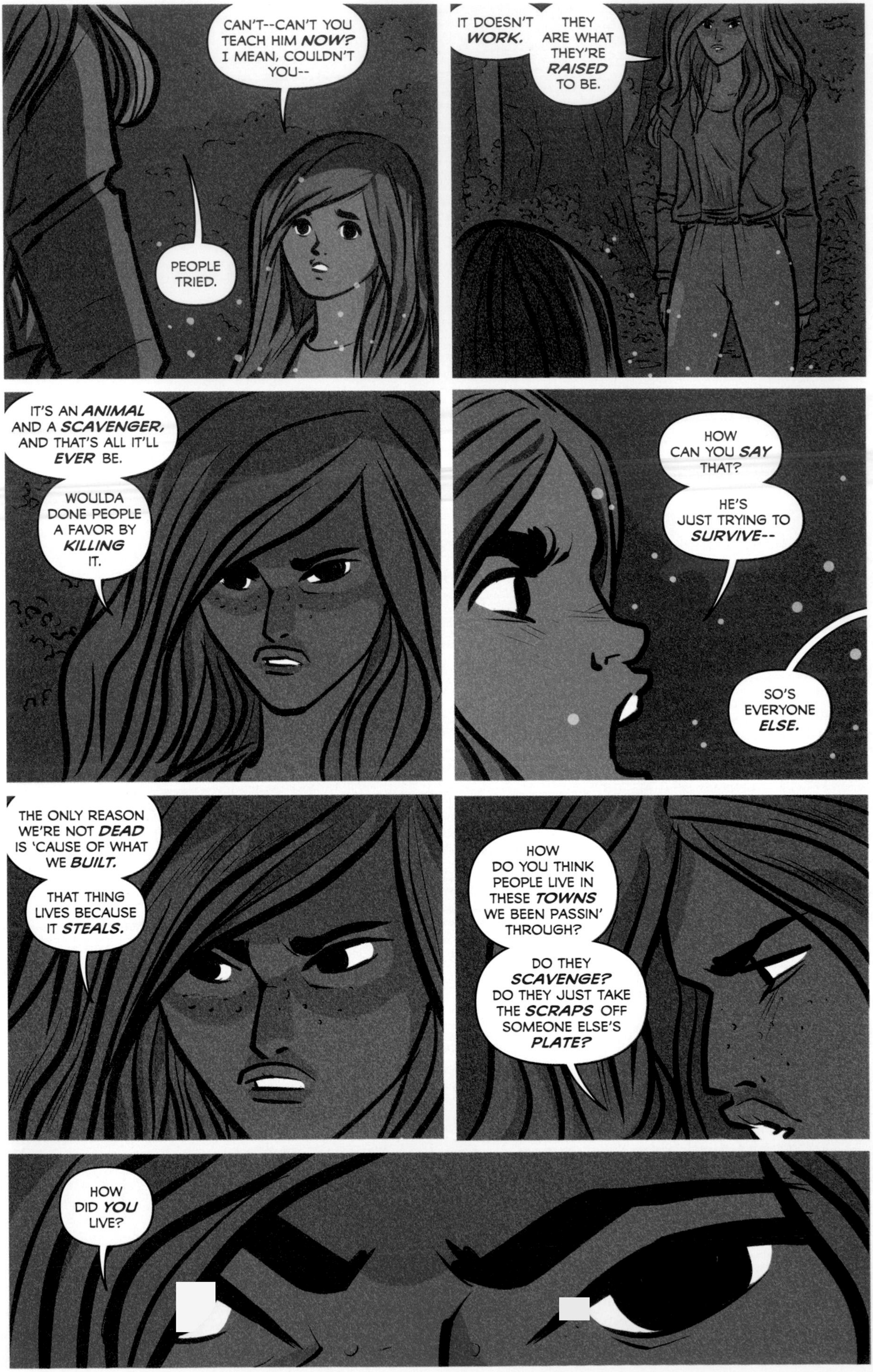
CAN'T--CAN'T YOU TEACH HIM NOW? I MEAN, COULDN'T YOU--
PEOPLE TRIED.
IT DOESN'T WORK.
THEY ARE WHAT THEY'RE RAISED TO BE.
IT'S AN ANIMAL AND A SCAVENGER, AND THAT'S ALL IT'LL EVER BE.
WOULDA DONE PEOPLE A FAVOR BY KILLING IT.
HOW CAN YOU SAY THAT?
HE'S JUST TRYING TO SURVIVE--
SO'S EVERYONE ELSE.
THE ONLY REASON WE'RE NOT DEAD IS 'CAUSE OF WHAT WE BUILT.
THAT THING LIVES BECAUSE IT STEALS.
HOW DO YOU THINK PEOPLE LIVE IN THESE TOWNS WE BEEN PASSIN' THROUGH?
DO THEY SCAVENGE? DO THEY JUST TAKE THE SCRAPS OFF SOMEONE ELSE'S PLATE?
HOW DID YOU LIVE?

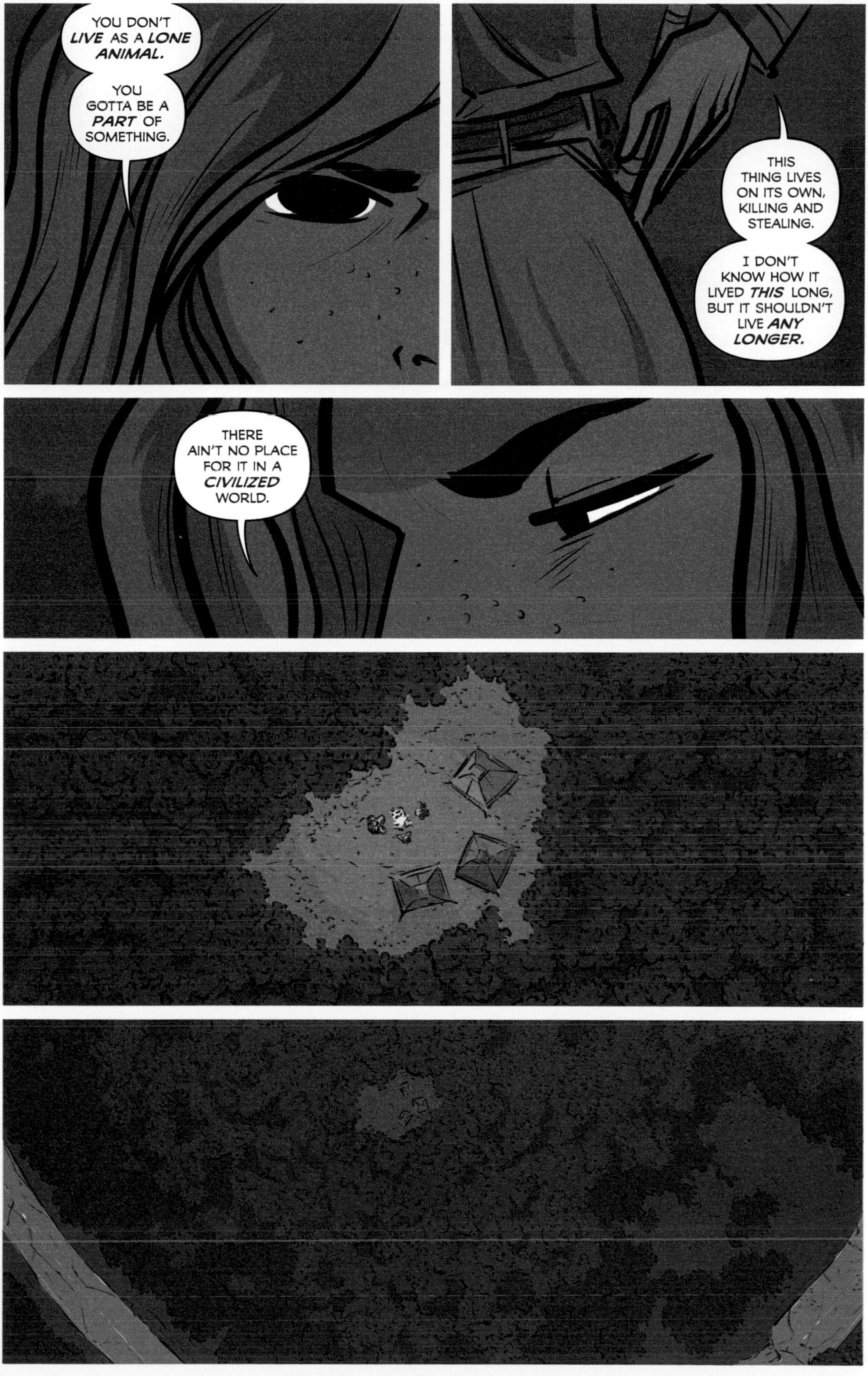
YOU DON'T LIVE AS A LONE ANIMAL.
YOU GOTTA BE A PART OF SOMETHING.
THIS THING LIVES ON ITS OWN, KILLING AND STEALING.
I DON'T KNOW HOW IT LIVED THIS LONG, BUT IT SHOULDN'T LIVE ANY LONGER.
THERE AIN'T NO PLACE FOR IT IN A CIVILIZED WORLD.

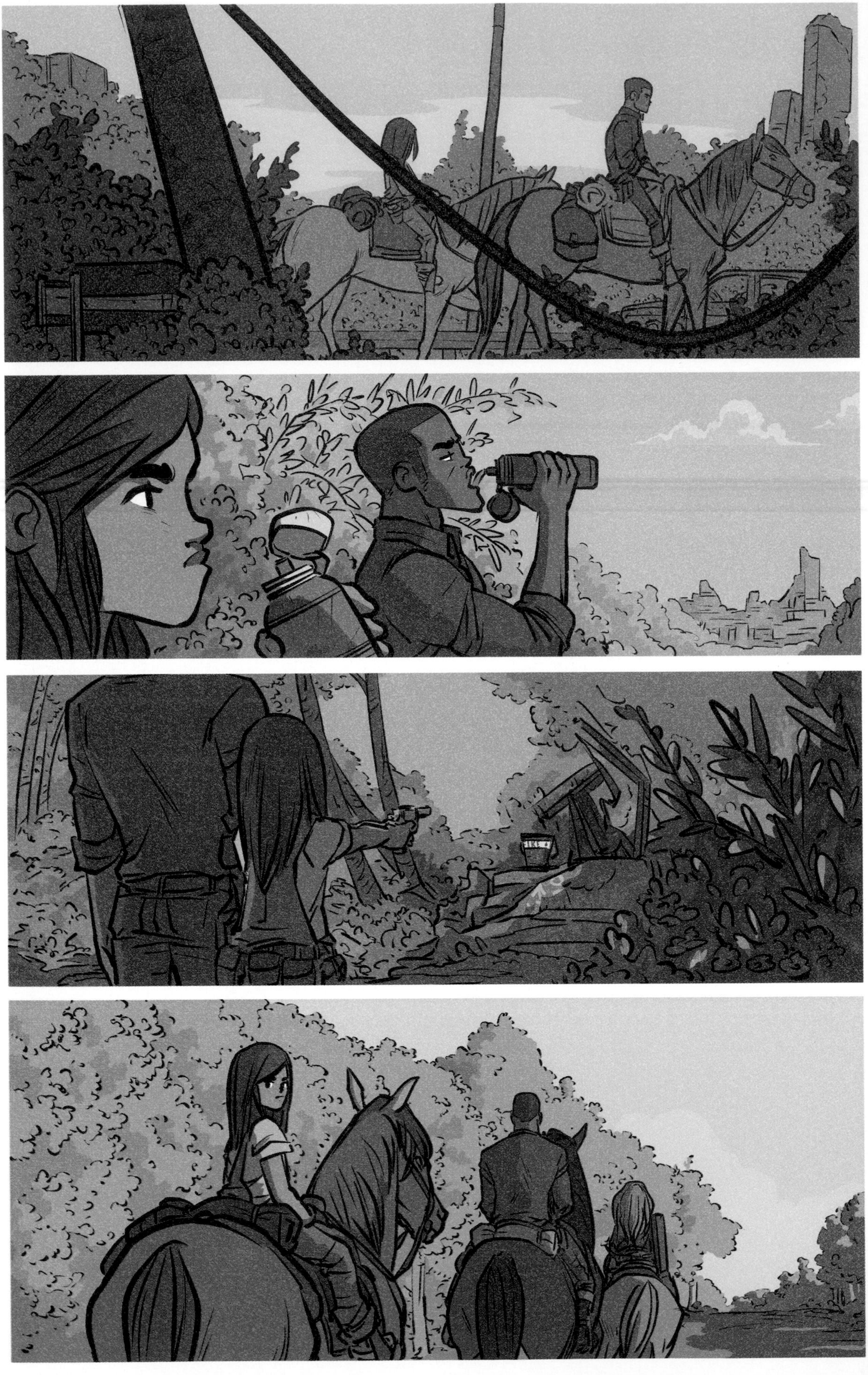

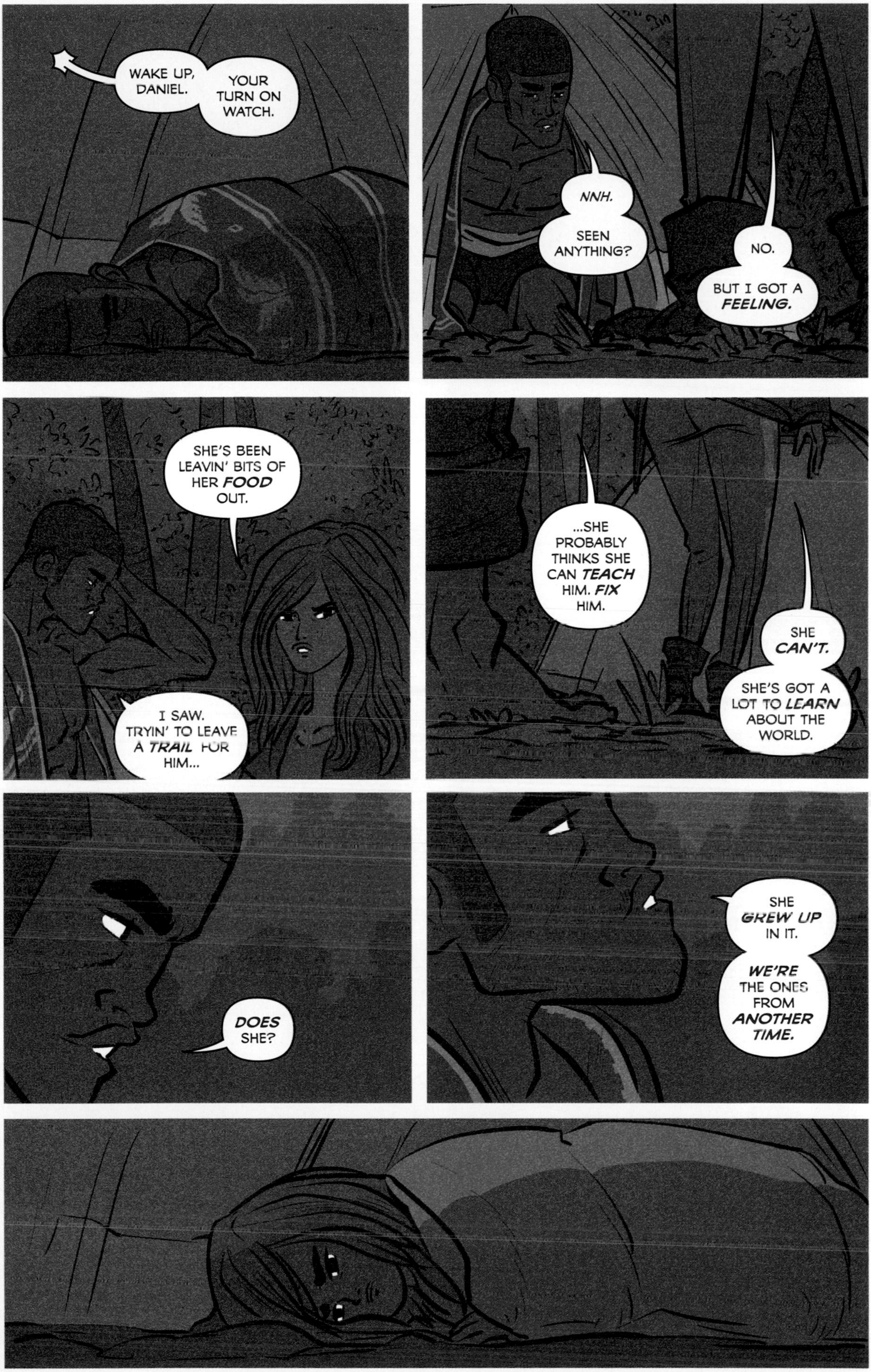
WAKE UP, DANIEL.
YOUR TURN ON WATCH.
NNH.
SEEN ANYTHING?
NO.
BUT I GOT A FEELING.
SHE'S BEEN LEAVIN' BITS OF HER FOOD OUT.
I SAW. TRYIN' TO LEAVE A TRAIL FOR HIM...
...SHE PROBABLY THINKS SHE CAN TEACH HIM. FIX HIM.
SHE CAN'T.
SHE'S GOT A LOT TO LEARN ABOUT THE WORLD.
DOES SHE?
SHE GREW UP IN IT.
WE'RE THE ONES FROM ANOTHER TIME.

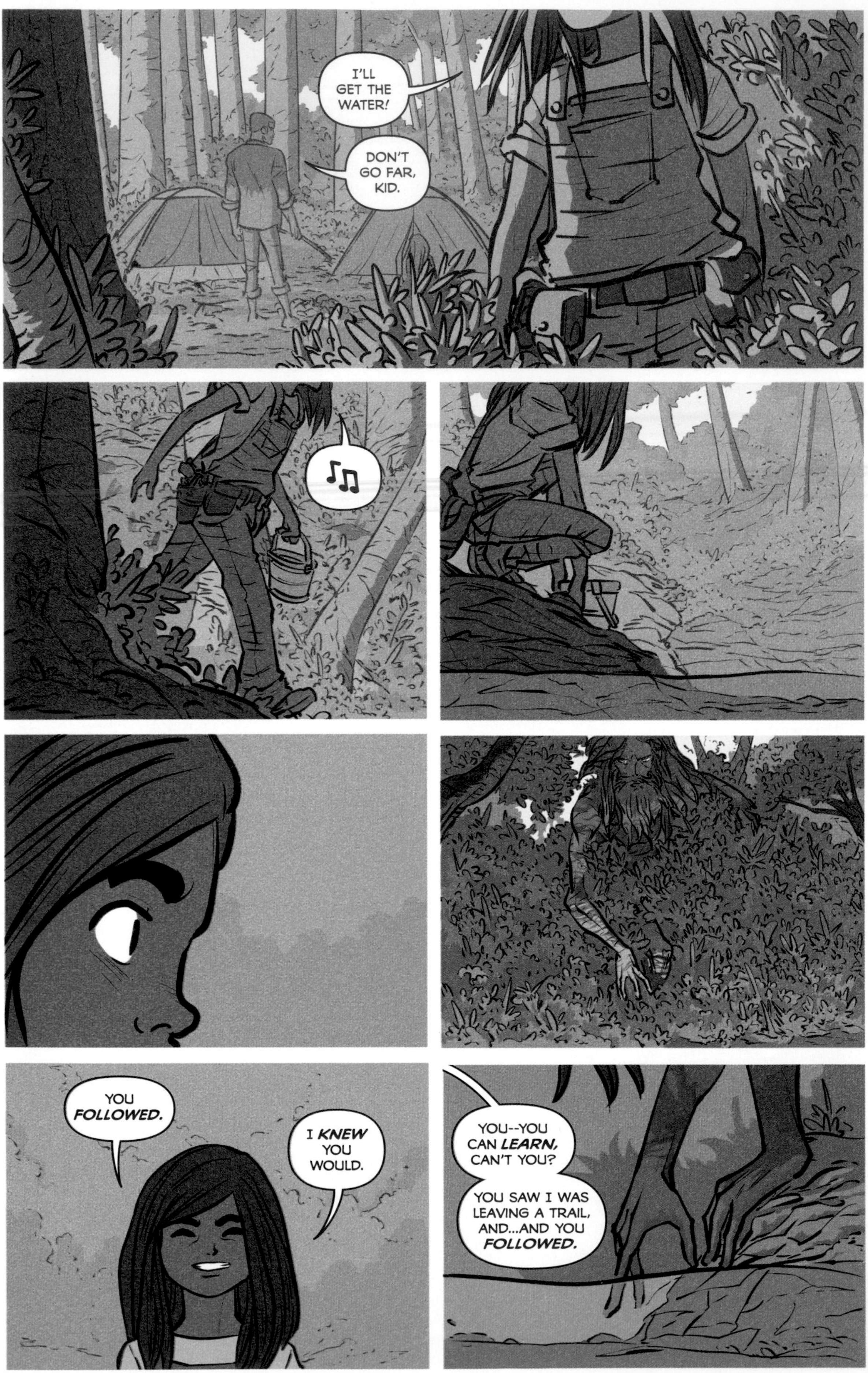
I'LL GET THE WATER!
DON'T GO FAR, KID.
♫♫
YOU FOLLOWED.
I KNEW YOU WOULD.
YOU--YOU CAN LEARN, CAN'T YOU?
YOU SAW I WAS LEAVING A TRAIL, AND...AND YOU FOLLOWED.

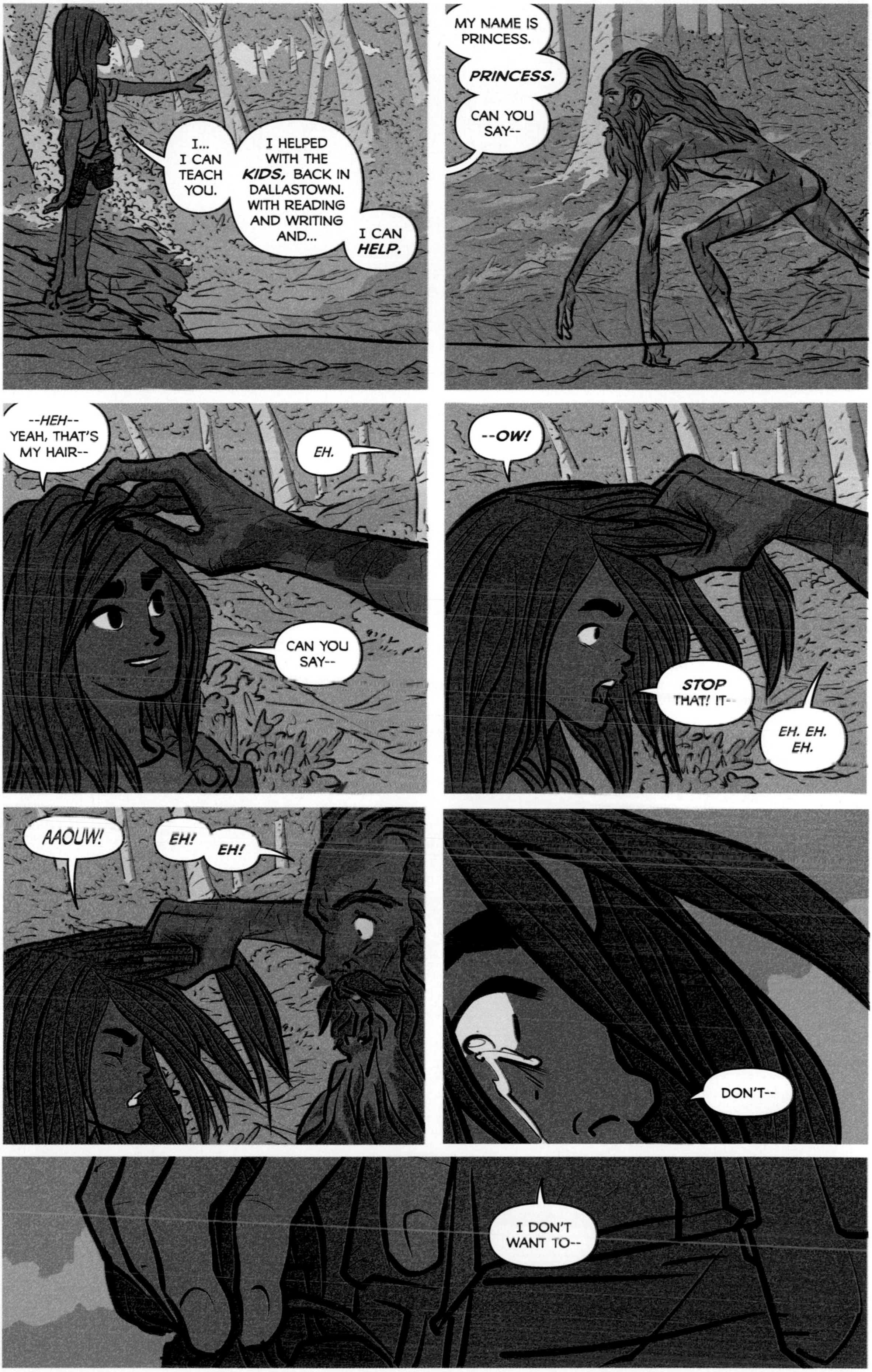
I... I CAN TEACH YOU.
I HELPED WITH THE KIDS, BACK IN DALLASTOWN. WITH READING AND WRITING AND...
I CAN HELP.
MY NAME IS PRINCESS.
PRINCESS.
CAN YOU SAY--
--HEH-- YEAH, THAT'S MY HAIR--
EH.
CAN YOU SAY--
--OW!
STOP THAT! IT--
EH. EH. EH.
AAOUW!
EH!
EH!
DON'T--
I DON'T WANT TO--

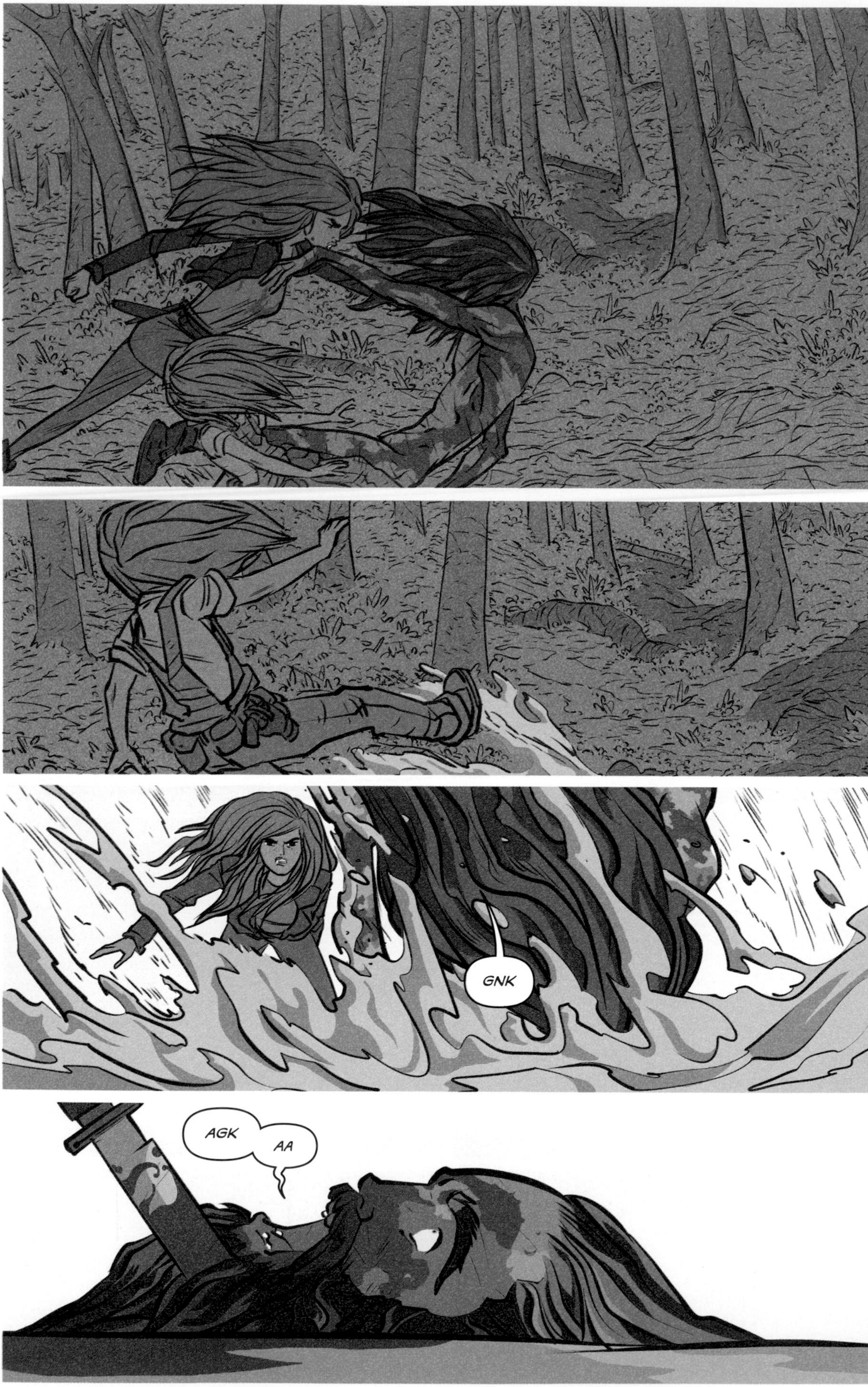
GNK
AGK
AA

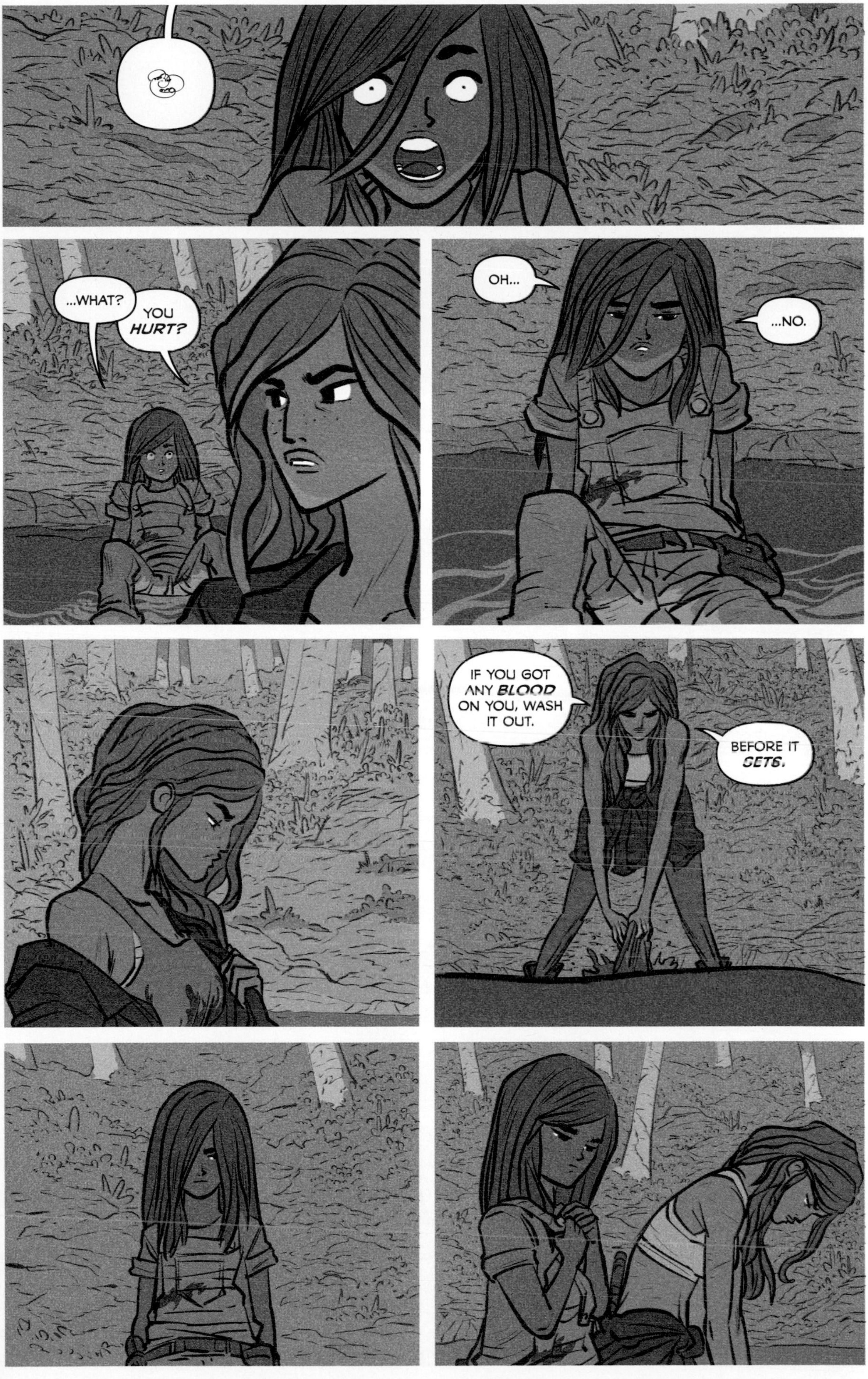
...WHAT?
YOU *HURT?*
OH...
...NO.
IF YOU GOT ANY *BLOOD* ON YOU, WASH IT OUT.
BEFORE IT *SETS.*

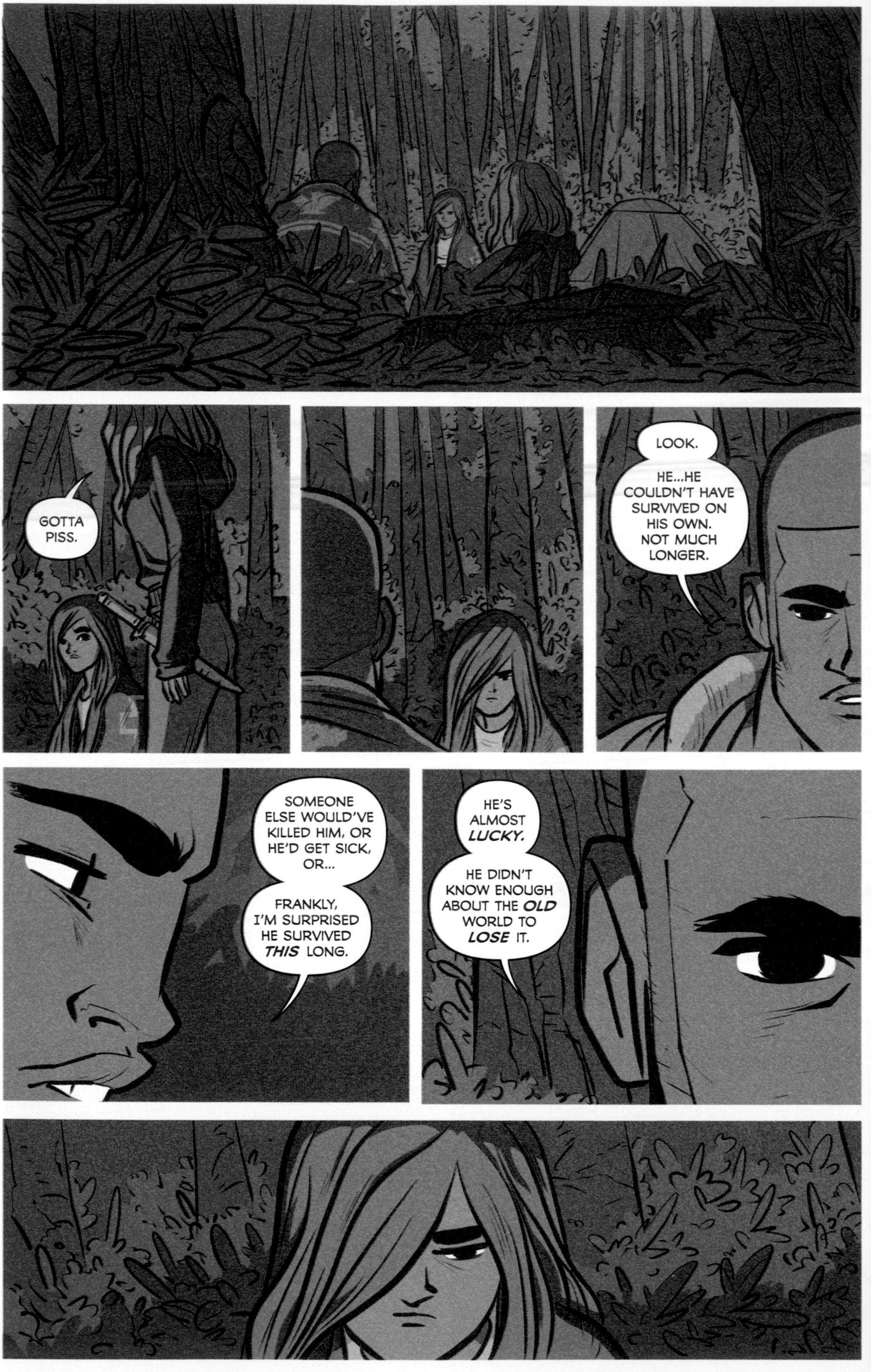
GOTTA PISS.
LOOK.
HE...HE COULDN'T HAVE SURVIVED ON HIS OWN. NOT MUCH LONGER.
SOMEONE ELSE WOULD'VE KILLED HIM, OR HE'D GET SICK, OR...
FRANKLY, I'M SURPRISED HE SURVIVED *THIS* LONG.
HE'S ALMOST *LUCKY.*
HE DIDN'T KNOW ENOUGH ABOUT THE *OLD* WORLD TO *LOSE* IT.

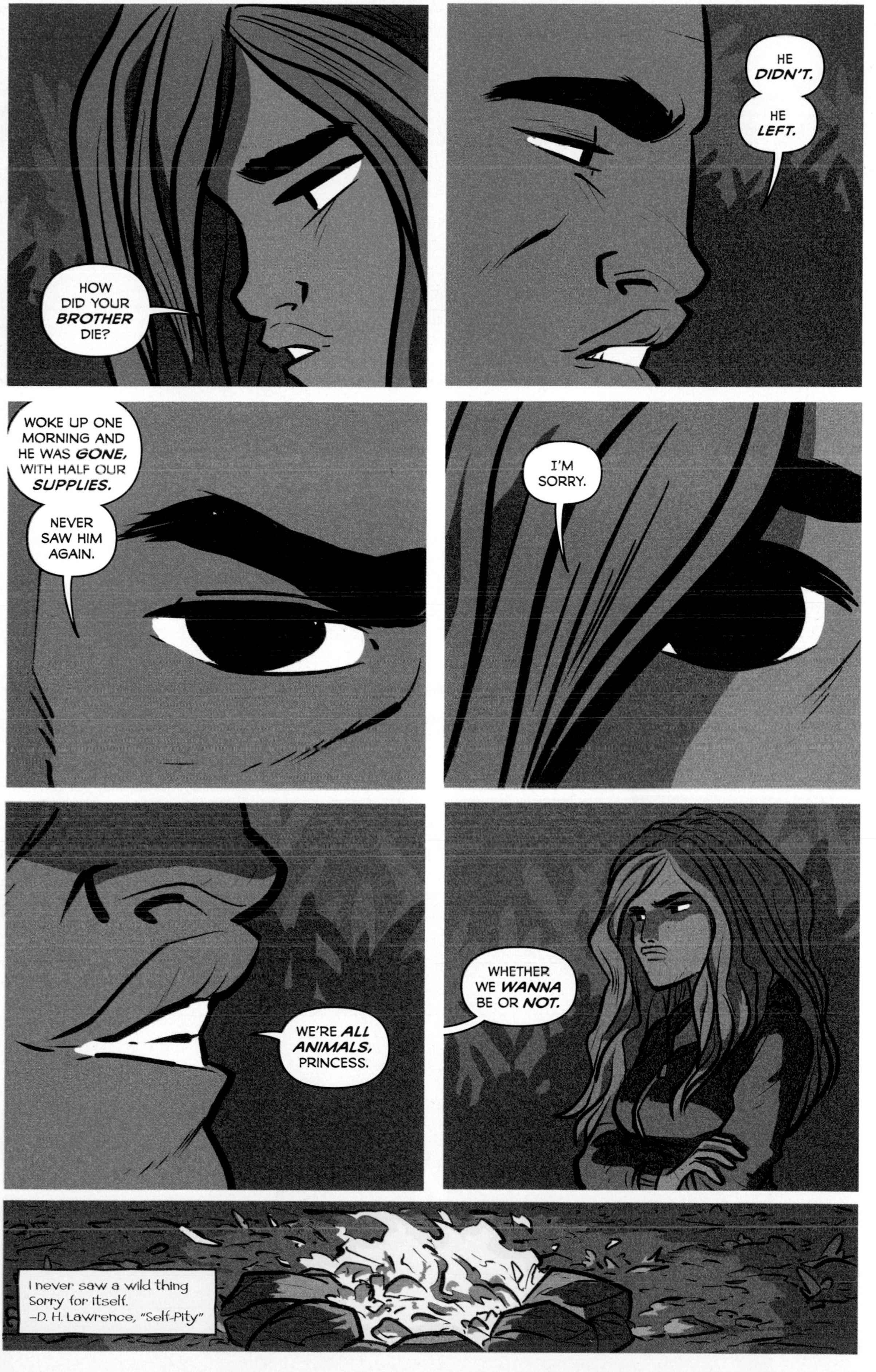
HOW DID YOUR BROTHER DIE?
HE DIDN'T.
HE LEFT.
WOKE UP ONE MORNING AND HE WAS GONE, WITH HALF OUR SUPPLIES.
NEVER SAW HIM AGAIN.
I'M SORRY.
WE'RE ALL ANIMALS, PRINCESS.
WHETHER WE WANNA BE OR NOT.
I never saw a wild thing
Sorry for itself.
–D. H. Lawrence, "Self-Pity"

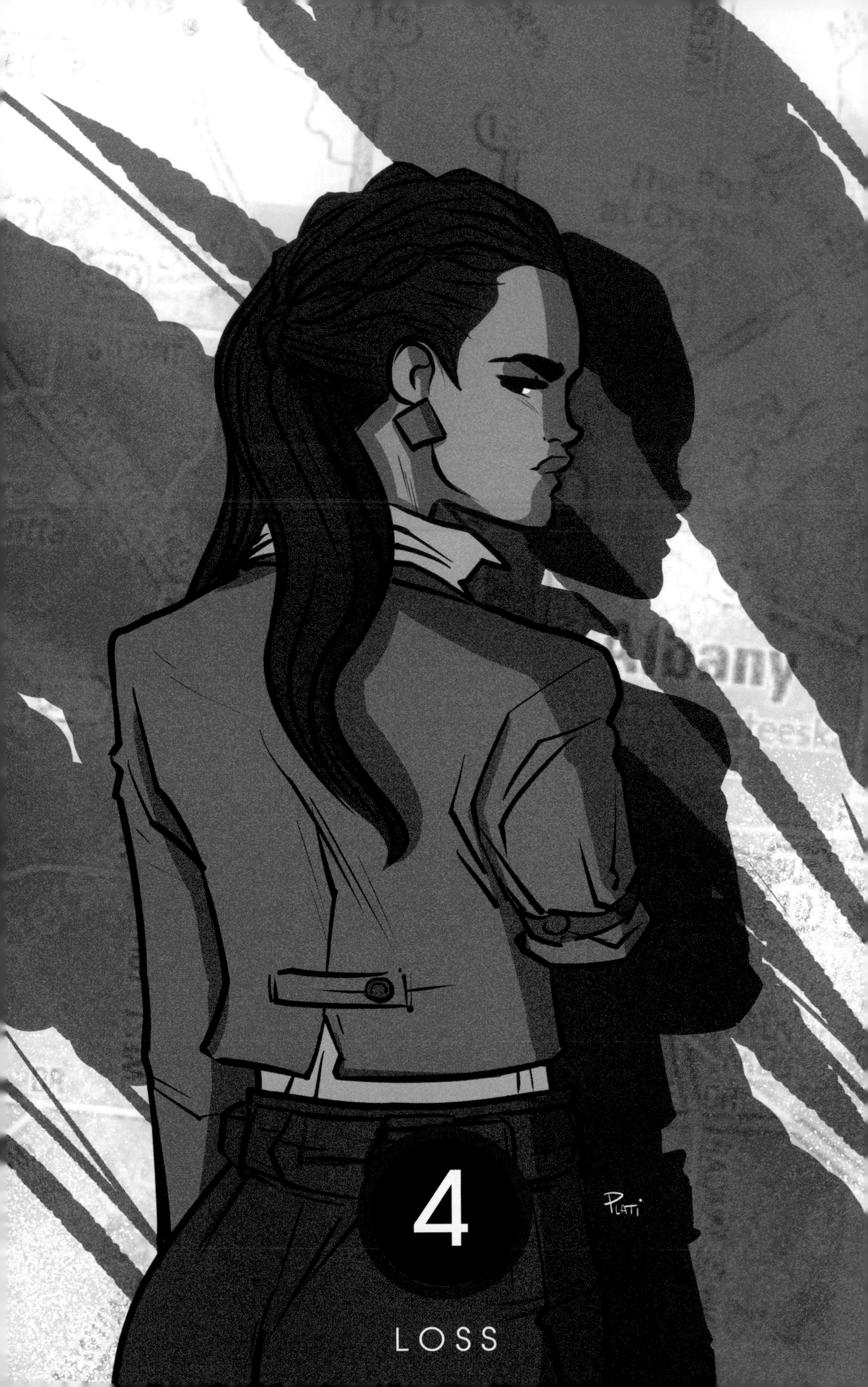
Albany
4
LOSS

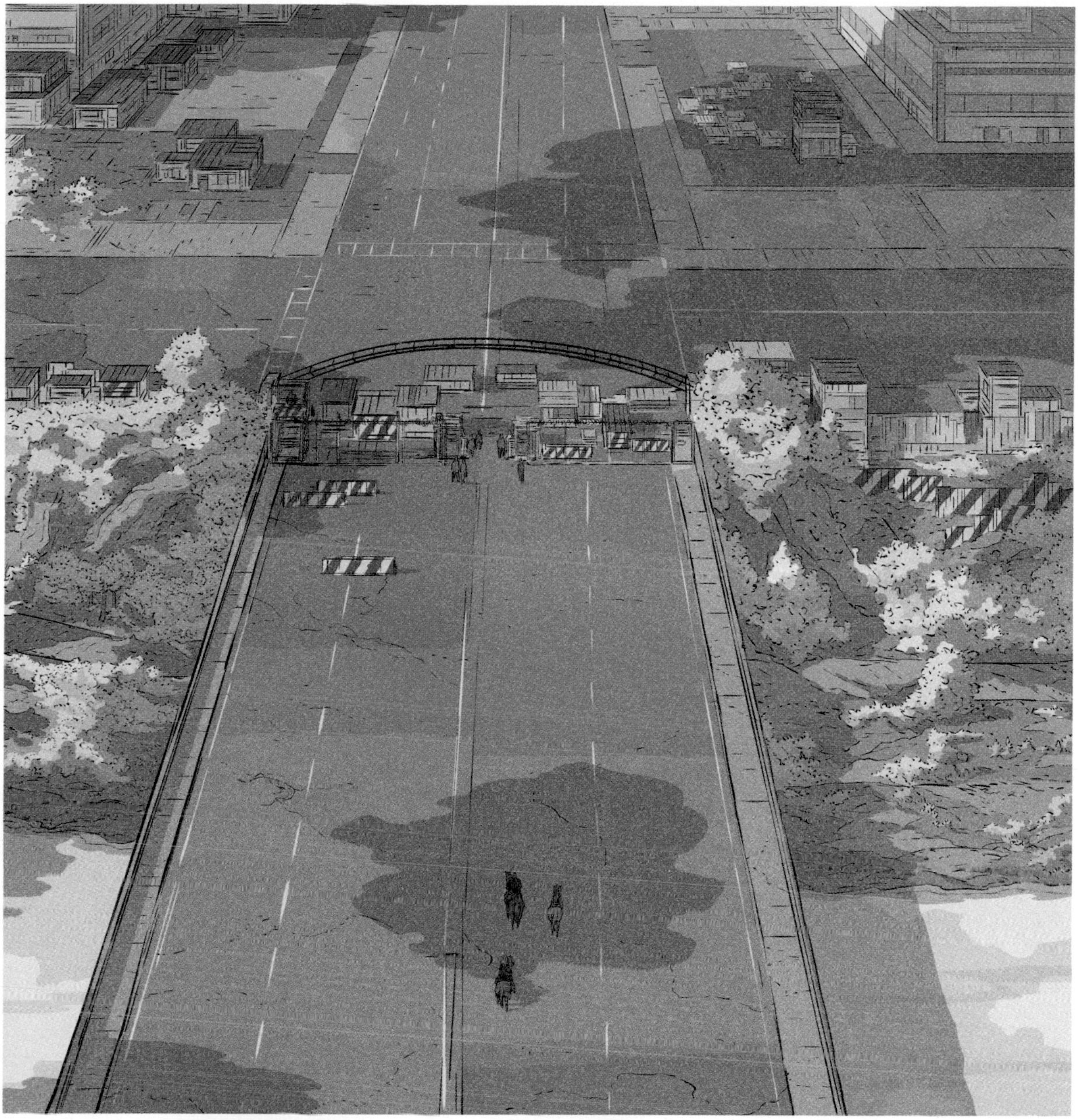

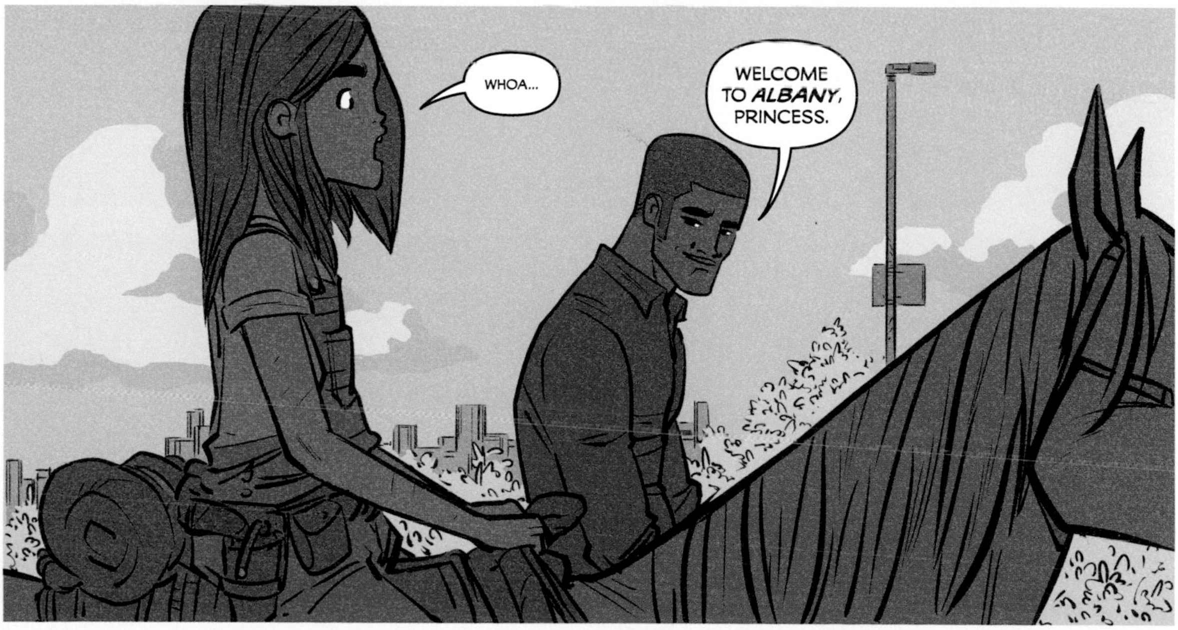
WHOA...
WELCOME TO *ALBANY*, PRINCESS.

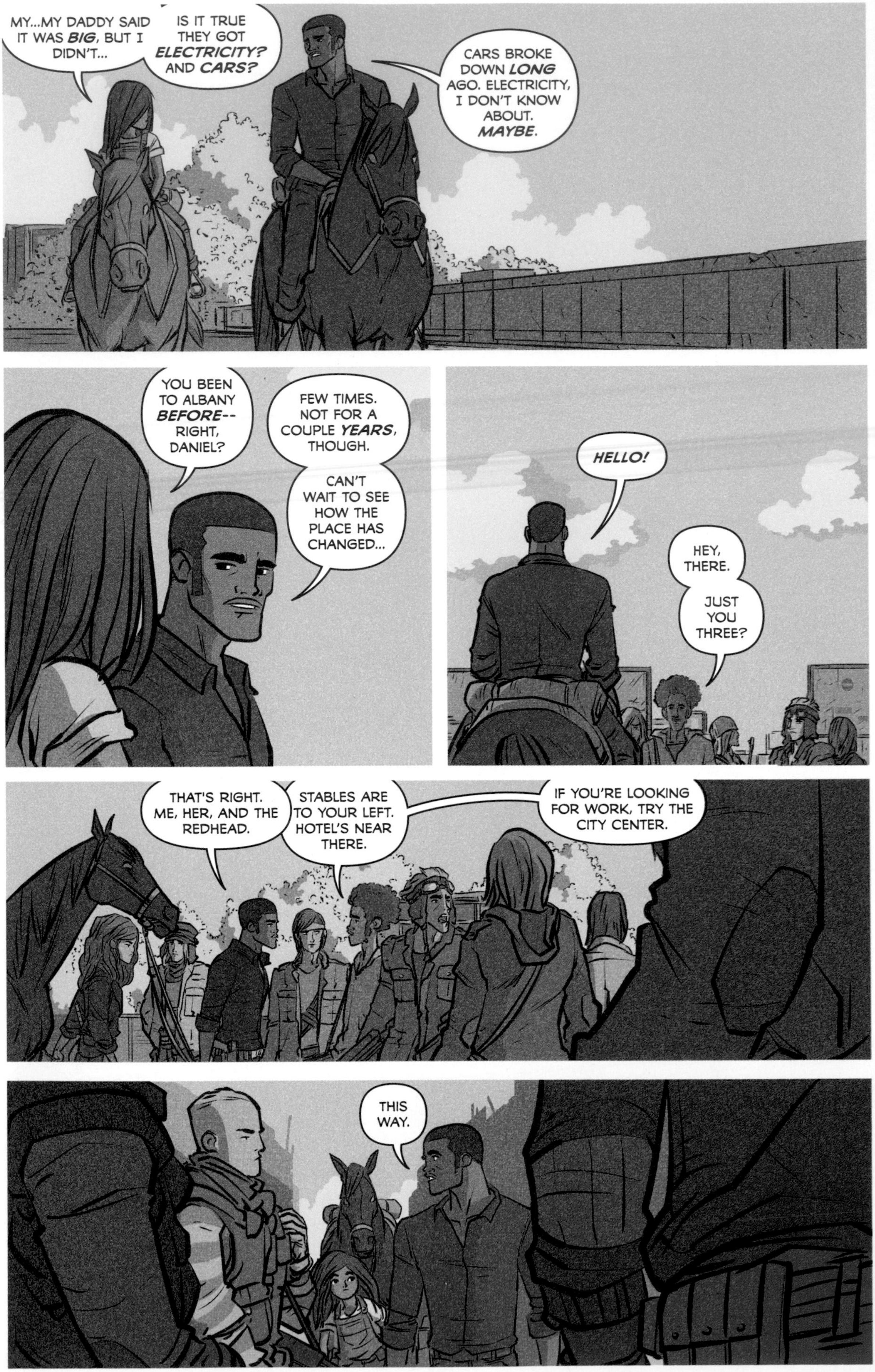

MY...MY DADDY SAID IT WAS BIG, BUT I DIDN'T...
IS IT TRUE THEY GOT ELECTRICITY? AND CARS?
CARS BROKE DOWN LONG AGO. ELECTRICITY, I DON'T KNOW ABOUT. MAYBE.
YOU BEEN TO ALBANY BEFORE-- RIGHT, DANIEL?
FEW TIMES. NOT FOR A COUPLE YEARS, THOUGH.
CAN'T WAIT TO SEE HOW THE PLACE HAS CHANGED...
HELLO!
HEY, THERE.
JUST YOU THREE?
THAT'S RIGHT. ME, HER, AND THE REDHEAD.
STABLES ARE TO YOUR LEFT. HOTEL'S NEAR THERE.
IF YOU'RE LOOKING FOR WORK, TRY THE CITY CENTER.
THIS WAY.

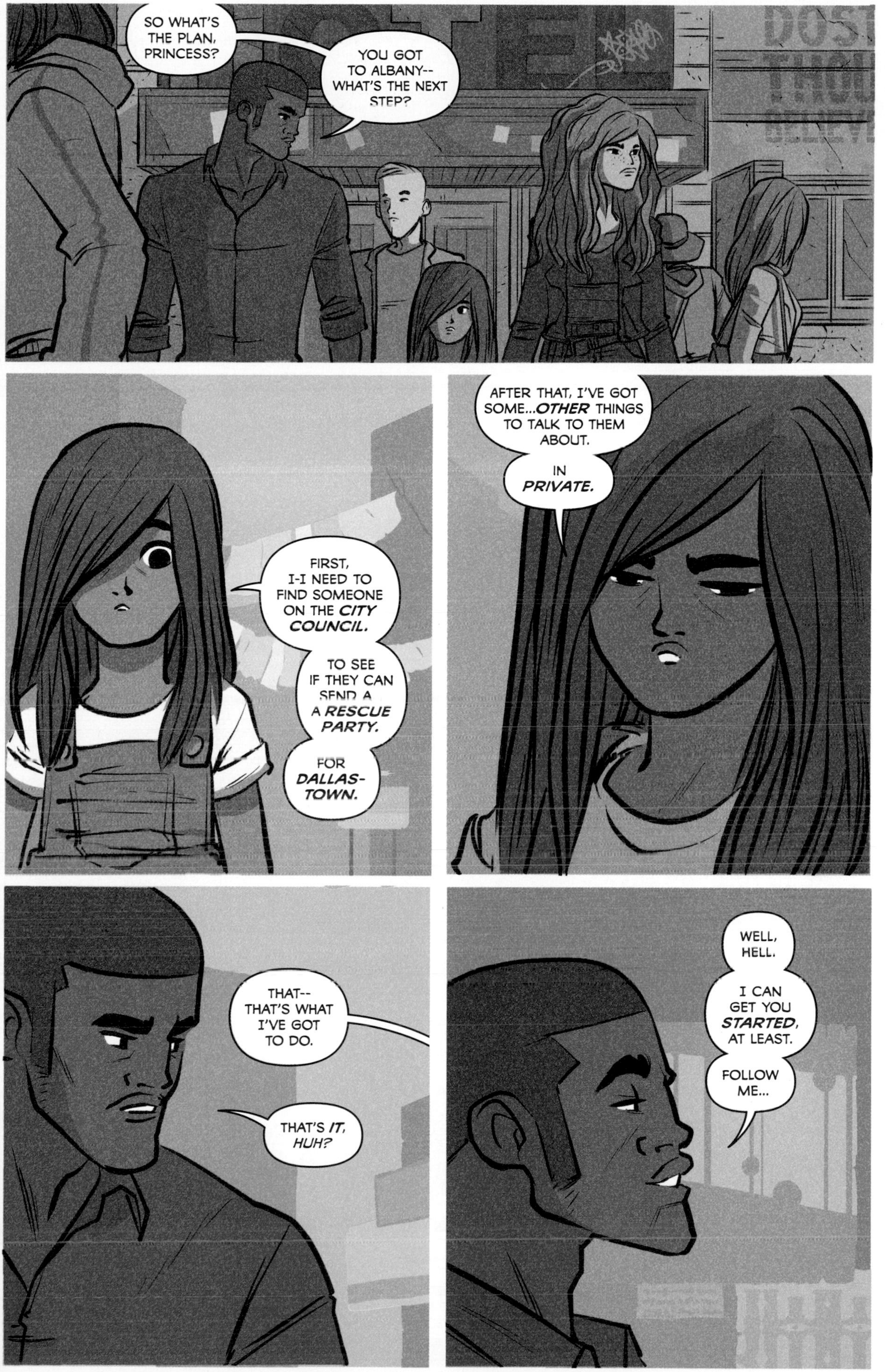
SO WHAT'S THE PLAN, PRINCESS?
YOU GOT TO ALBANY-- WHAT'S THE NEXT STEP?
FIRST, I-I NEED TO FIND SOMEONE ON THE *CITY COUNCIL.*
TO SEE IF THEY CAN SEND A A *RESCUE PARTY.*
FOR *DALLAS-TOWN.*
AFTER THAT, I'VE GOT SOME...*OTHER* THINGS TO TALK TO THEM ABOUT.
IN *PRIVATE.*
THAT-- THAT'S WHAT I'VE GOT TO DO.
THAT'S *IT,* HUH?
WELL, HELL.
I CAN GET YOU *STARTED*, AT LEAST.
FOLLOW ME...

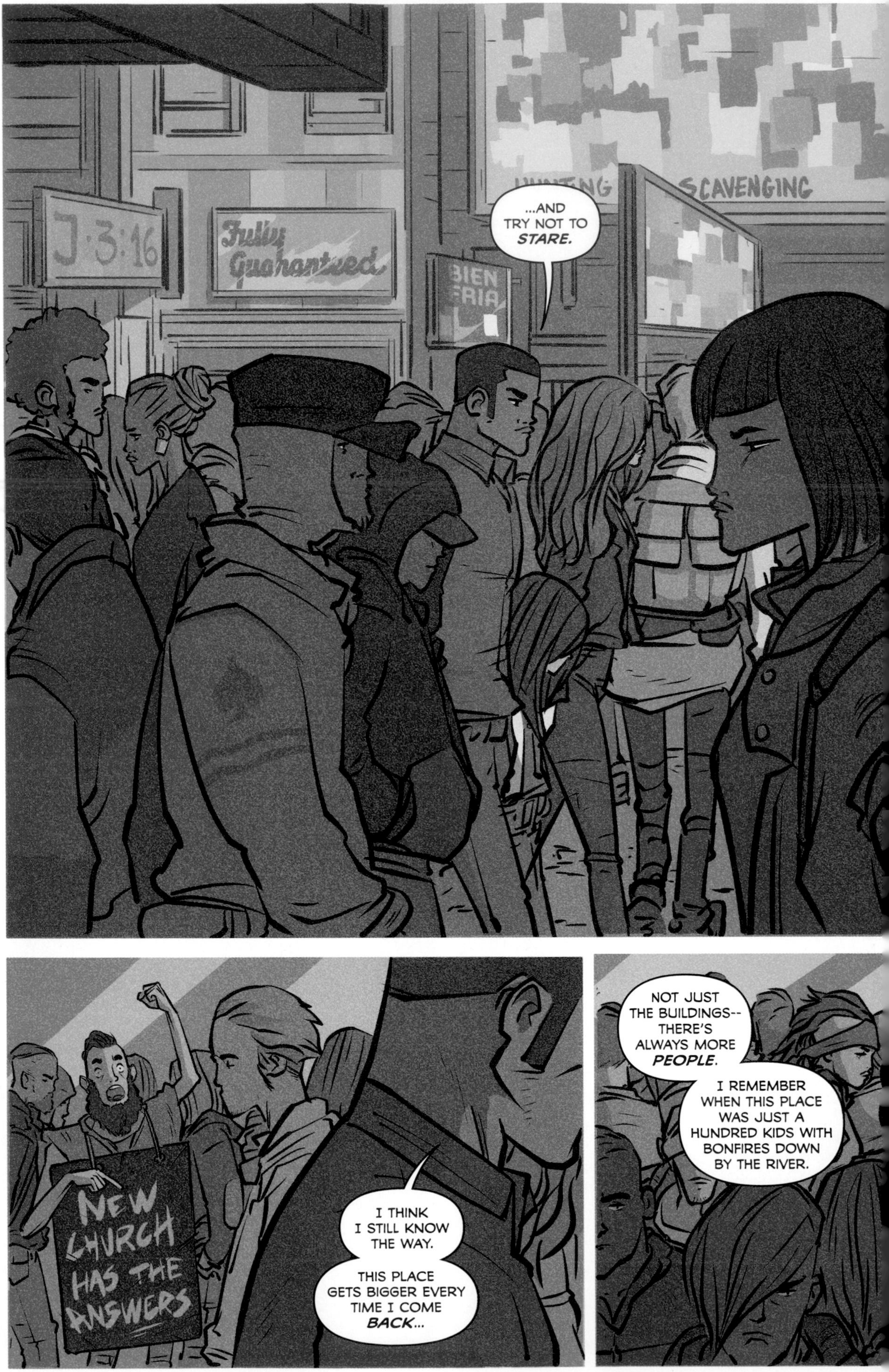
J·3:16
Fully Guaranteed
BIEN FRIA
SCAVENGING
...AND TRY NOT TO STARE.
NEW CHURCH HAS THE ANSWERS
I THINK I STILL KNOW THE WAY.
THIS PLACE GETS BIGGER EVERY TIME I COME BACK...
NOT JUST THE BUILDINGS-- THERE'S ALWAYS MORE PEOPLE.
I REMEMBER WHEN THIS PLACE WAS JUST A HUNDRED KIDS WITH BONFIRES DOWN BY THE RIVER.

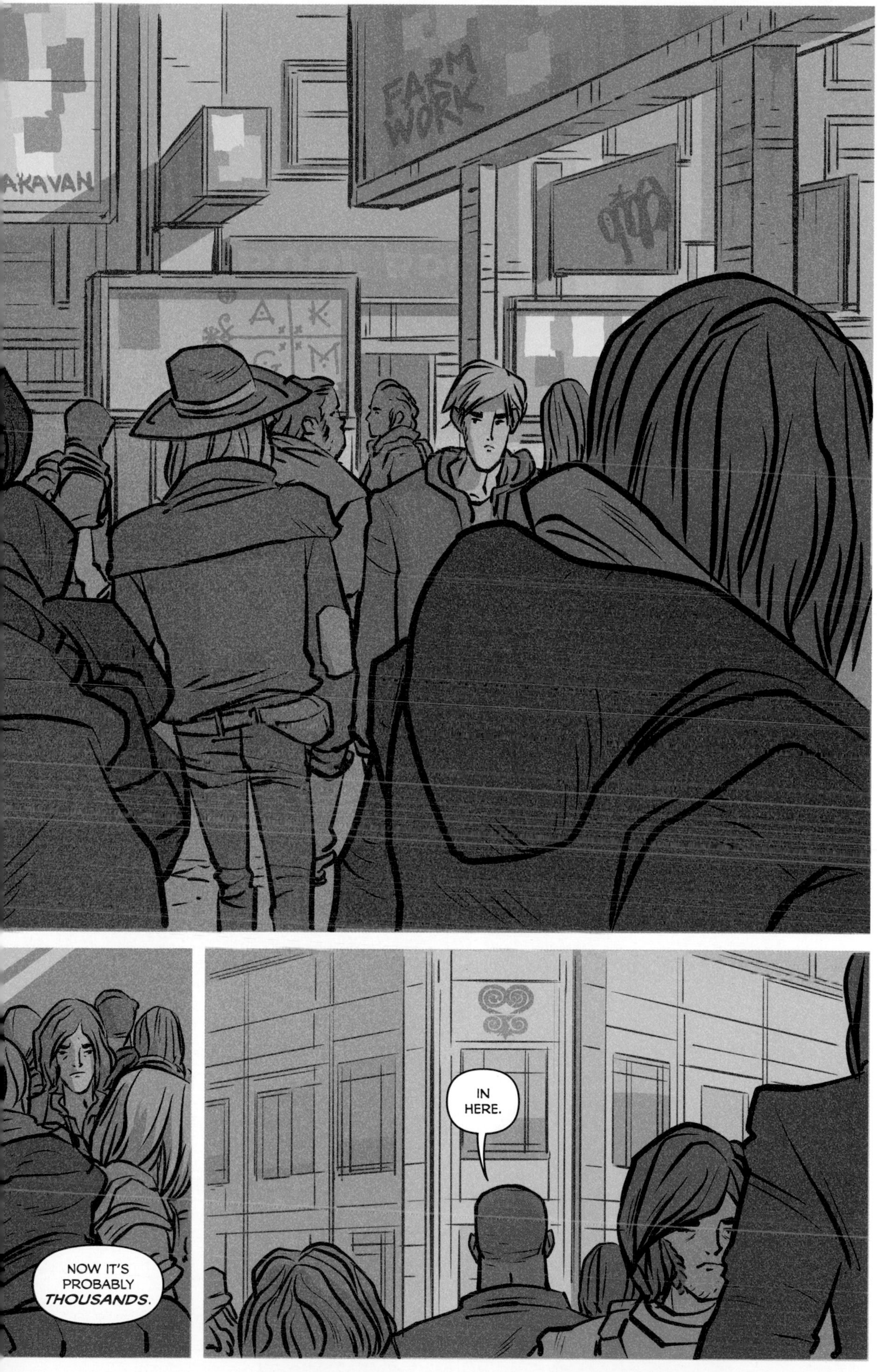
AKAVAN
FARM WORK
NOW IT'S PROBABLY *THOUSANDS*.
IN HERE.

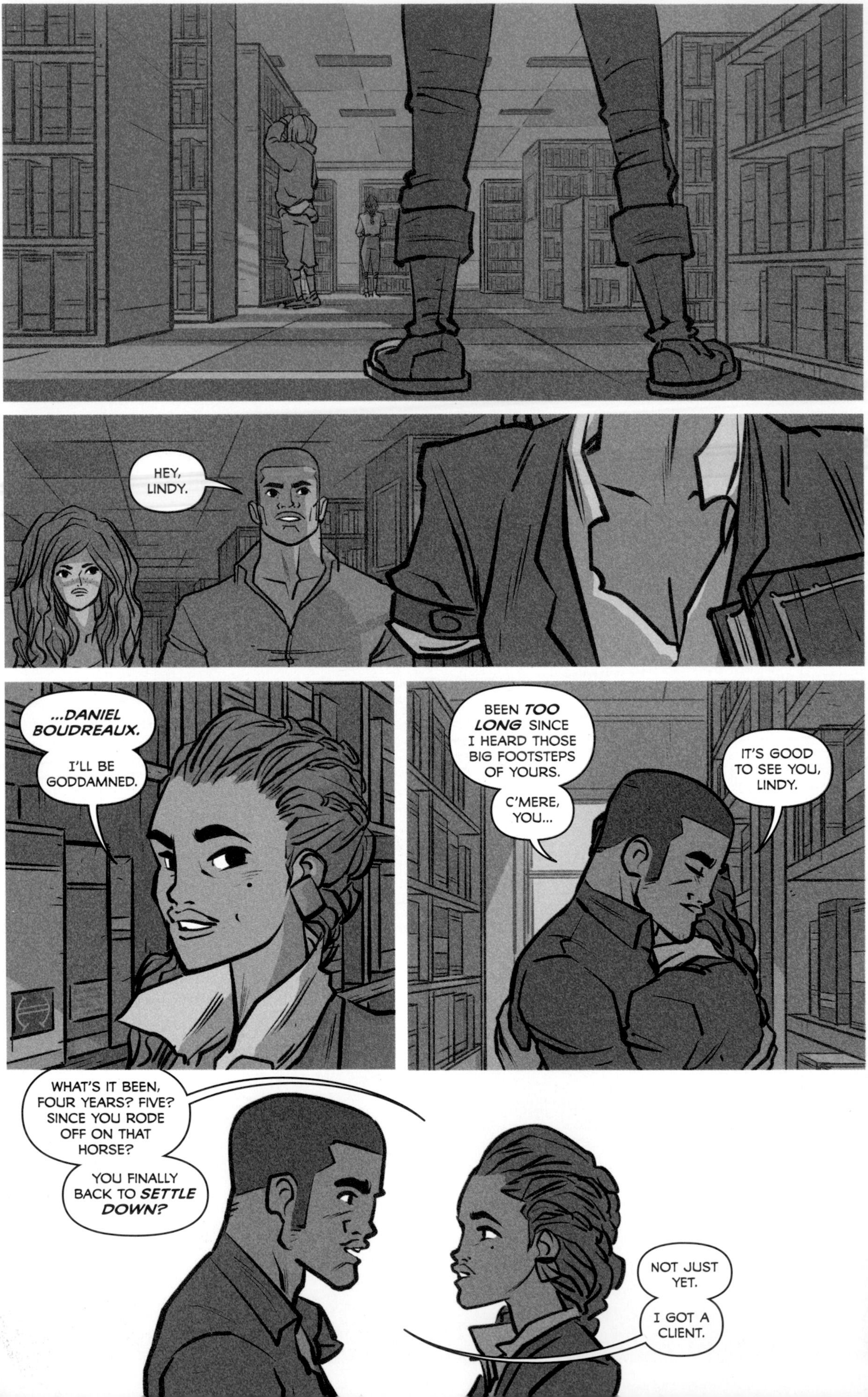
HEY, LINDY.
...DANIEL BOUDREAUX.
I'LL BE GODDAMNED.
BEEN TOO LONG SINCE I HEARD THOSE BIG FOOTSTEPS OF YOURS.
C'MERE, YOU...
IT'S GOOD TO SEE YOU, LINDY.
WHAT'S IT BEEN, FOUR YEARS? FIVE? SINCE YOU RODE OFF ON THAT HORSE?
YOU FINALLY BACK TO SETTLE DOWN?
NOT JUST YET.
I GOT A CLIENT.

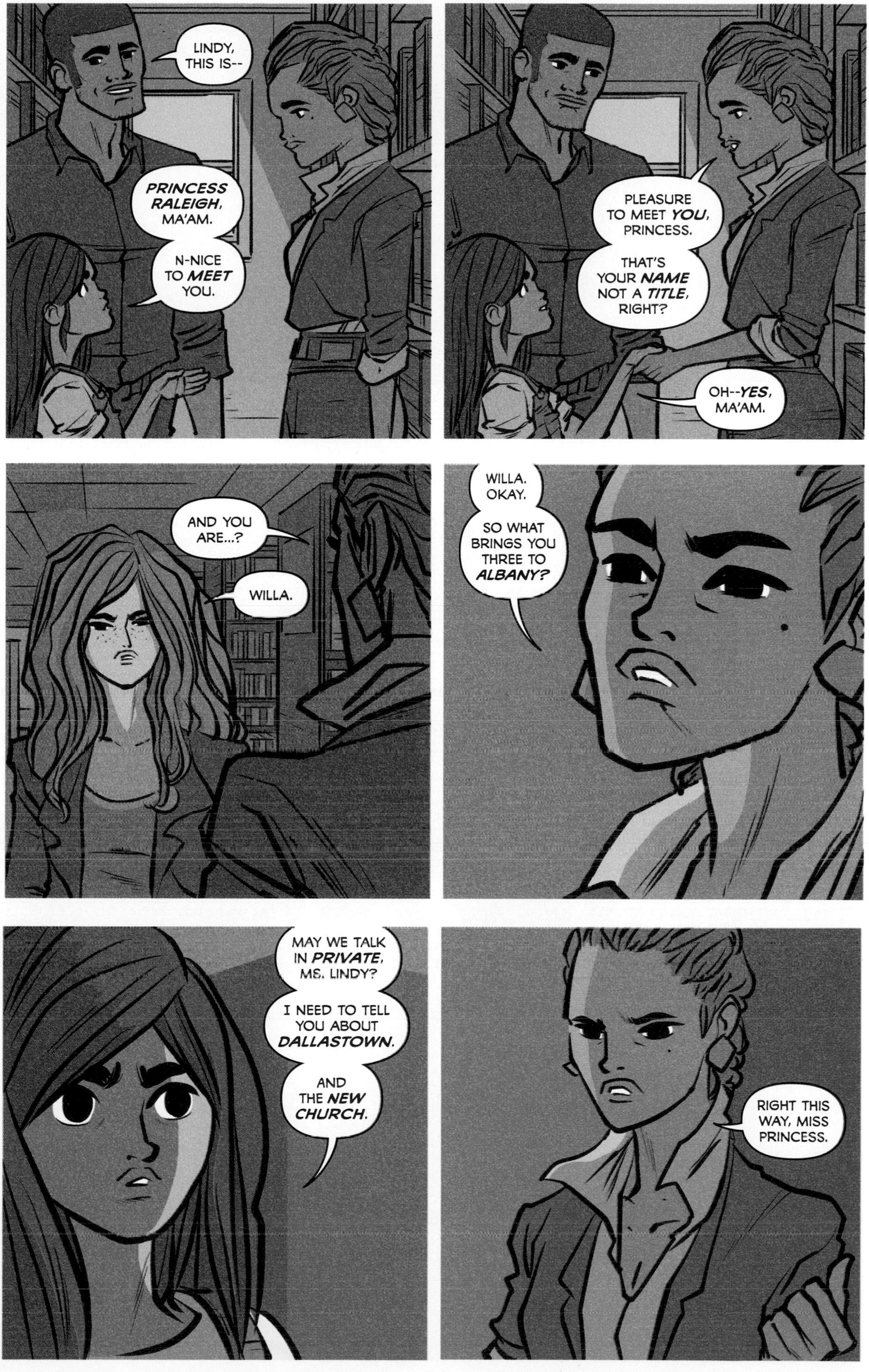
LINDY, THIS IS--
PRINCESS RALEIGH, MA'AM.
N-NICE TO *MEET* YOU.
PLEASURE TO MEET *YOU*, PRINCESS.
THAT'S YOUR *NAME* NOT A *TITLE*, RIGHT?
OH--*YES*, MA'AM.
AND YOU ARE...?
WILLA.
WILLA. OKAY.
SO WHAT BRINGS YOU THREE TO *ALBANY?*
MAY WE TALK IN *PRIVATE*, MS. LINDY?
I NEED TO TELL YOU ABOUT *DALLASTOWN*.
AND THE *NEW CHURCH*.
RIGHT THIS WAY, MISS PRINCESS.

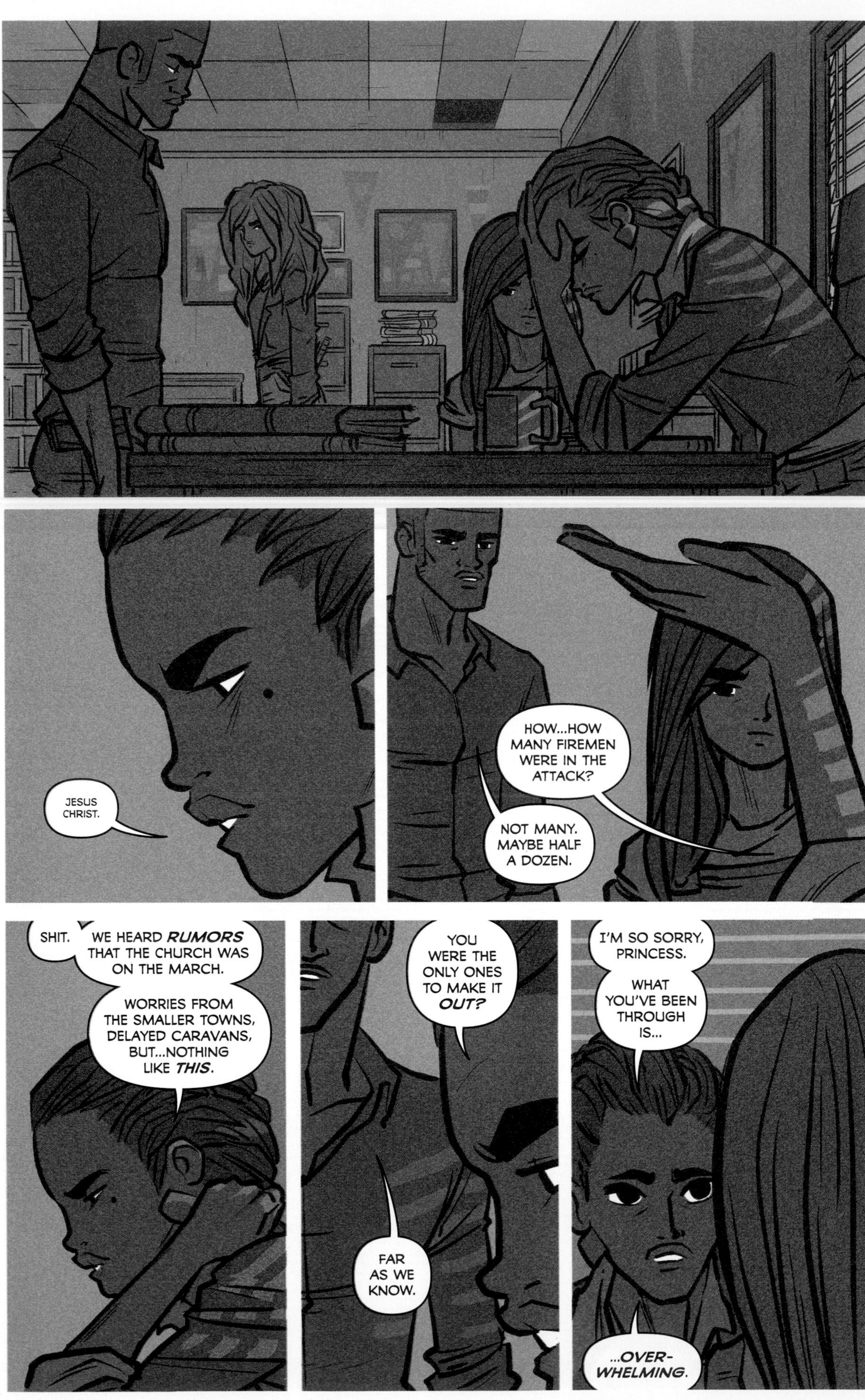
JESUS CHRIST.
HOW...HOW MANY FIREMEN WERE IN THE ATTACK?
NOT MANY. MAYBE HALF A DOZEN.
SHIT.
WE HEARD RUMORS THAT THE CHURCH WAS ON THE MARCH.
WORRIES FROM THE SMALLER TOWNS, DELAYED CARAVANS, BUT...NOTHING LIKE THIS.
YOU WERE THE ONLY ONES TO MAKE IT OUT?
FAR AS WE KNOW.
I'M SO SORRY, PRINCESS.
WHAT YOU'VE BEEN THROUGH IS...
...OVER-WHELMING.

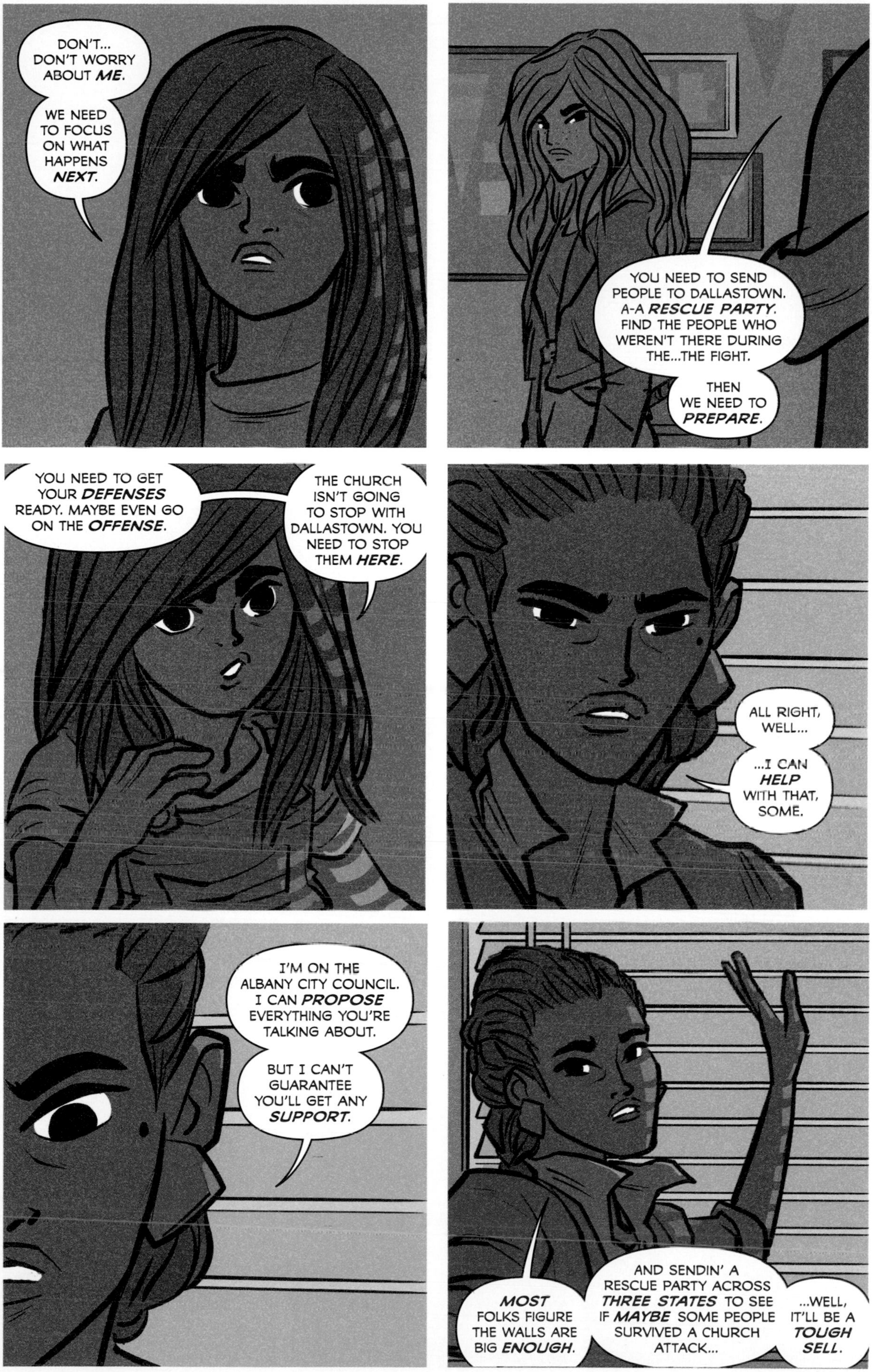

DON'T... DON'T WORRY ABOUT ME.
WE NEED TO FOCUS ON WHAT HAPPENS NEXT.
YOU NEED TO SEND PEOPLE TO DALLASTOWN. A-A RESCUE PARTY. FIND THE PEOPLE WHO WEREN'T THERE DURING THE...THE FIGHT.
THEN WE NEED TO PREPARE.
YOU NEED TO GET YOUR DEFENSES READY. MAYBE EVEN GO ON THE OFFENSE.
THE CHURCH ISN'T GOING TO STOP WITH DALLASTOWN. YOU NEED TO STOP THEM HERE.
ALL RIGHT, WELL...
...I CAN HELP WITH THAT, SOME.
I'M ON THE ALBANY CITY COUNCIL. I CAN PROPOSE EVERYTHING YOU'RE TALKING ABOUT.
BUT I CAN'T GUARANTEE YOU'LL GET ANY SUPPORT.
MOST FOLKS FIGURE THE WALLS ARE BIG ENOUGH.
AND SENDIN' A RESCUE PARTY ACROSS THREE STATES TO SEE IF MAYBE SOME PEOPLE SURVIVED A CHURCH ATTACK...
...WELL, IT'LL BE A TOUGH SELL.

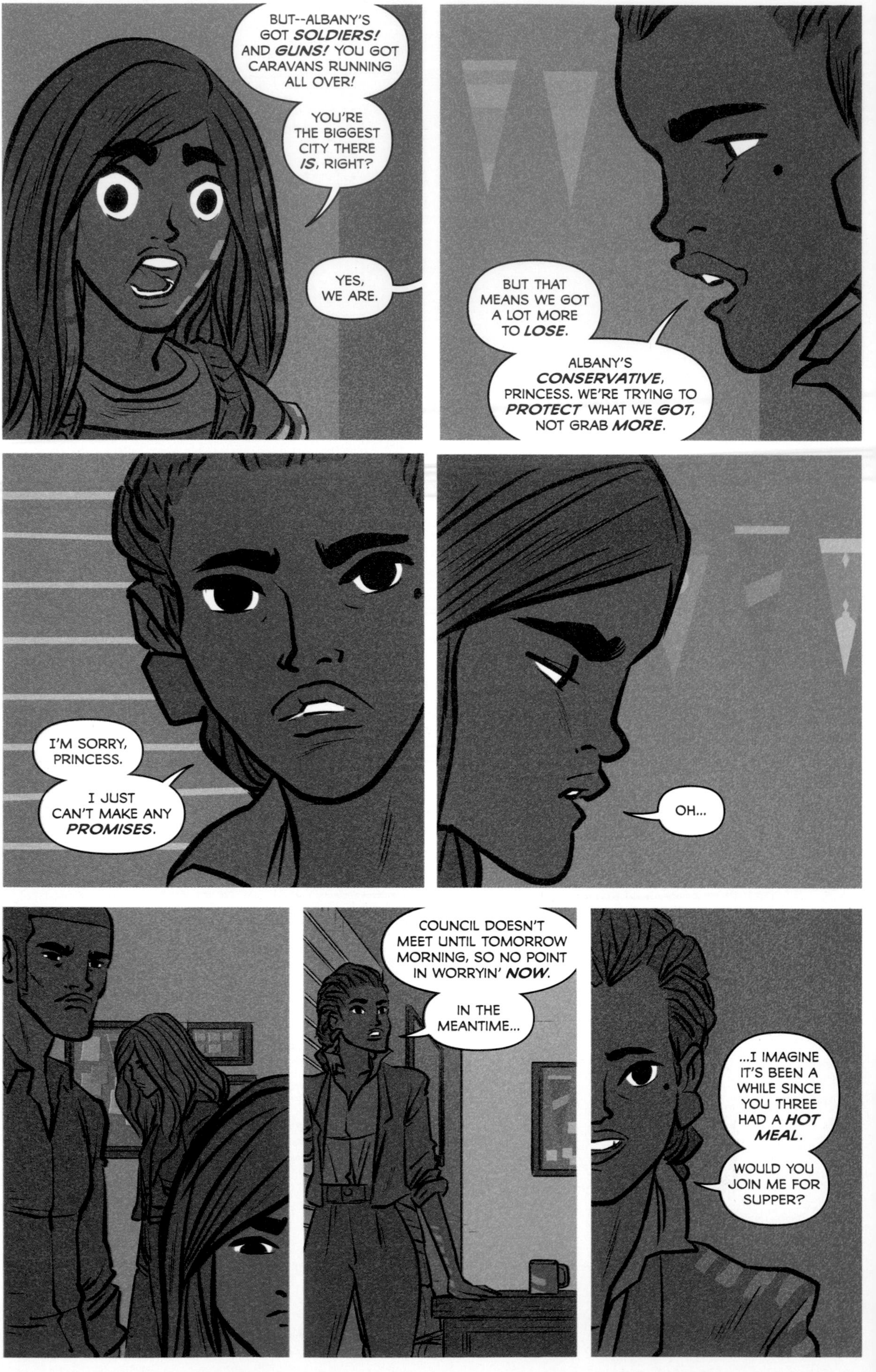
BUT--ALBANY'S GOT SOLDIERS! AND GUNS! YOU GOT CARAVANS RUNNING ALL OVER!
YOU'RE THE BIGGEST CITY THERE IS, RIGHT?
YES, WE ARE.
BUT THAT MEANS WE GOT A LOT MORE TO LOSE.
ALBANY'S CONSERVATIVE, PRINCESS. WE'RE TRYING TO PROTECT WHAT WE GOT, NOT GRAB MORE.
I'M SORRY, PRINCESS.
I JUST CAN'T MAKE ANY PROMISES.
OH...
COUNCIL DOESN'T MEET UNTIL TOMORROW MORNING, SO NO POINT IN WORRYIN' NOW.
IN THE MEANTIME...
...I IMAGINE IT'S BEEN A WHILE SINCE YOU THREE HAD A HOT MEAL.
WOULD YOU JOIN ME FOR SUPPER?

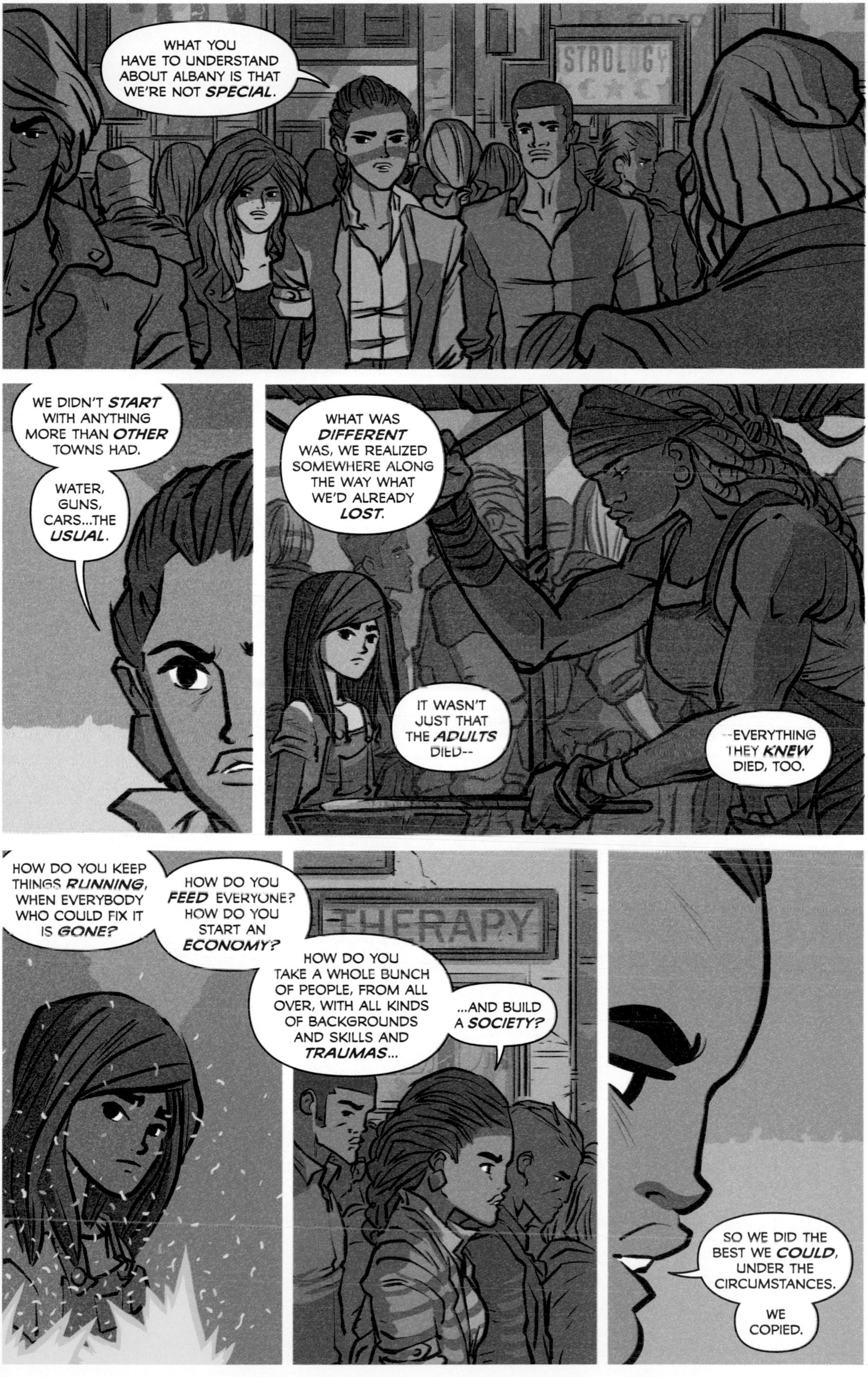
WHAT YOU HAVE TO UNDERSTAND ABOUT ALBANY IS THAT WE'RE NOT *SPECIAL*.
STROLOGY
WE DIDN'T *START* WITH ANYTHING MORE THAN *OTHER* TOWNS HAD.
WATER, GUNS, CARS...THE *USUAL*.
WHAT WAS *DIFFERENT* WAS, WE REALIZED SOMEWHERE ALONG THE WAY WHAT WE'D ALREADY *LOST*.
IT WASN'T JUST THAT THE *ADULTS* DIED--
--EVERYTHING THEY *KNEW* DIED, TOO.
HOW DO YOU KEEP THINGS *RUNNING*, WHEN EVERYBODY WHO COULD FIX IT IS *GONE?*
HOW DO YOU *FEED* EVERYONE? HOW DO YOU START AN *ECONOMY?*
THERAPY
HOW DO YOU TAKE A WHOLE BUNCH OF PEOPLE, FROM ALL OVER, WITH ALL KINDS OF BACKGROUNDS AND SKILLS AND *TRAUMAS*...
...AND BUILD A *SOCIETY?*
SO WE DID THE BEST WE *COULD*, UNDER THE CIRCUMSTANCES.
WE COPIED.

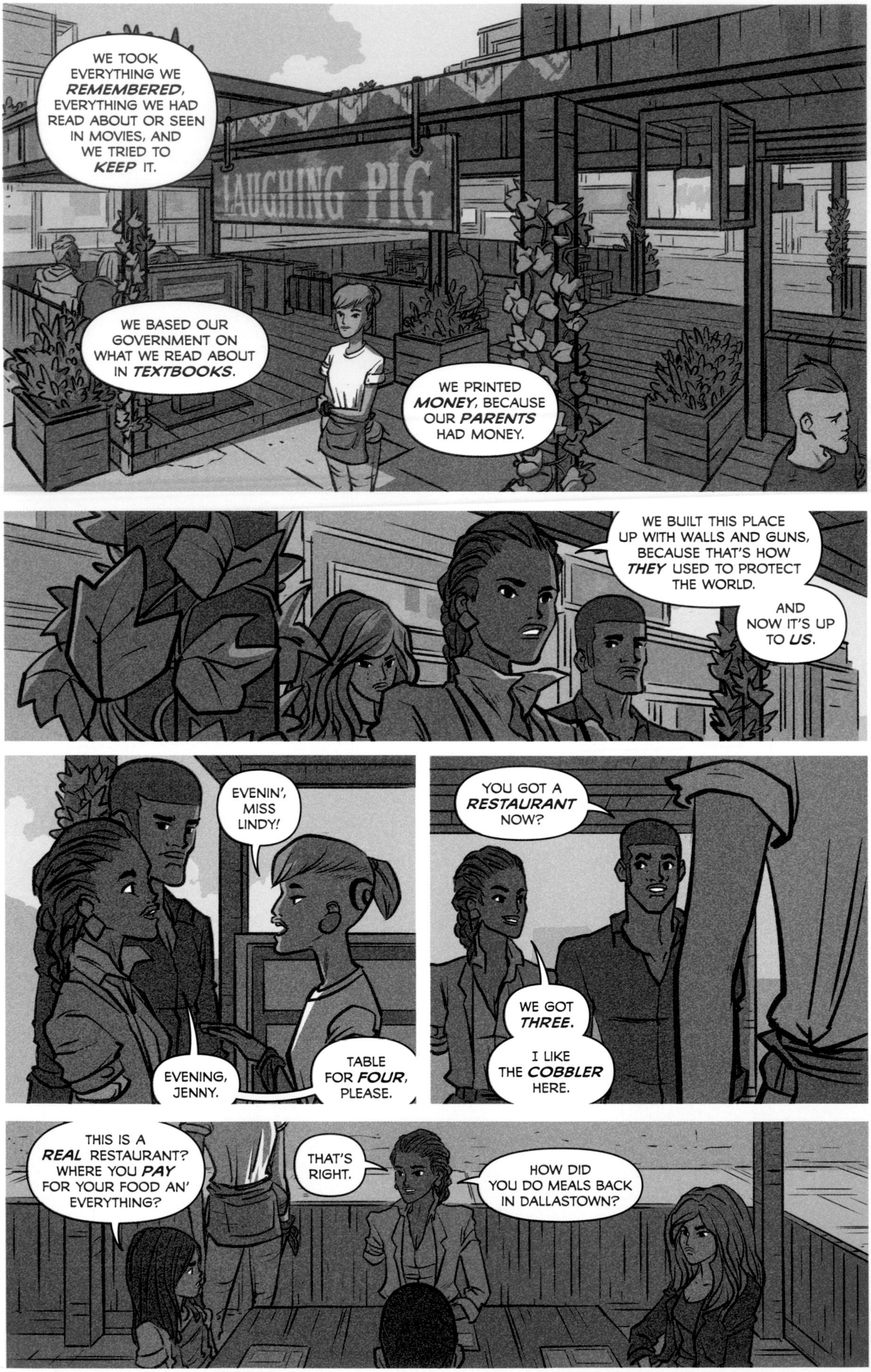
WE TOOK EVERYTHING WE REMEMBERED, EVERYTHING WE HAD READ ABOUT OR SEEN IN MOVIES, AND WE TRIED TO KEEP IT.
LAUGHING PIG
WE BASED OUR GOVERNMENT ON WHAT WE READ ABOUT IN TEXTBOOKS.
WE PRINTED MONEY, BECAUSE OUR PARENTS HAD MONEY.
WE BUILT THIS PLACE UP WITH WALLS AND GUNS, BECAUSE THAT'S HOW THEY USED TO PROTECT THE WORLD.
AND NOW IT'S UP TO US.
EVENIN', MISS LINDY!
EVENING, JENNY.
TABLE FOR FOUR, PLEASE.
YOU GOT A RESTAURANT NOW?
WE GOT THREE.
I LIKE THE COBBLER HERE.
THIS IS A REAL RESTAURANT? WHERE YOU PAY FOR YOUR FOOD AN' EVERYTHING?
THAT'S RIGHT.
HOW DID YOU DO MEALS BACK IN DALLASTOWN?

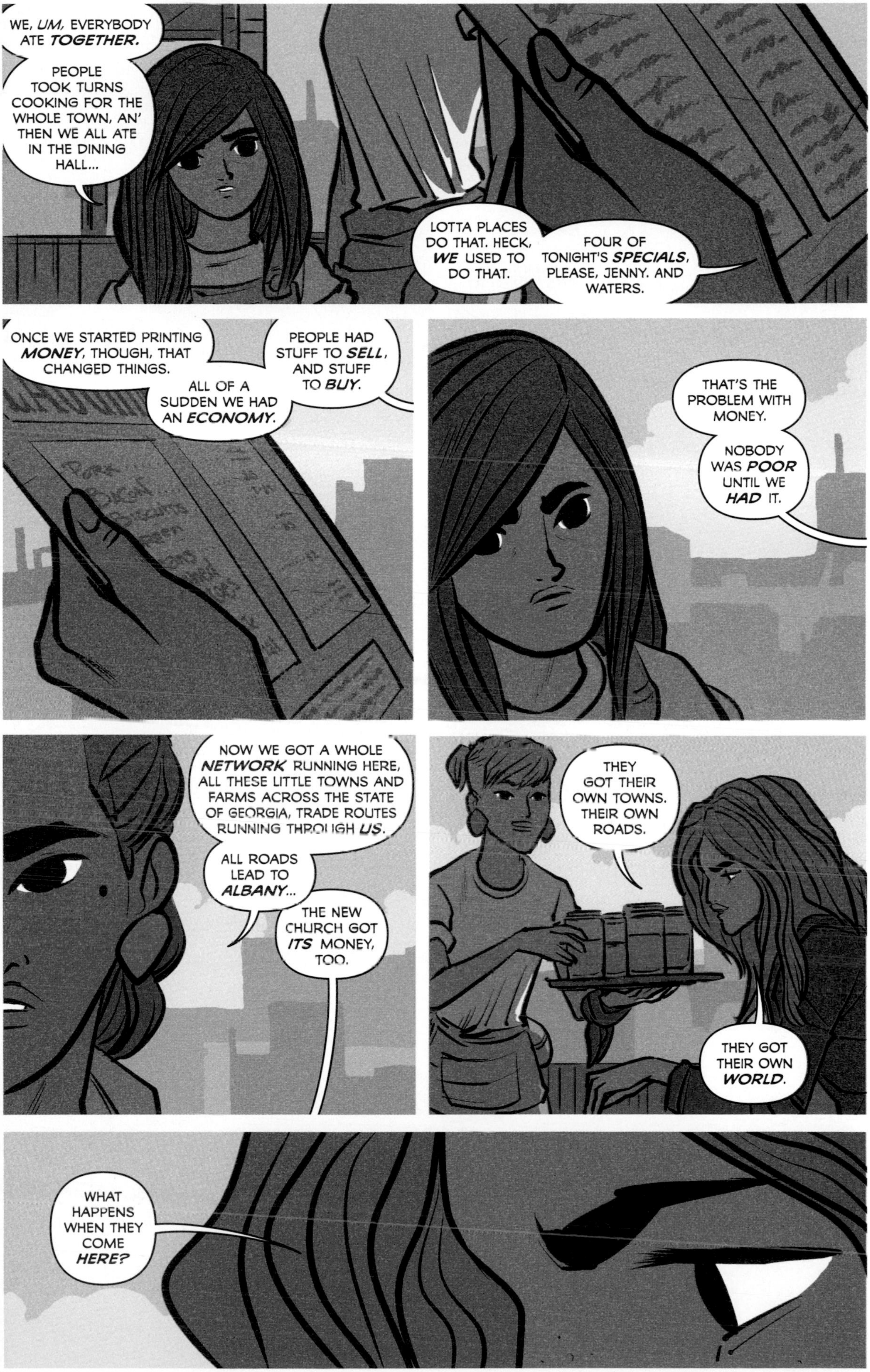

WE, UM, EVERYBODY ATE TOGETHER.
PEOPLE TOOK TURNS COOKING FOR THE WHOLE TOWN, AN' THEN WE ALL ATE IN THE DINING HALL...
LOTTA PLACES DO THAT. HECK, WE USED TO DO THAT.
FOUR OF TONIGHT'S SPECIALS, PLEASE, JENNY. AND WATERS.
ONCE WE STARTED PRINTING MONEY, THOUGH, THAT CHANGED THINGS.
ALL OF A SUDDEN WE HAD AN ECONOMY.
PEOPLE HAD STUFF TO SELL, AND STUFF TO BUY.
THAT'S THE PROBLEM WITH MONEY.
NOBODY WAS POOR UNTIL WE HAD IT.
NOW WE GOT A WHOLE NETWORK RUNNING HERE, ALL THESE LITTLE TOWNS AND FARMS ACROSS THE STATE OF GEORGIA, TRADE ROUTES RUNNING THROUGH US.
ALL ROADS LEAD TO ALBANY...
THE NEW CHURCH GOT ITS MONEY, TOO.
THEY GOT THEIR OWN TOWNS. THEIR OWN ROADS.
THEY GOT THEIR OWN WORLD.
WHAT HAPPENS WHEN THEY COME HERE?

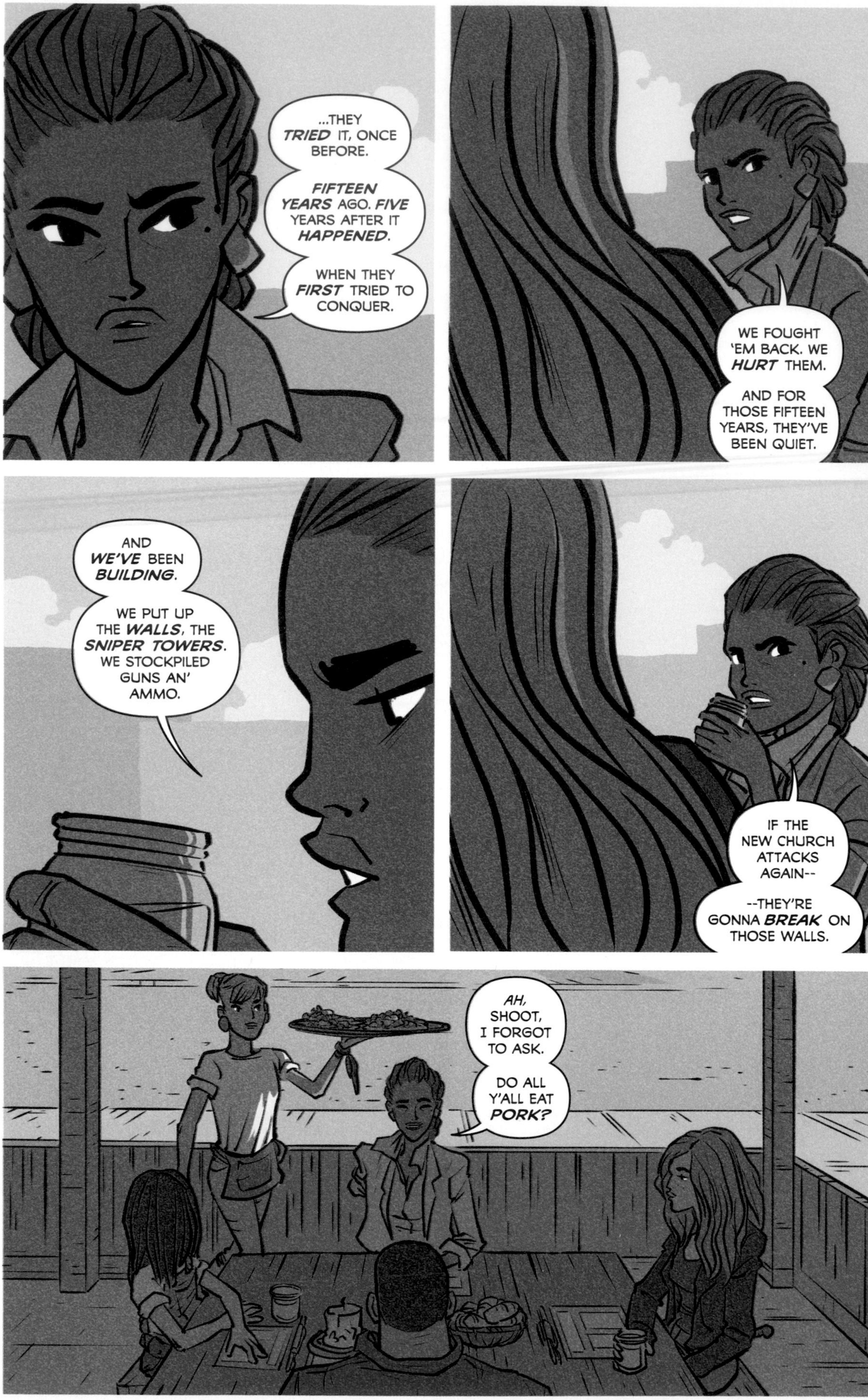
...THEY *TRIED* IT, ONCE BEFORE.
FIFTEEN YEARS AGO. *FIVE* YEARS AFTER IT *HAPPENED*.
WHEN THEY *FIRST* TRIED TO CONQUER.
WE FOUGHT 'EM BACK. WE *HURT* THEM.
AND FOR THOSE FIFTEEN YEARS, THEY'VE BEEN QUIET.
AND *WE'VE* BEEN *BUILDING*.
WE PUT UP THE *WALLS*, THE *SNIPER TOWERS*. WE STOCKPILED GUNS AN' AMMO.
IF THE NEW CHURCH ATTACKS AGAIN--
--THEY'RE GONNA *BREAK* ON THOSE WALLS.
AH, SHOOT, I FORGOT TO ASK.
DO ALL Y'ALL EAT *PORK?*

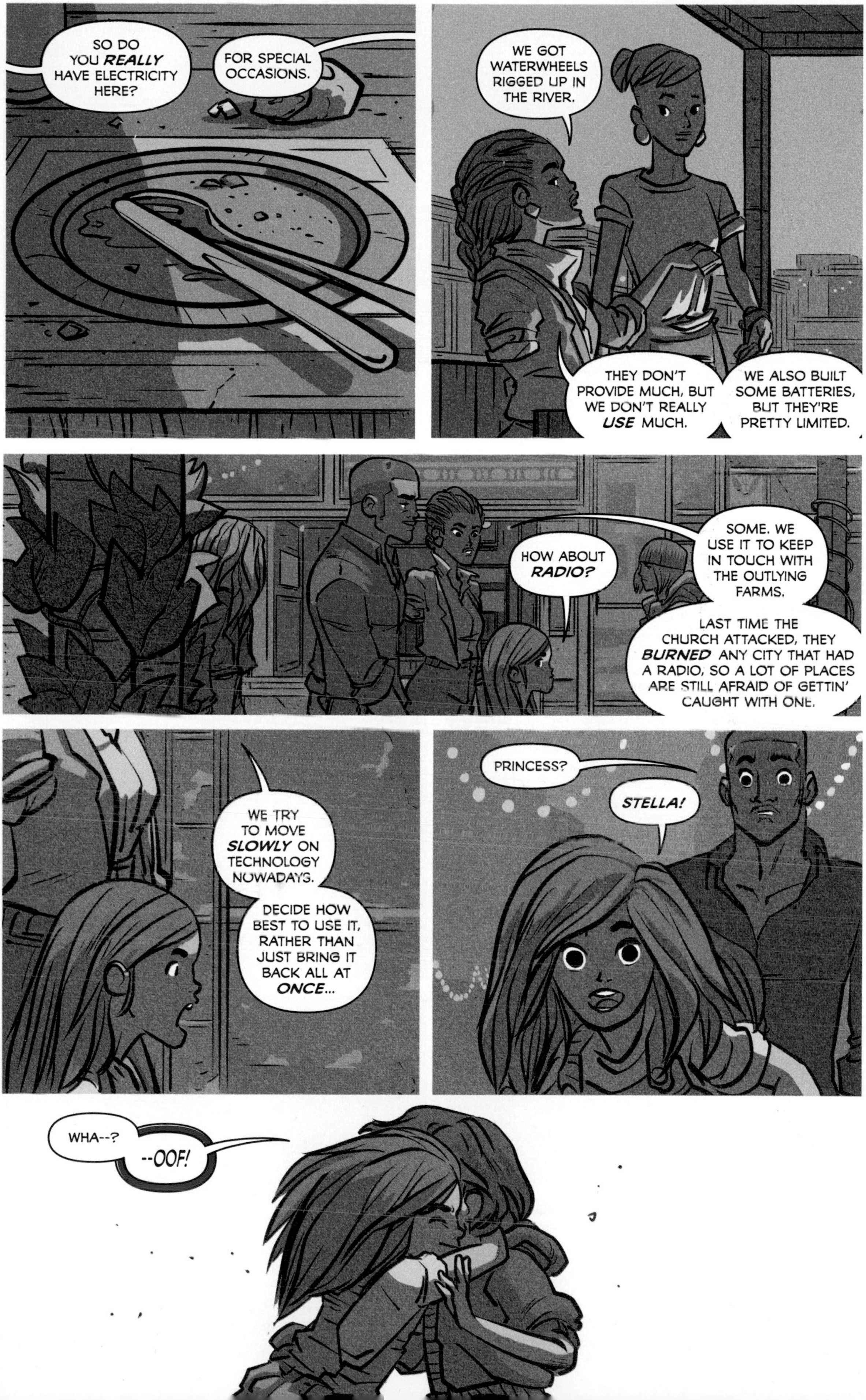
SO DO YOU REALLY HAVE ELECTRICITY HERE?
FOR SPECIAL OCCASIONS.
WE GOT WATERWHEELS RIGGED UP IN THE RIVER.
THEY DON'T PROVIDE MUCH, BUT WE DON'T REALLY USE MUCH.
WE ALSO BUILT SOME BATTERIES, BUT THEY'RE PRETTY LIMITED.
HOW ABOUT RADIO?
SOME. WE USE IT TO KEEP IN TOUCH WITH THE OUTLYING FARMS.
LAST TIME THE CHURCH ATTACKED, THEY BURNED ANY CITY THAT HAD A RADIO, SO A LOT OF PLACES ARE STILL AFRAID OF GETTIN' CAUGHT WITH ONE.
WE TRY TO MOVE SLOWLY ON TECHNOLOGY NOWADAYS.
DECIDE HOW BEST TO USE IT, RATHER THAN JUST BRING IT BACK ALL AT ONCE...
PRINCESS?
STELLA!
WHA--?
--OOF!

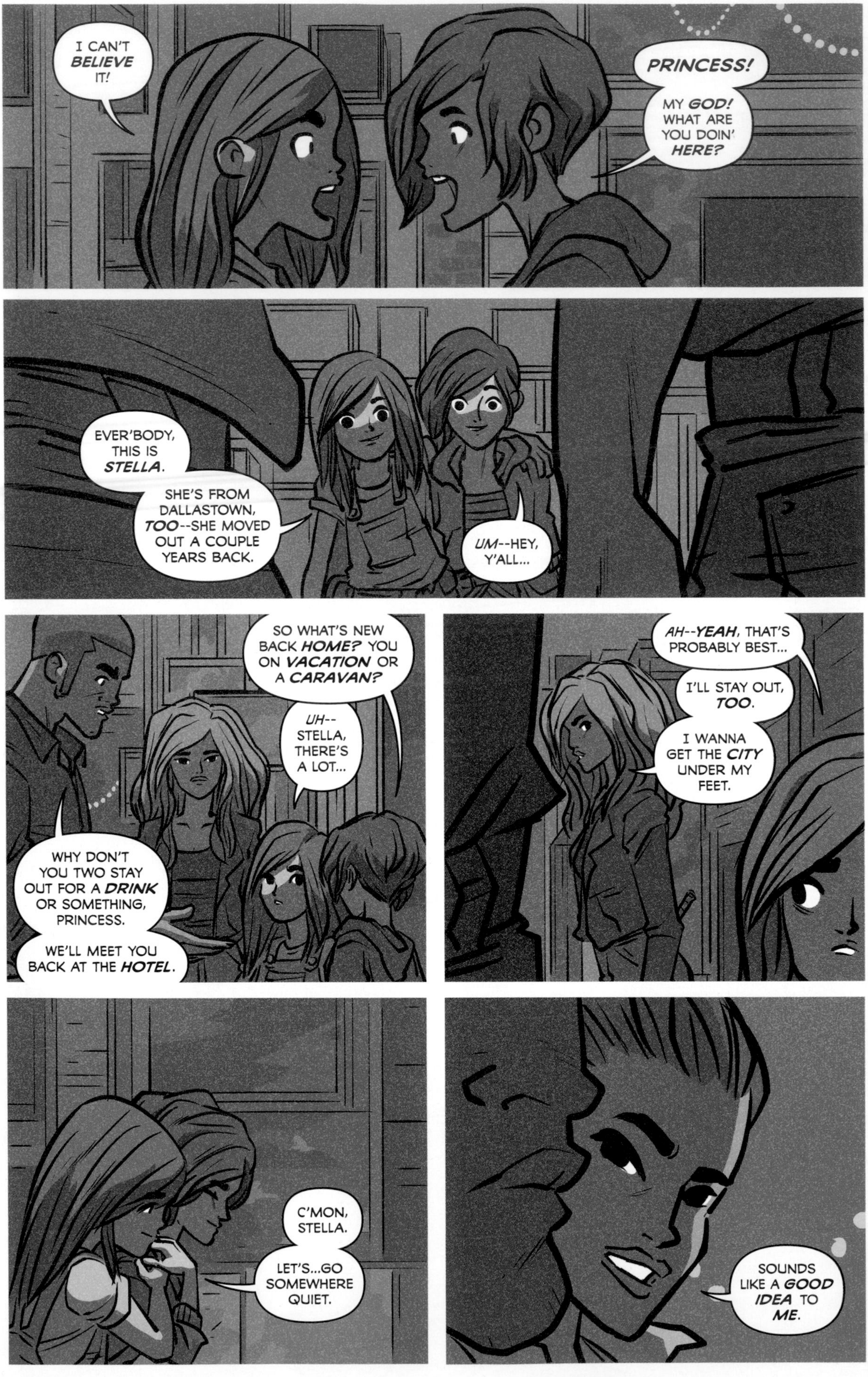
I CAN'T *BELIEVE* IT!
PRINCESS!
MY *GOD!* WHAT ARE YOU DOIN' *HERE?*
EVER'BODY, THIS IS *STELLA*.
SHE'S FROM DALLASTOWN, *TOO*--SHE MOVED OUT A COUPLE YEARS BACK.
UM--HEY, Y'ALL...
SO WHAT'S NEW BACK *HOME?* YOU ON *VACATION* OR A *CARAVAN?*
UH-- STELLA, THERE'S A LOT...
WHY DON'T YOU TWO STAY OUT FOR A *DRINK* OR SOMETHING, PRINCESS.
WE'LL MEET YOU BACK AT THE *HOTEL*.
AH--*YEAH*, THAT'S PROBABLY BEST...
I'LL STAY OUT, *TOO*.
I WANNA GET THE *CITY* UNDER MY FEET.
C'MON, STELLA.
LET'S...GO SOMEWHERE QUIET.
SOUNDS LIKE A *GOOD IDEA* TO *ME*.

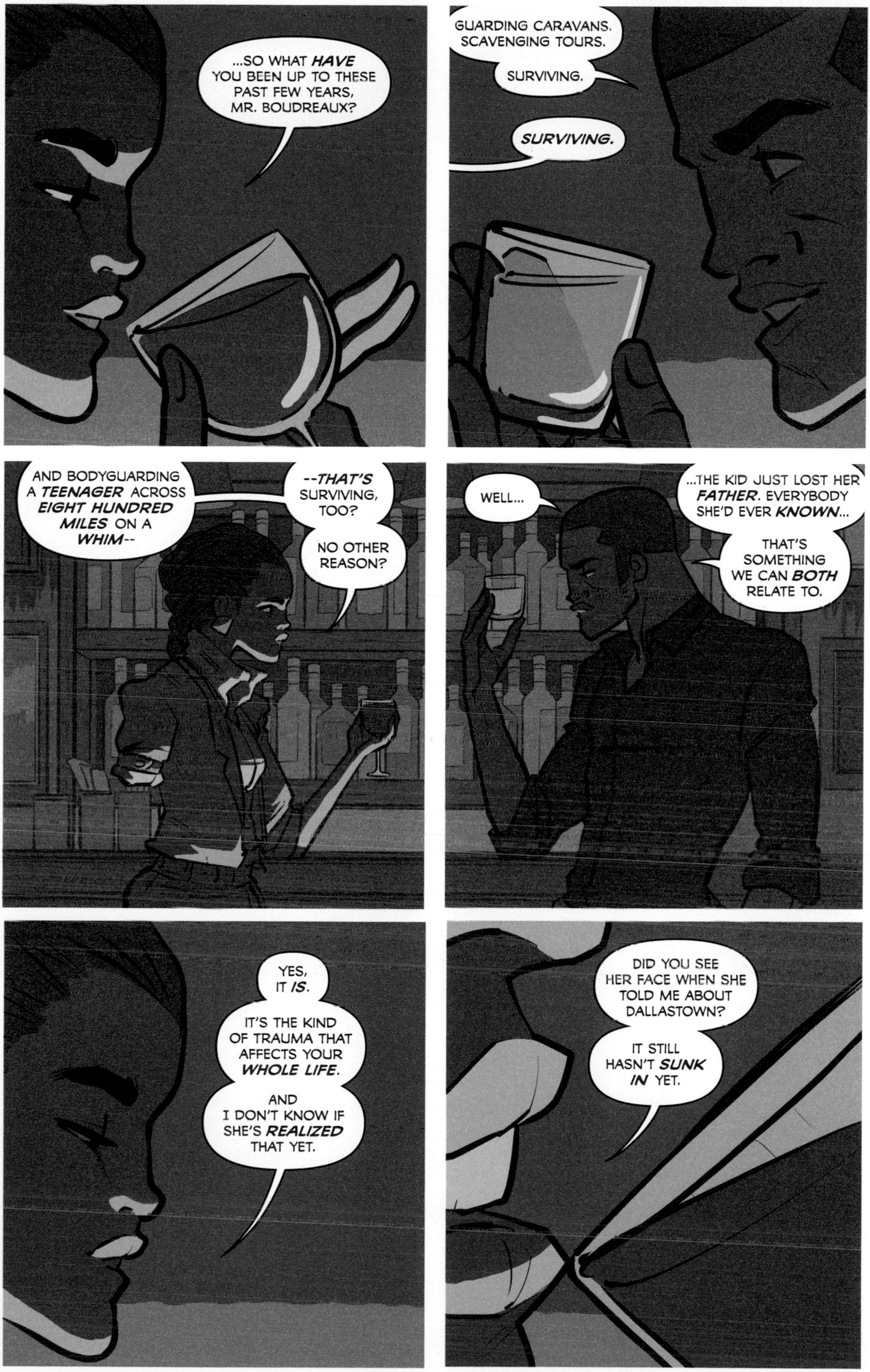
...SO WHAT *HAVE* YOU BEEN UP TO THESE PAST FEW YEARS, MR. BOUDREAUX?
GUARDING CARAVANS. SCAVENGING TOURS.
SURVIVING.
SURVIVING.
AND BODYGUARDING A *TEENAGER* ACROSS *EIGHT HUNDRED MILES* ON A *WHIM*--
--THAT'S SURVIVING, TOO?
NO OTHER REASON?
WELL...
...THE KID JUST LOST HER *FATHER*. EVERYBODY SHE'D EVER *KNOWN*...
THAT'S SOMETHING WE CAN *BOTH* RELATE TO.
YES, IT *IS*.
IT'S THE KIND OF TRAUMA THAT AFFECTS YOUR *WHOLE LIFE*.
AND I DON'T KNOW IF SHE'S *REALIZED* THAT YET.
DID YOU SEE HER FACE WHEN SHE TOLD ME ABOUT DALLASTOWN?
IT STILL HASN'T *SUNK IN* YET.

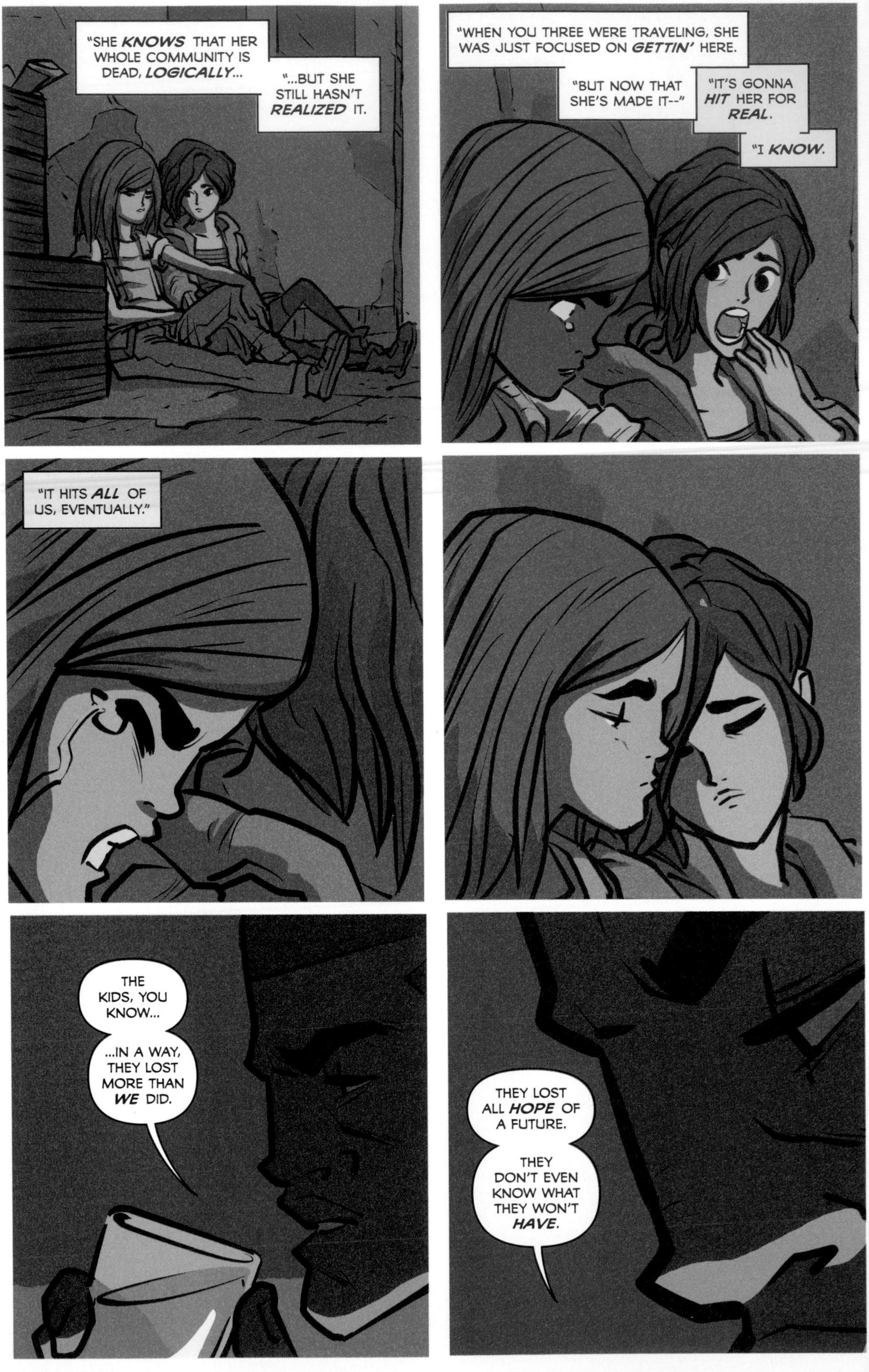
"SHE KNOWS THAT HER WHOLE COMMUNITY IS DEAD, LOGICALLY...
"...BUT SHE STILL HASN'T REALIZED IT.
"WHEN YOU THREE WERE TRAVELING, SHE WAS JUST FOCUSED ON GETTIN' HERE.
"BUT NOW THAT SHE'S MADE IT--"
"IT'S GONNA HIT HER FOR REAL.
"I KNOW.
"IT HITS ALL OF US, EVENTUALLY."
THE KIDS, YOU KNOW...
...IN A WAY, THEY LOST MORE THAN WE DID.
THEY LOST ALL HOPE OF A FUTURE.
THEY DON'T EVEN KNOW WHAT THEY WON'T HAVE.

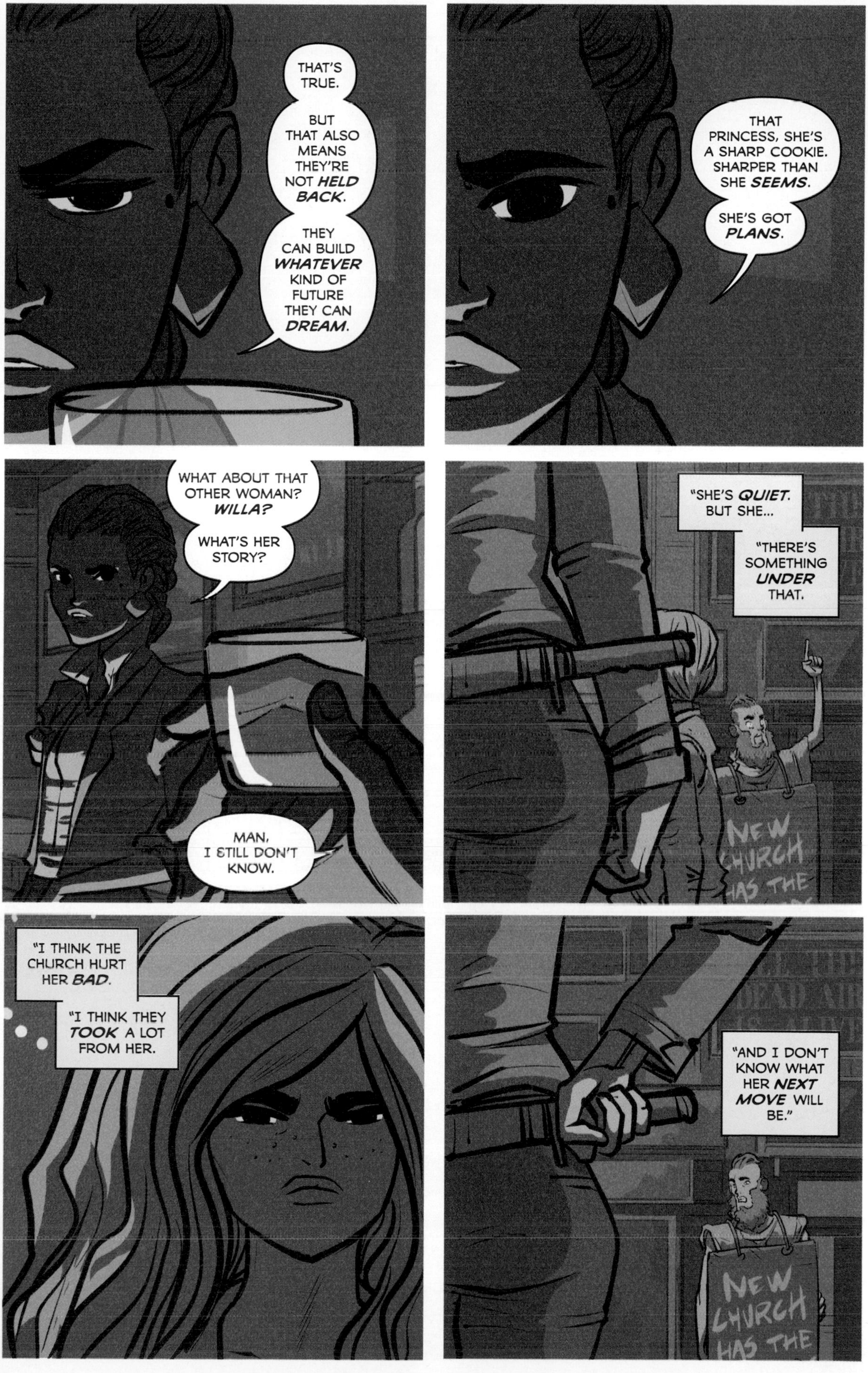
THAT'S TRUE.
BUT THAT ALSO MEANS THEY'RE NOT *HELD BACK*.
THEY CAN BUILD *WHATEVER* KIND OF FUTURE THEY CAN *DREAM*.
THAT PRINCESS, SHE'S A SHARP COOKIE. SHARPER THAN SHE *SEEMS*.
SHE'S GOT *PLANS*.
WHAT ABOUT THAT OTHER WOMAN? *WILLA?*
WHAT'S HER STORY?
MAN, I STILL DON'T KNOW.
"SHE'S *QUIET*. BUT SHE...
"THERE'S SOMETHING *UNDER* THAT.
NEW CHURCH HAS THE
"I THINK THE CHURCH HURT HER *BAD*.
"I THINK THEY *TOOK* A LOT FROM HER.
"AND I DON'T KNOW WHAT HER *NEXT MOVE* WILL BE."
NEW CHURCH HAS THE

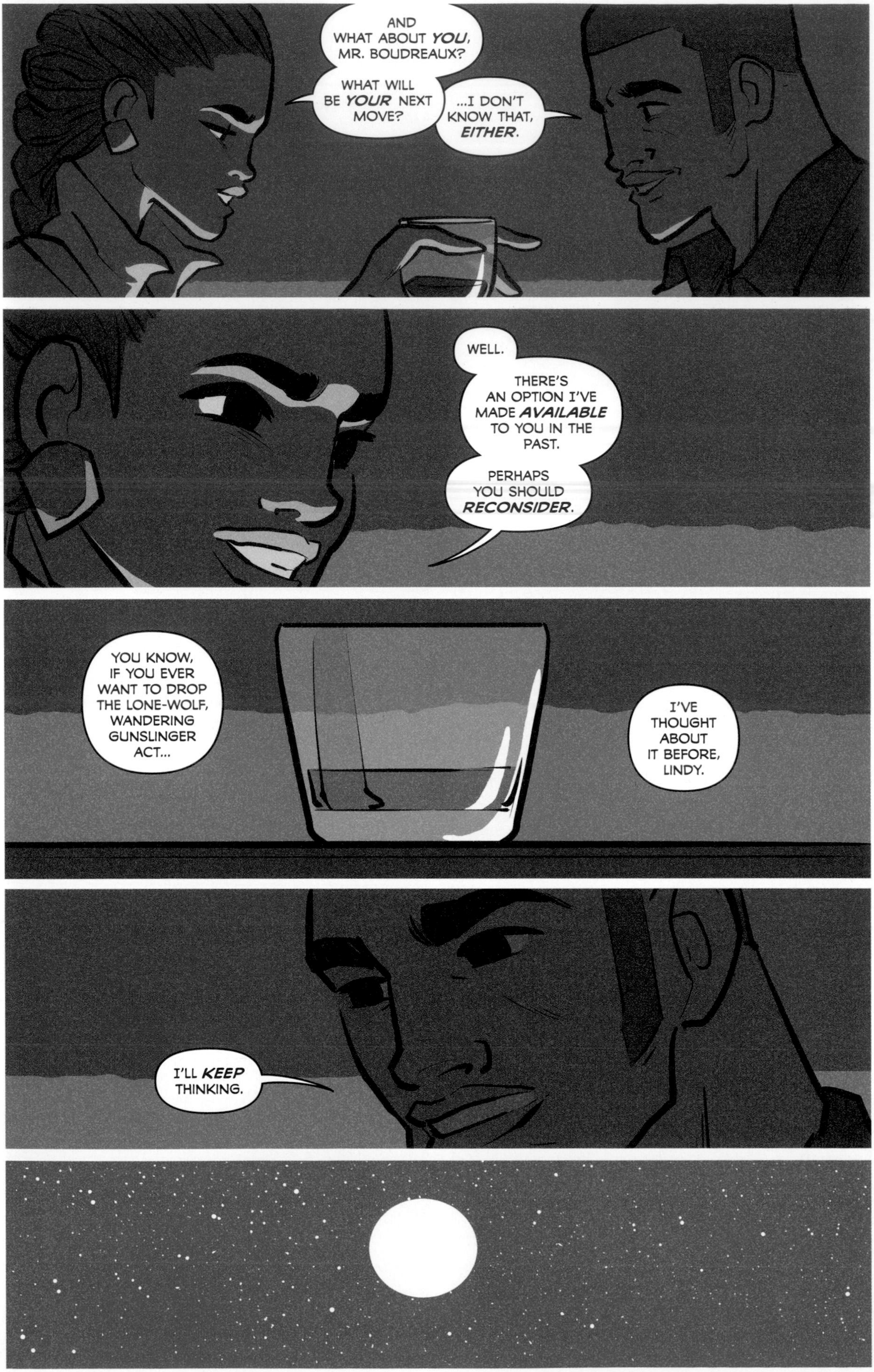
AND WHAT ABOUT *YOU*, MR. BOUDREAUX?
WHAT WILL BE *YOUR* NEXT MOVE?
...I DON'T KNOW THAT, *EITHER*.
WELL.
THERE'S AN OPTION I'VE MADE *AVAILABLE* TO YOU IN THE PAST.
PERHAPS YOU SHOULD *RECONSIDER*.
YOU KNOW, IF YOU EVER WANT TO DROP THE LONE-WOLF, WANDERING GUNSLINGER ACT...
I'VE THOUGHT ABOUT IT BEFORE, LINDY.
I'LL *KEEP* THINKING.

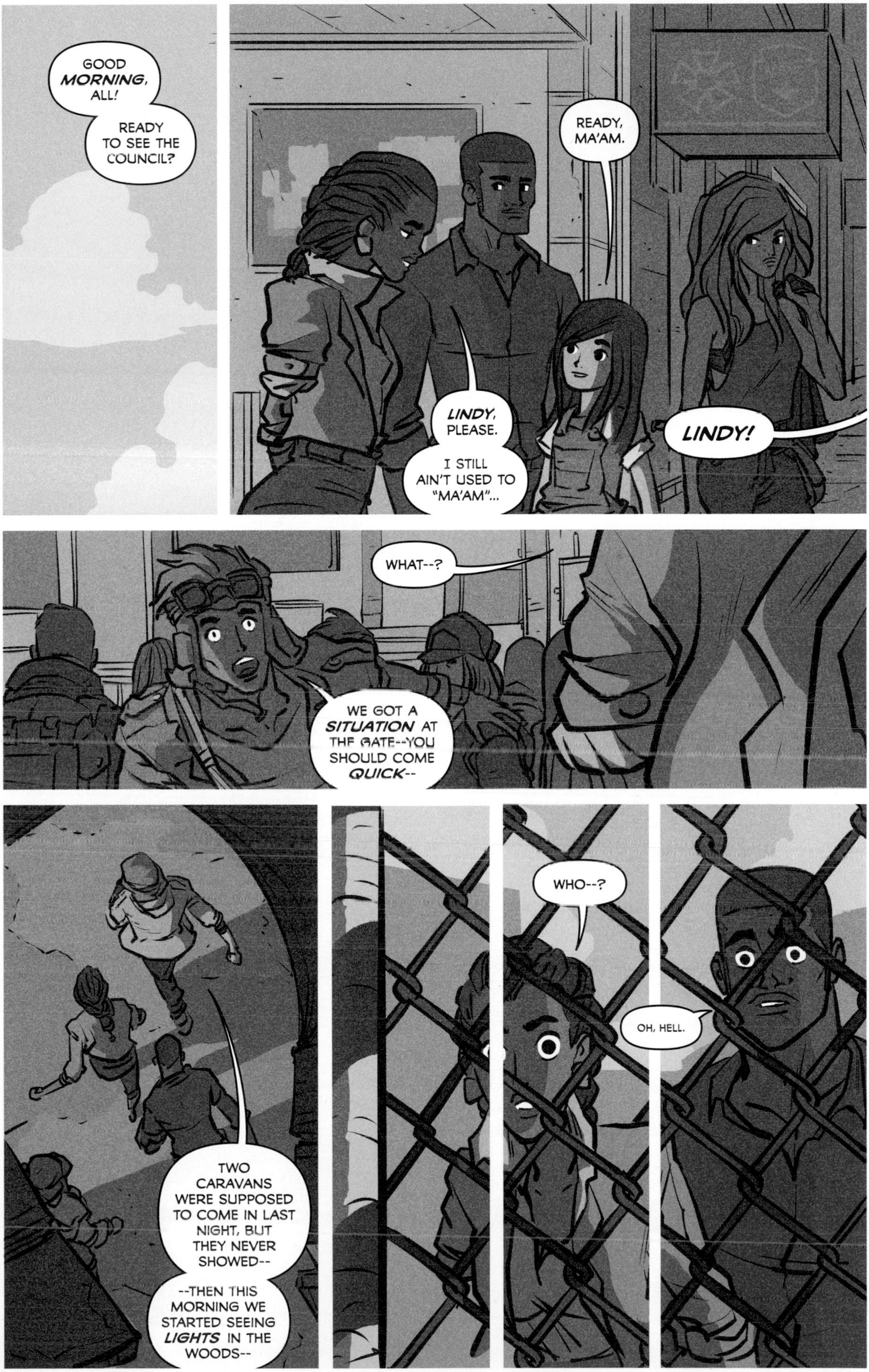
GOOD MORNING, ALL!
READY TO SEE THE COUNCIL?
READY, MA'AM.
LINDY, PLEASE.
I STILL AIN'T USED TO "MA'AM"...
LINDY!
WHAT--?
WE GOT A SITUATION AT THE GATE--YOU SHOULD COME QUICK--
TWO CARAVANS WERE SUPPOSED TO COME IN LAST NIGHT, BUT THEY NEVER SHOWED--
--THEN THIS MORNING WE STARTED SEEING LIGHTS IN THE WOODS--
WHO--?
OH, HELL.

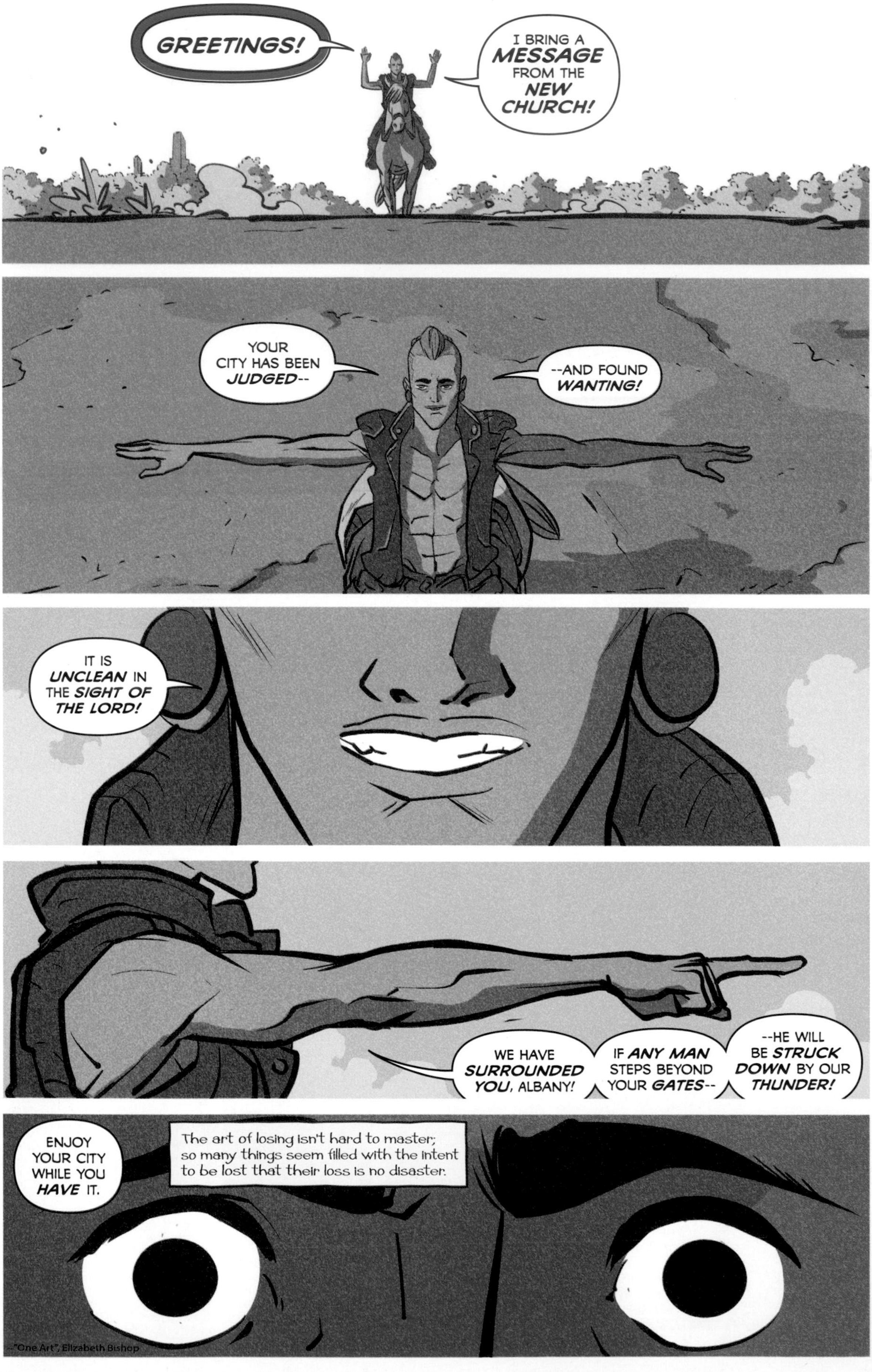
GREETINGS!
I BRING A MESSAGE FROM THE NEW CHURCH!
YOUR CITY HAS BEEN JUDGED--
--AND FOUND WANTING!
IT IS UNCLEAN IN THE SIGHT OF THE LORD!
WE HAVE SURROUNDED YOU, ALBANY!
IF ANY MAN STEPS BEYOND YOUR GATES--
--HE WILL BE STRUCK DOWN BY OUR THUNDER!
ENJOY YOUR CITY WHILE YOU HAVE IT.
The art of losing isn't hard to master; so many things seem filled with the intent to be lost that their loss is no disaster.
"One Art", Elizabeth Bishop

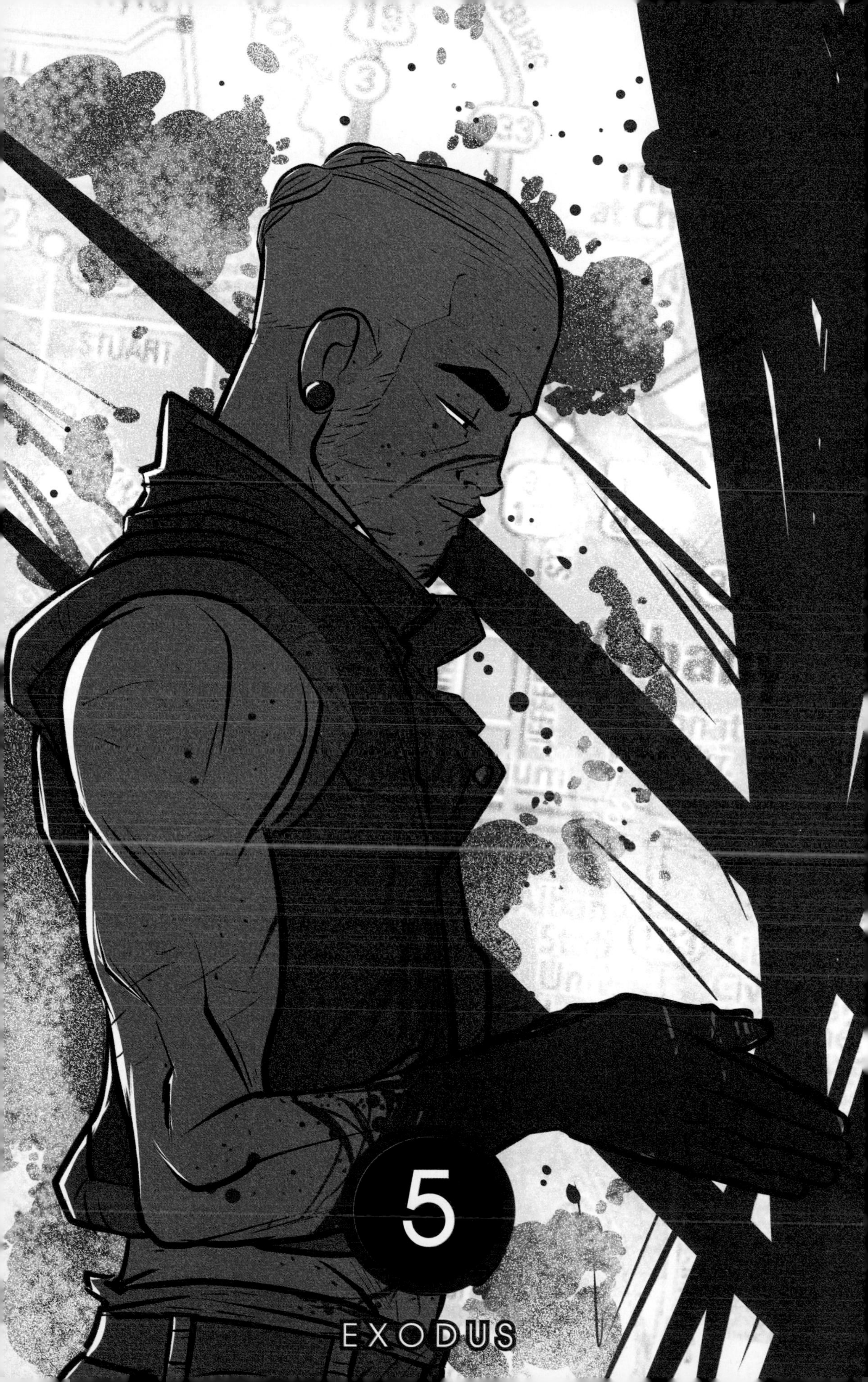

5

EXODUS

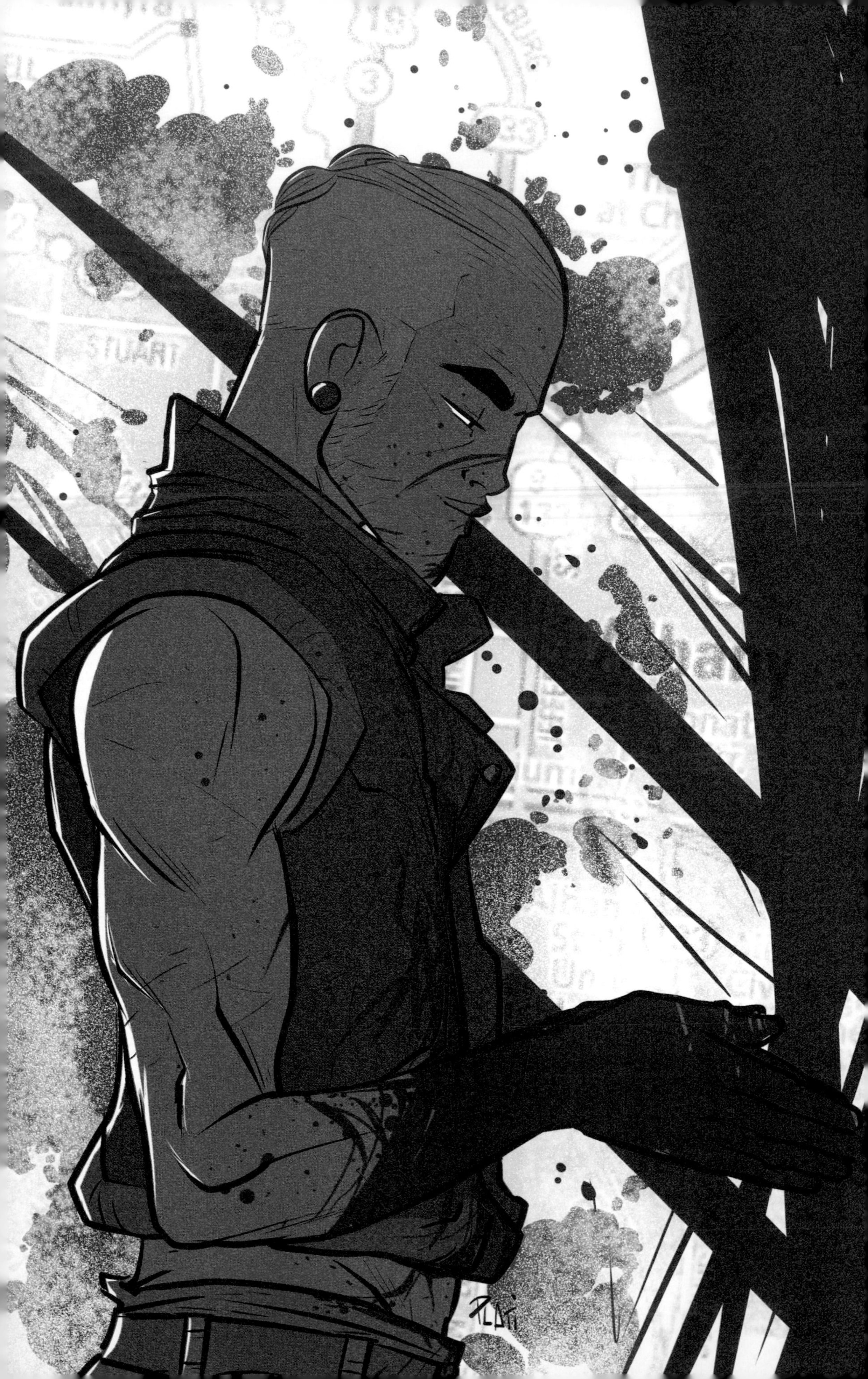
STUART

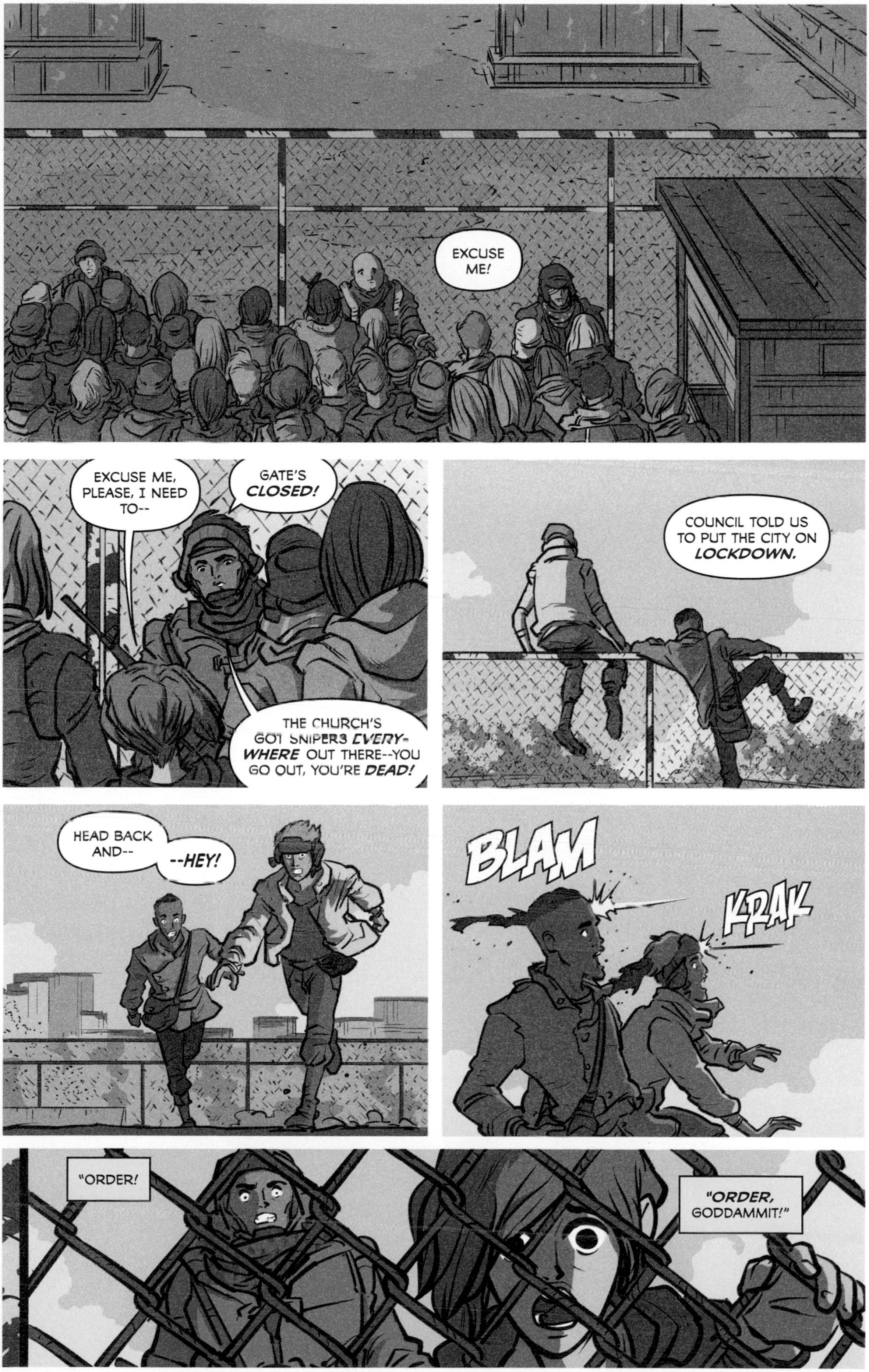
EXCUSE ME!
EXCUSE ME, PLEASE, I NEED TO--
GATE'S *CLOSED!*
THE CHURCH'S GOT SNIPERS *EVERY-WHERE* OUT THERE--YOU GO OUT, YOU'RE *DEAD!*
COUNCIL TOLD US TO PUT THE CITY ON *LOCKDOWN.*
HEAD BACK AND--
--HEY!
BLAM
KRAK
"ORDER!
"*ORDER,* GODDAMMIT!"

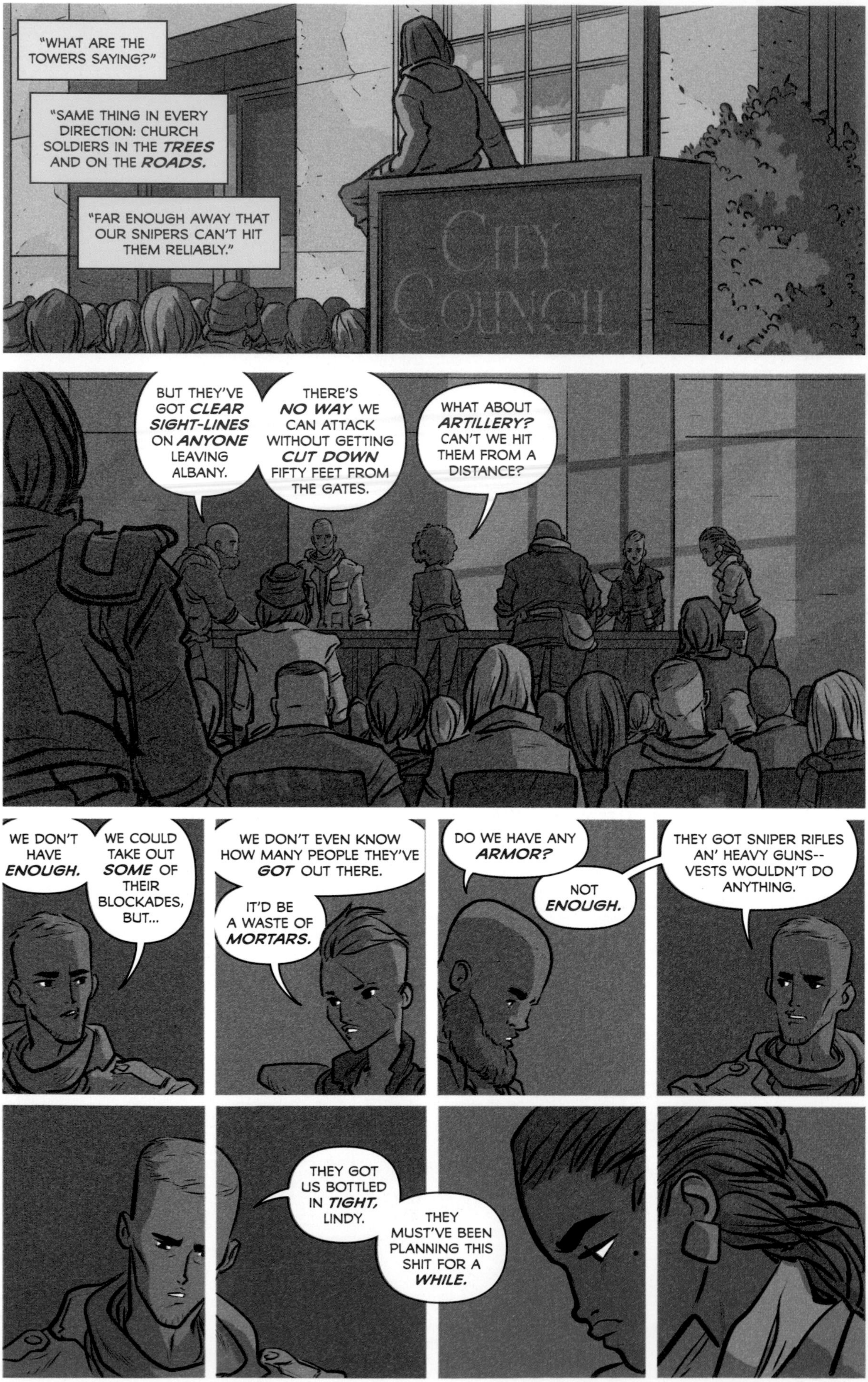
"WHAT ARE THE TOWERS SAYING?"
"SAME THING IN EVERY DIRECTION: CHURCH SOLDIERS IN THE TREES AND ON THE ROADS.
"FAR ENOUGH AWAY THAT OUR SNIPERS CAN'T HIT THEM RELIABLY."
CITY COUNCIL
BUT THEY'VE GOT CLEAR SIGHT-LINES ON ANYONE LEAVING ALBANY.
THERE'S NO WAY WE CAN ATTACK WITHOUT GETTING CUT DOWN FIFTY FEET FROM THE GATES.
WHAT ABOUT ARTILLERY? CAN'T WE HIT THEM FROM A DISTANCE?
WE DON'T HAVE ENOUGH.
WE COULD TAKE OUT SOME OF THEIR BLOCKADES, BUT...
WE DON'T EVEN KNOW HOW MANY PEOPLE THEY'VE GOT OUT THERE.
IT'D BE A WASTE OF MORTARS.
DO WE HAVE ANY ARMOR?
NOT ENOUGH.
THEY GOT SNIPER RIFLES AN' HEAVY GUNS-- VESTS WOULDN'T DO ANYTHING.
THEY GOT US BOTTLED IN TIGHT, LINDY.
THEY MUST'VE BEEN PLANNING THIS SHIT FOR A WHILE.

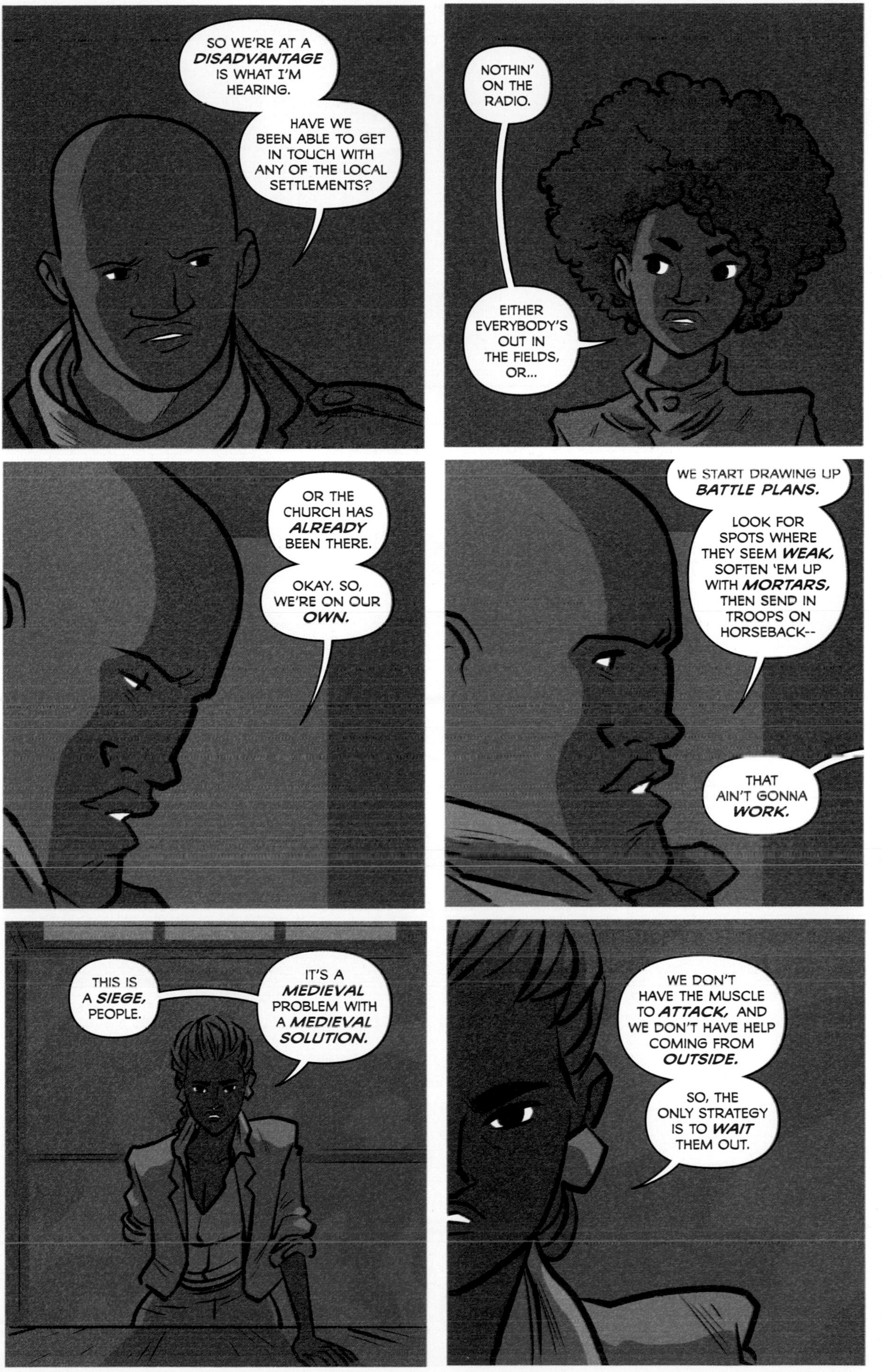
SO WE'RE AT A *DISADVANTAGE* IS WHAT I'M HEARING.
HAVE WE BEEN ABLE TO GET IN TOUCH WITH ANY OF THE LOCAL SETTLEMENTS?
NOTHIN' ON THE RADIO.
EITHER EVERYBODY'S OUT IN THE FIELDS, OR...
OR THE CHURCH HAS *ALREADY* BEEN THERE.
OKAY. SO, WE'RE ON OUR *OWN.*
WE START DRAWING UP *BATTLE PLANS.*
LOOK FOR SPOTS WHERE THEY SEEM *WEAK,* SOFTEN 'EM UP WITH *MORTARS,* THEN SEND IN TROOPS ON HORSEBACK--
THAT AIN'T GONNA *WORK.*
THIS IS A *SIEGE,* PEOPLE.
IT'S A *MEDIEVAL* PROBLEM WITH A *MEDIEVAL SOLUTION.*
WE DON'T HAVE THE MUSCLE TO *ATTACK,* AND WE DON'T HAVE HELP COMING FROM *OUTSIDE.*
SO, THE ONLY STRATEGY IS TO *WAIT* THEM OUT.

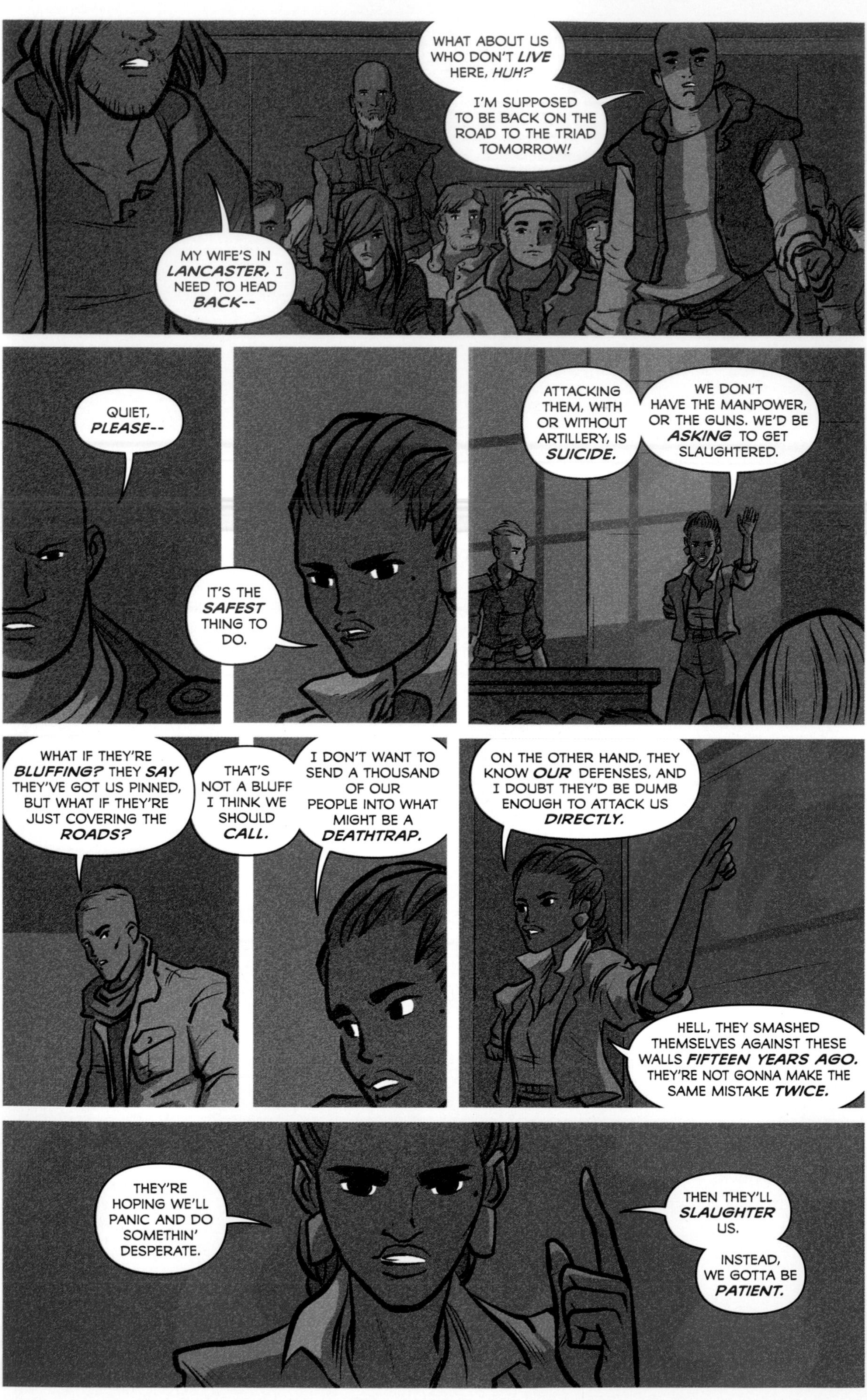
WHAT ABOUT US WHO DON'T *LIVE* HERE, *HUH?*
I'M SUPPOSED TO BE BACK ON THE ROAD TO THE TRIAD TOMORROW!
MY WIFE'S IN *LANCASTER,* I NEED TO HEAD *BACK--*
QUIET, *PLEASE--*
IT'S THE *SAFEST* THING TO DO.
ATTACKING THEM, WITH OR WITHOUT ARTILLERY, IS *SUICIDE.*
WE DON'T HAVE THE MANPOWER, OR THE GUNS. WE'D BE *ASKING* TO GET SLAUGHTERED.
WHAT IF THEY'RE *BLUFFING?* THEY *SAY* THEY'VE GOT US PINNED, BUT WHAT IF THEY'RE JUST COVERING THE *ROADS?*
THAT'S NOT A BLUFF I THINK WE SHOULD *CALL.*
I DON'T WANT TO SEND A THOUSAND OF OUR PEOPLE INTO WHAT MIGHT BE A *DEATHTRAP.*
ON THE OTHER HAND, THEY KNOW *OUR* DEFENSES, AND I DOUBT THEY'D BE DUMB ENOUGH TO ATTACK US *DIRECTLY.*
HELL, THEY SMASHED THEMSELVES AGAINST THESE WALLS *FIFTEEN YEARS AGO.* THEY'RE NOT GONNA MAKE THE SAME MISTAKE *TWICE.*
THEY'RE HOPING WE'LL PANIC AND DO SOMETHIN' DESPERATE.
THEN THEY'LL *SLAUGHTER* US.
INSTEAD, WE GOTTA BE *PATIENT.*

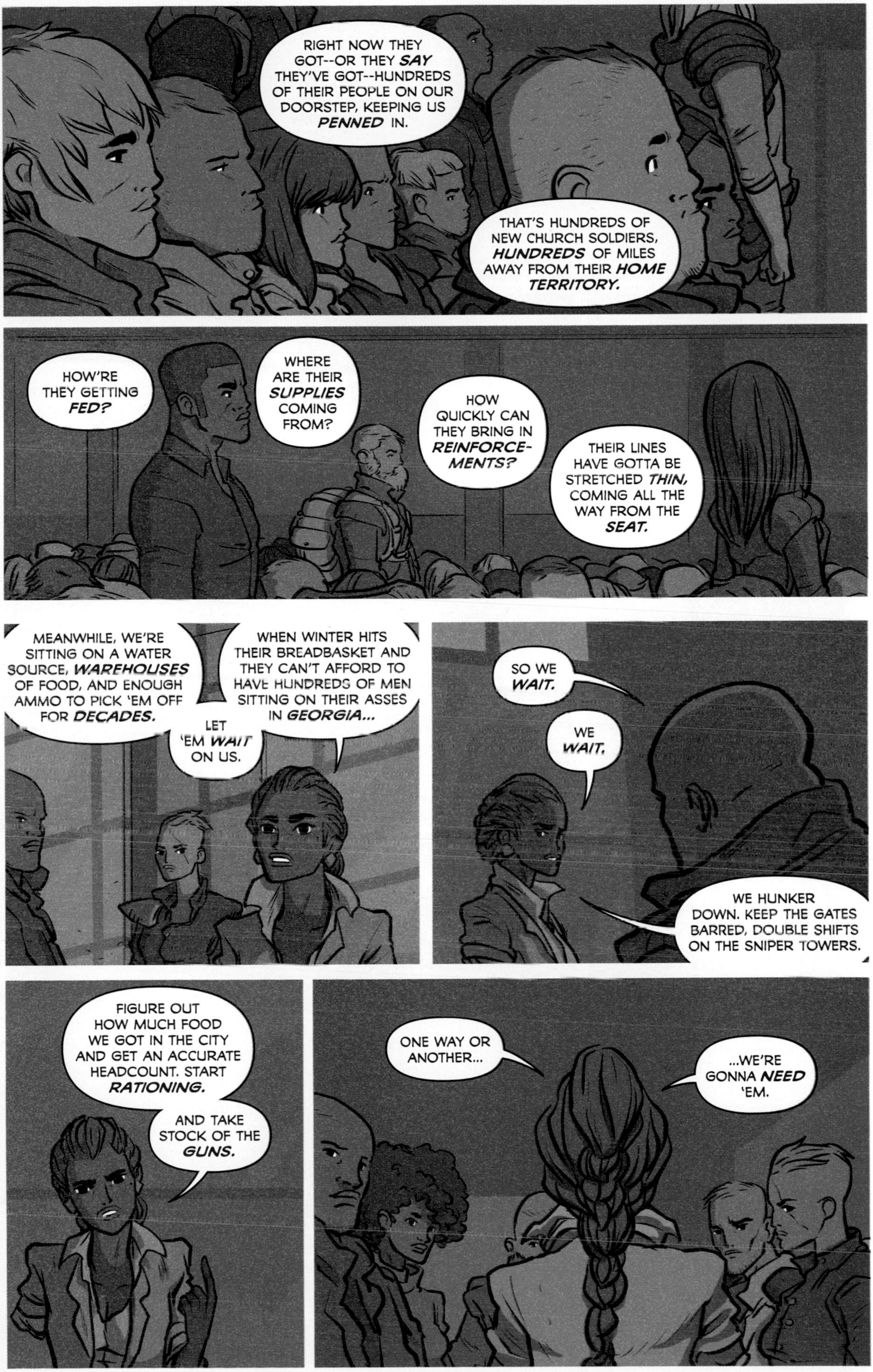
RIGHT NOW THEY GOT--OR THEY *SAY* THEY'VE GOT--HUNDREDS OF THEIR PEOPLE ON OUR DOORSTEP, KEEPING US *PENNED* IN.
THAT'S HUNDREDS OF NEW CHURCH SOLDIERS, *HUNDREDS* OF MILES AWAY FROM THEIR *HOME TERRITORY.*
HOW'RE THEY GETTING *FED?*
WHERE ARE THEIR *SUPPLIES* COMING FROM?
HOW QUICKLY CAN THEY BRING IN *REINFORCE-MENTS?*
THEIR LINES HAVE GOTTA BE STRETCHED *THIN,* COMING ALL THE WAY FROM THE *SEAT.*
MEANWHILE, WE'RE SITTING ON A WATER SOURCE, *WAREHOUSES* OF FOOD, AND ENOUGH AMMO TO PICK 'EM OFF FOR *DECADES.*
WHEN WINTER HITS THEIR BREADBASKET AND THEY CAN'T AFFORD TO HAVE HUNDREDS OF MEN SITTING ON THEIR ASSES IN *GEORGIA...*
LET 'EM *WAIT* ON US.
SO WE *WAIT.*
WE *WAIT.*
WE HUNKER DOWN. KEEP THE GATES BARRED, DOUBLE SHIFTS ON THE SNIPER TOWERS.
FIGURE OUT HOW MUCH FOOD WE GOT IN THE CITY AND GET AN ACCURATE HEADCOUNT. START *RATIONING.*
AND TAKE STOCK OF THE *GUNS.*
ONE WAY OR ANOTHER...
...WE'RE GONNA *NEED* 'EM.

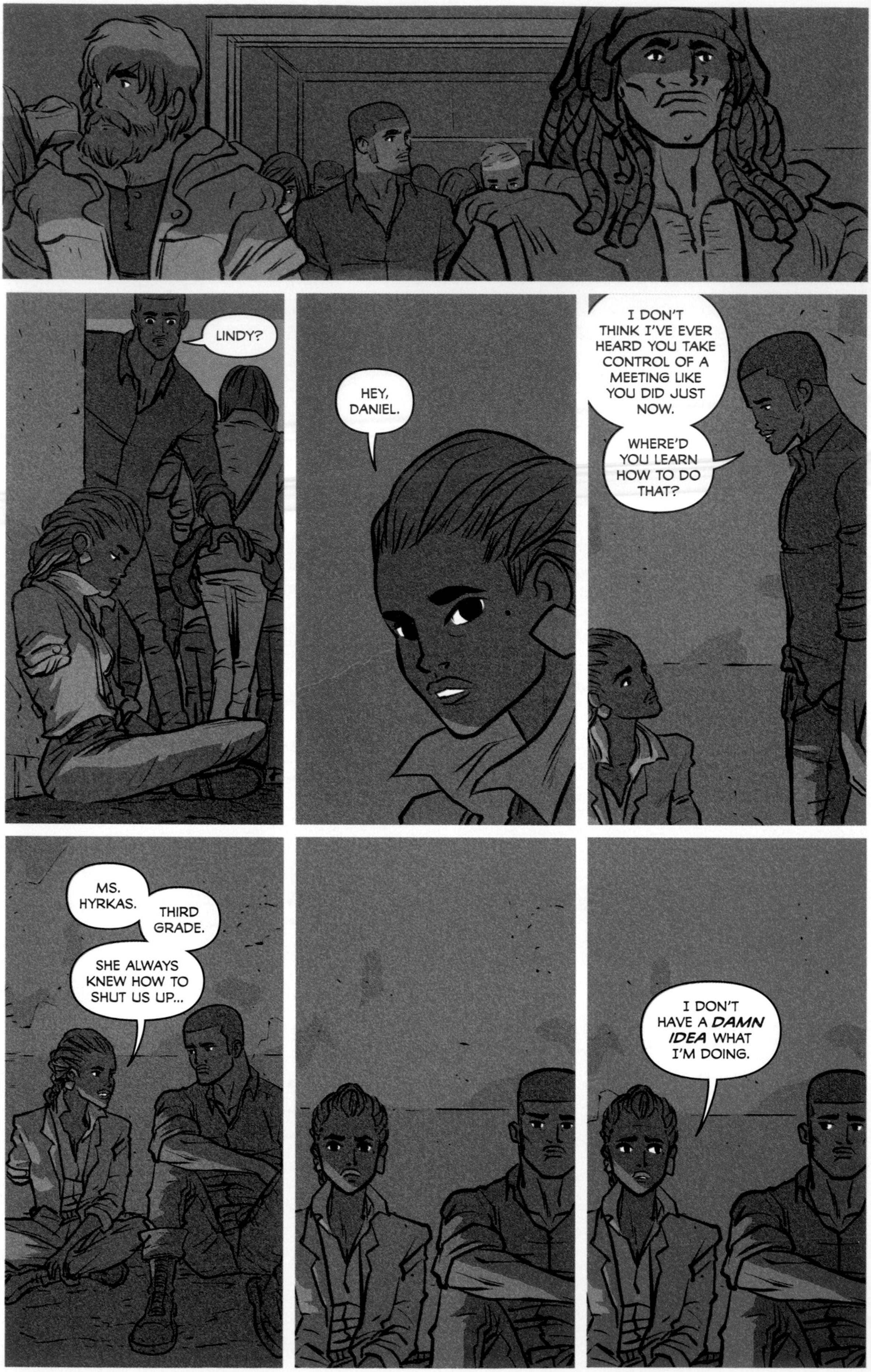
LINDY?
HEY, DANIEL.
I DON'T THINK I'VE EVER HEARD YOU TAKE CONTROL OF A MEETING LIKE YOU DID JUST NOW.
WHERE'D YOU LEARN HOW TO DO THAT?
MS. HYRKAS.
THIRD GRADE.
SHE ALWAYS KNEW HOW TO SHUT US UP...
I DON'T HAVE A *DAMN IDEA* WHAT I'M DOING.

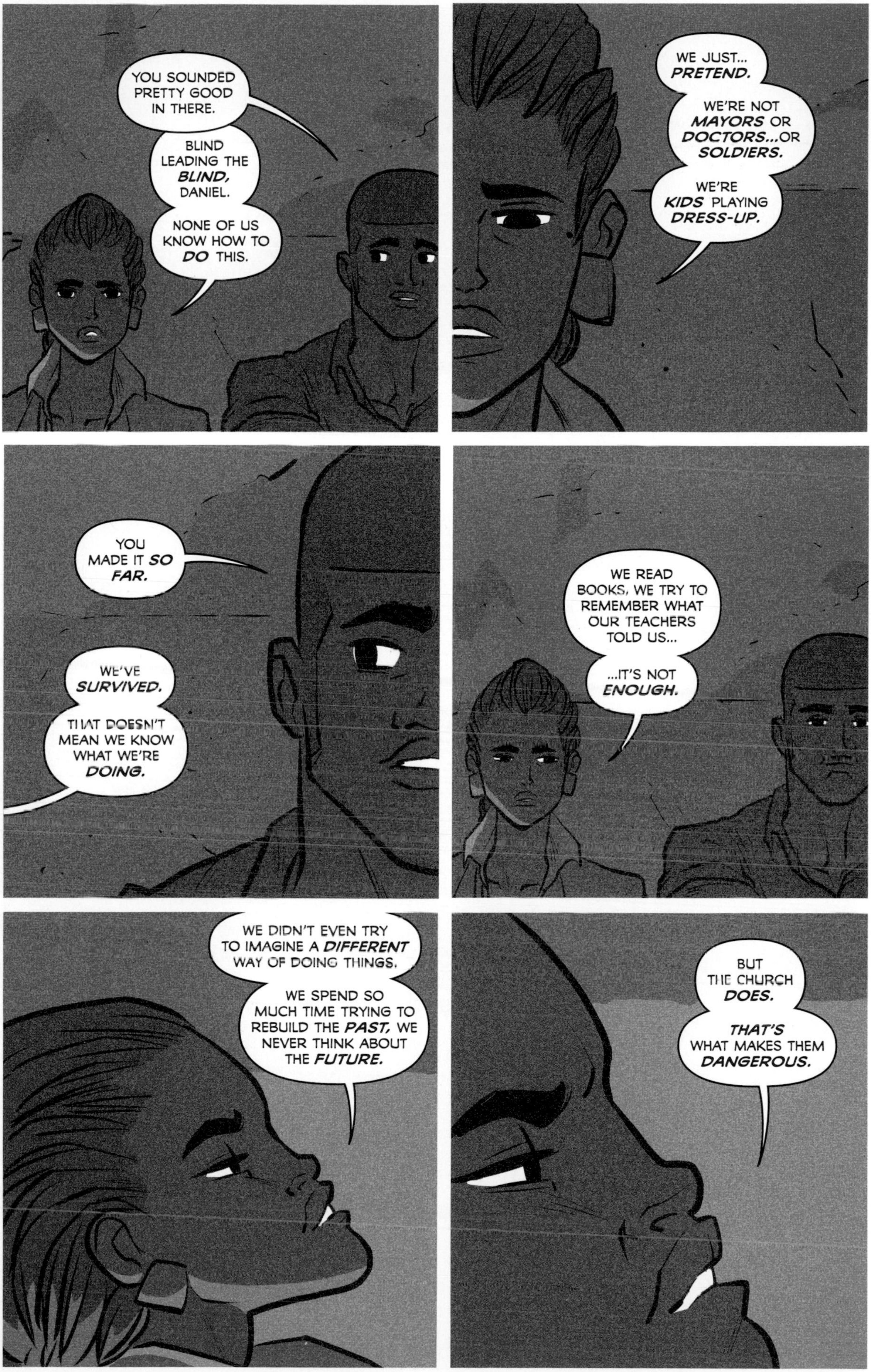
YOU SOUNDED PRETTY GOOD IN THERE.
BLIND LEADING THE BLIND, DANIEL.
NONE OF US KNOW HOW TO DO THIS.
WE JUST... PRETEND.
WE'RE NOT MAYORS OR DOCTORS...OR SOLDIERS.
WE'RE KIDS PLAYING DRESS-UP.
YOU MADE IT SO FAR.
WE'VE SURVIVED.
THAT DOESN'T MEAN WE KNOW WHAT WE'RE DOING.
WE READ BOOKS, WE TRY TO REMEMBER WHAT OUR TEACHERS TOLD US...
...IT'S NOT ENOUGH.
WE DIDN'T EVEN TRY TO IMAGINE A DIFFERENT WAY OF DOING THINGS.
WE SPEND SO MUCH TIME TRYING TO REBUILD THE PAST, WE NEVER THINK ABOUT THE FUTURE.
BUT THE CHURCH DOES.
THAT'S WHAT MAKES THEM DANGEROUS.

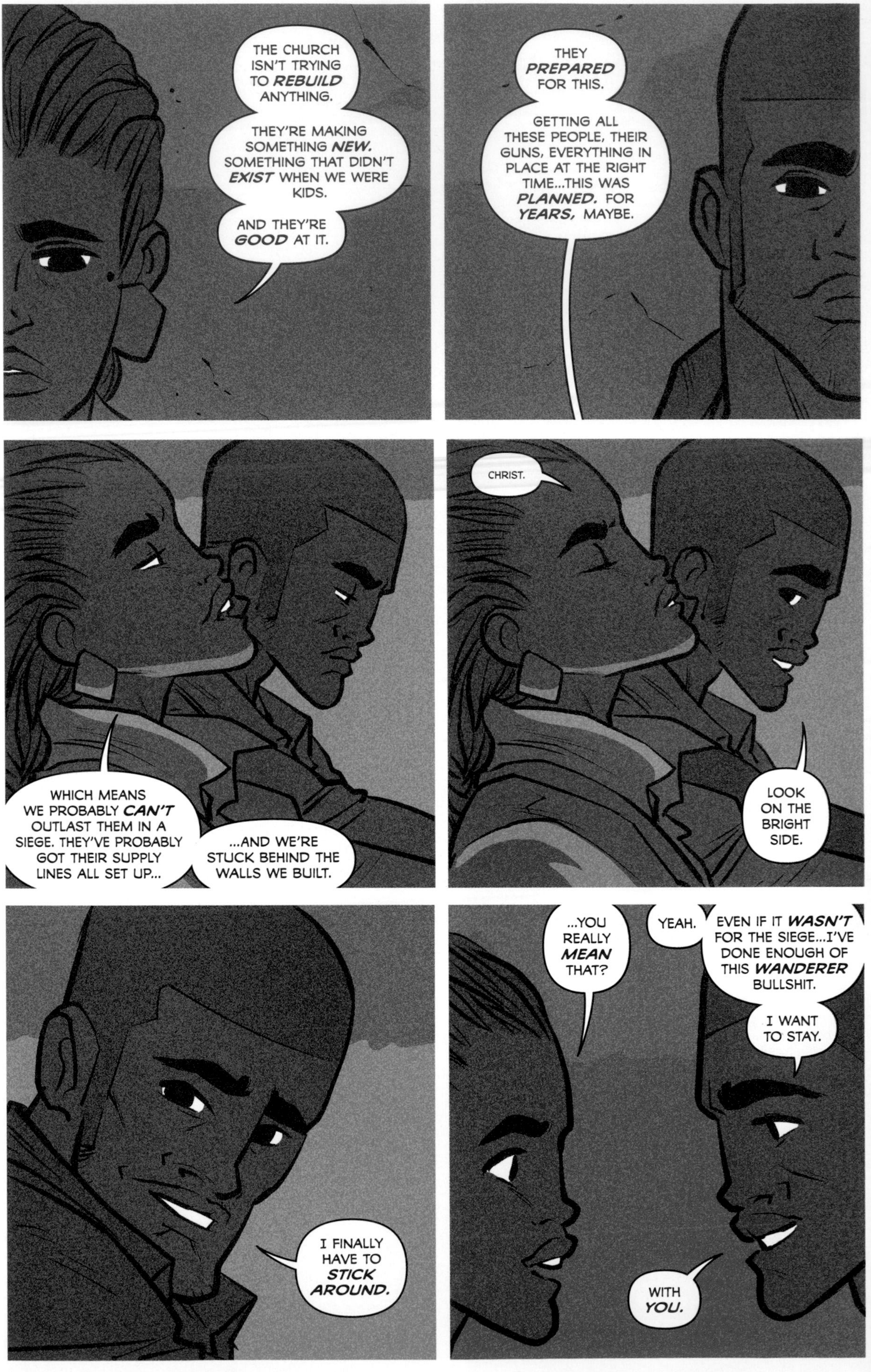
THE CHURCH ISN'T TRYING TO *REBUILD* ANYTHING.
THEY'RE MAKING SOMETHING *NEW.* SOMETHING THAT DIDN'T *EXIST* WHEN WE WERE KIDS.
AND THEY'RE *GOOD* AT IT.
THEY *PREPARED* FOR THIS.
GETTING ALL THESE PEOPLE, THEIR GUNS, EVERYTHING IN PLACE AT THE RIGHT TIME...THIS WAS *PLANNED.* FOR *YEARS,* MAYBE.
WHICH MEANS WE PROBABLY *CAN'T* OUTLAST THEM IN A SIEGE. THEY'VE PROBABLY GOT THEIR SUPPLY LINES ALL SET UP...
...AND WE'RE STUCK BEHIND THE WALLS WE BUILT.
CHRIST.
LOOK ON THE BRIGHT SIDE.
I FINALLY HAVE TO *STICK AROUND.*
...YOU REALLY *MEAN* THAT?
YEAH.
EVEN IF IT *WASN'T* FOR THE SIEGE...I'VE DONE ENOUGH OF THIS *WANDERER* BULLSHIT.
I WANT TO STAY.
WITH *YOU.*

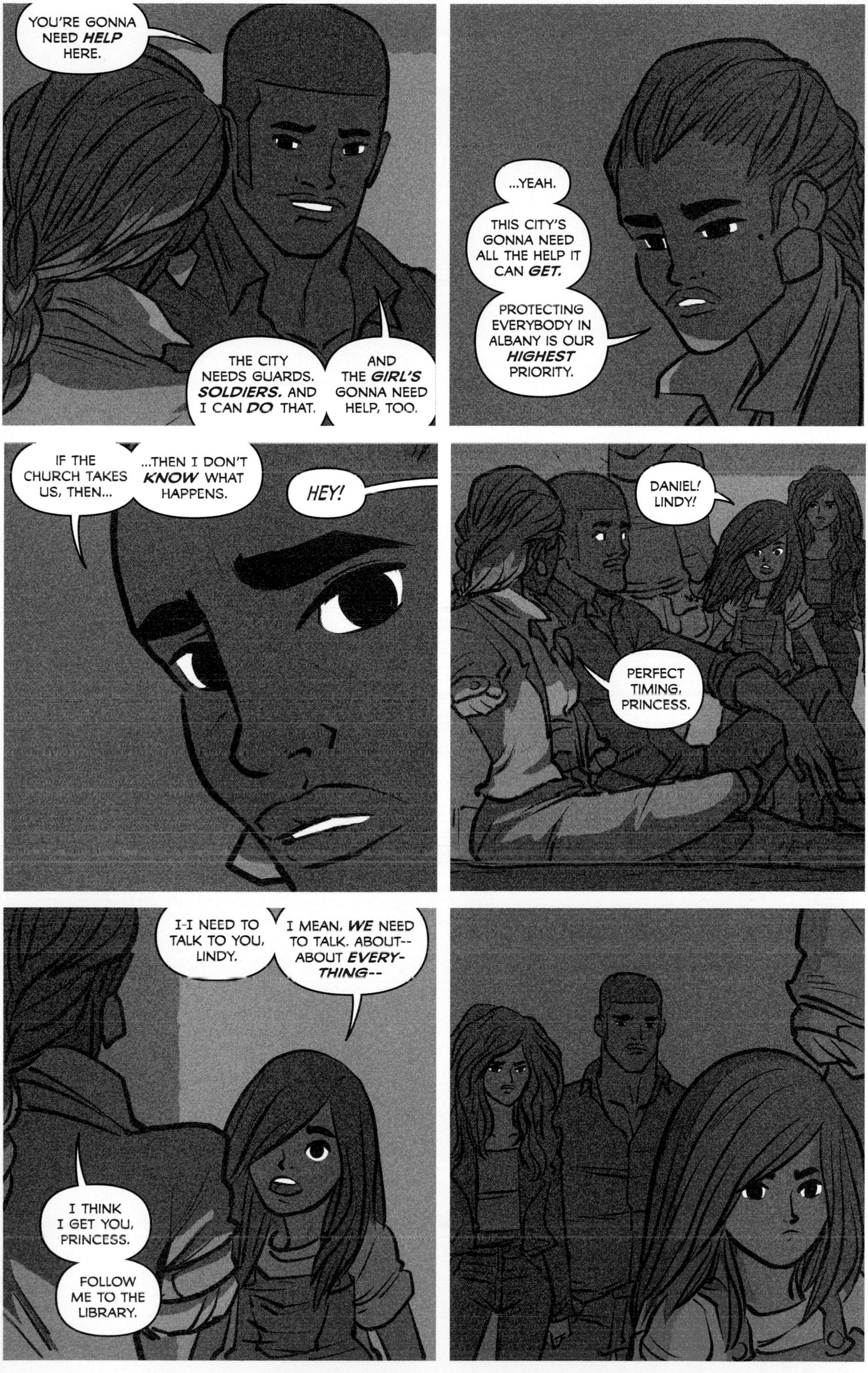
YOU'RE GONNA NEED *HELP* HERE.
THE CITY NEEDS GUARDS. ***SOLDIERS.*** AND I CAN *DO* THAT.
AND THE *GIRL'S* GONNA NEED HELP, TOO.
...YEAH.
THIS CITY'S GONNA NEED ALL THE HELP IT CAN *GET.*
PROTECTING EVERYBODY IN ALBANY IS OUR ***HIGHEST*** PRIORITY.
IF THE CHURCH TAKES US, THEN...
...THEN I DON'T ***KNOW*** WHAT HAPPENS.
HEY!
DANIEL! LINDY!
PERFECT TIMING, PRINCESS.
I-I NEED TO TALK TO YOU, LINDY.
I MEAN, ***WE*** NEED TO TALK. ABOUT-- ABOUT ***EVERY-THING***--
I THINK I GET YOU, PRINCESS.
FOLLOW ME TO THE LIBRARY.

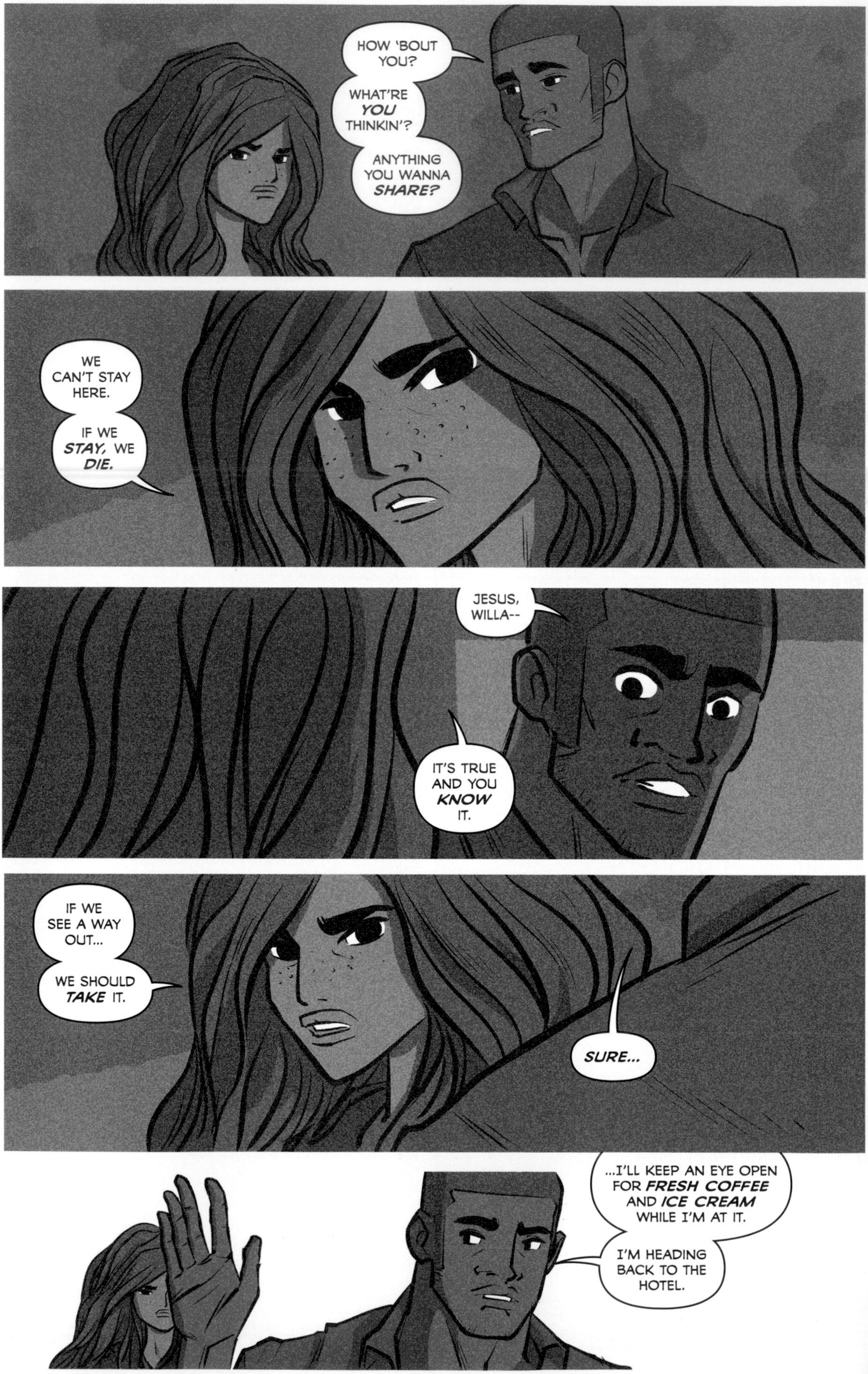
HOW 'BOUT YOU?
WHAT'RE *YOU* THINKIN'?
ANYTHING YOU WANNA *SHARE?*
WE CAN'T STAY HERE.
IF WE *STAY,* WE *DIE.*
JESUS, WILLA--
IT'S TRUE AND YOU *KNOW* IT.
IF WE SEE A WAY OUT...
WE SHOULD *TAKE* IT.
SURE...
...I'LL KEEP AN EYE OPEN FOR *FRESH COFFEE* AND *ICE CREAM* WHILE I'M AT IT.
I'M HEADING BACK TO THE HOTEL.

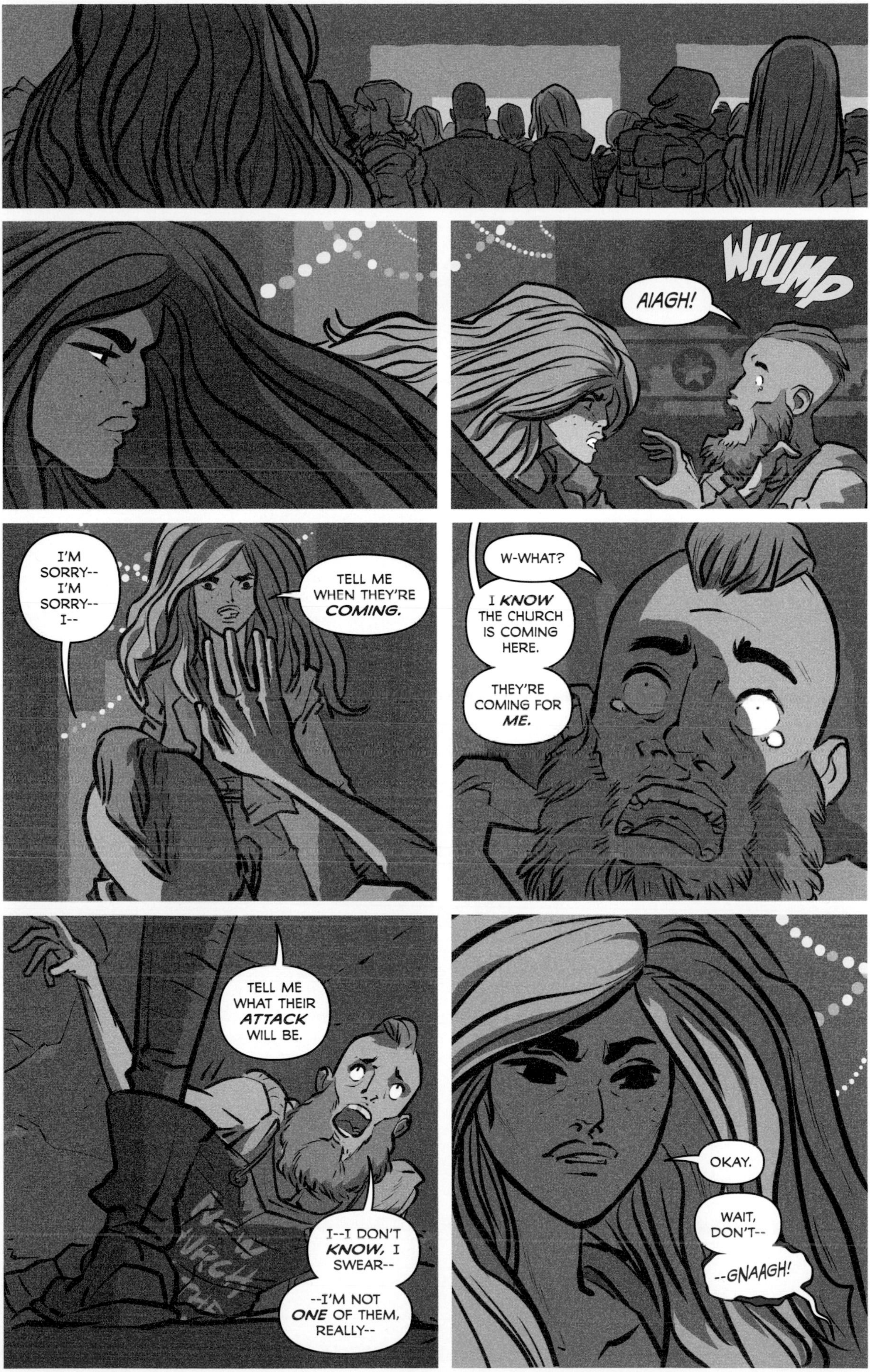
WHUMP
AIAGH!
I'M SORRY-- I'M SORRY-- I--
TELL ME WHEN THEY'RE *COMING.*
W-WHAT?
I *KNOW* THE CHURCH IS COMING HERE.
THEY'RE COMING FOR *ME.*
TELL ME WHAT THEIR *ATTACK* WILL BE.
I--I DON'T *KNOW,* I SWEAR--
--I'M NOT *ONE* OF THEM, REALLY--
OKAY.
WAIT, DON'T--
--GNAAGH!

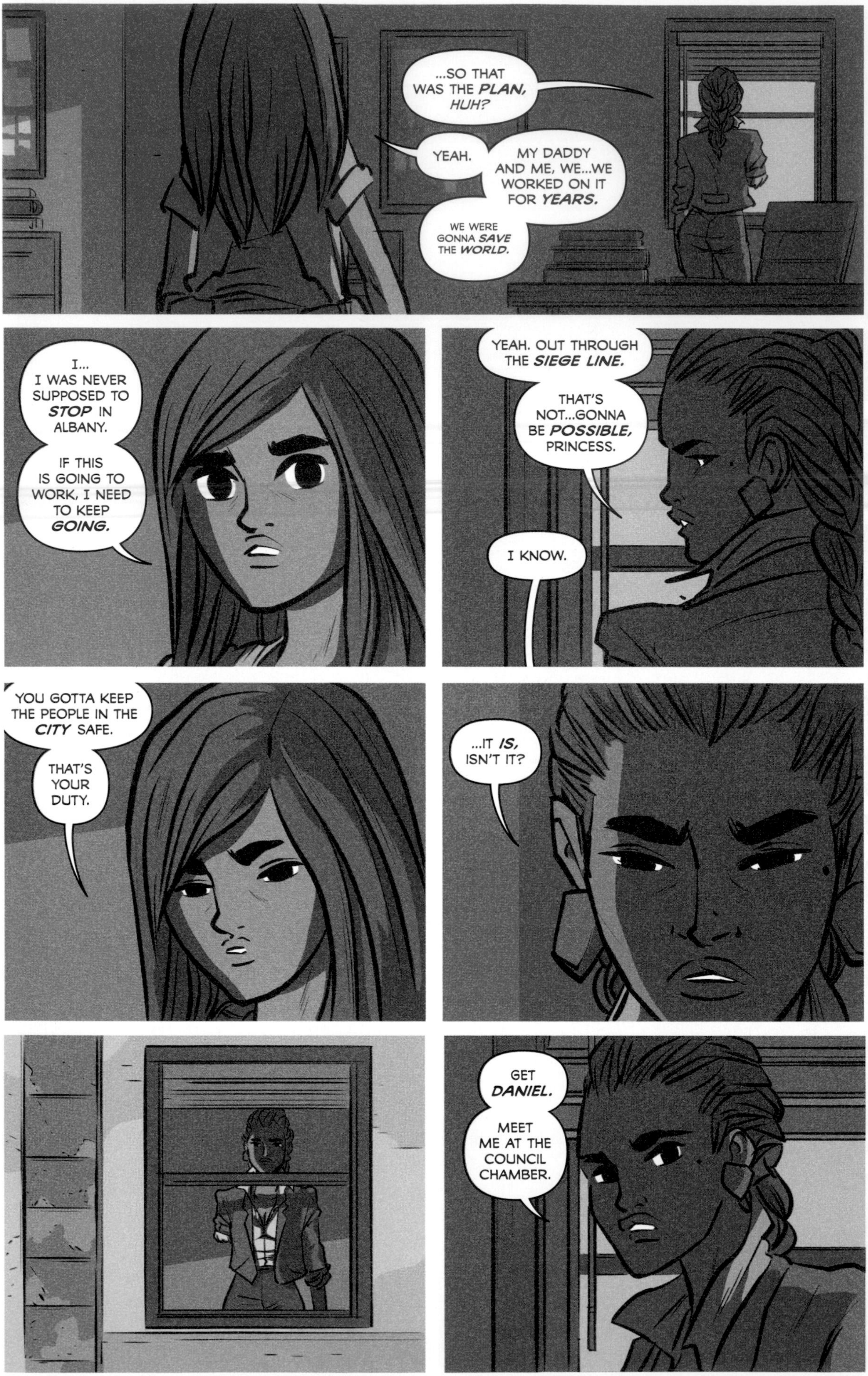
...SO THAT WAS THE PLAN, HUH?
YEAH.
MY DADDY AND ME, WE...WE WORKED ON IT FOR YEARS.
WE WERE GONNA SAVE THE WORLD.
I... I WAS NEVER SUPPOSED TO STOP IN ALBANY.
IF THIS IS GOING TO WORK, I NEED TO KEEP GOING.
YEAH. OUT THROUGH THE SIEGE LINE.
THAT'S NOT...GONNA BE POSSIBLE, PRINCESS.
I KNOW.
YOU GOTTA KEEP THE PEOPLE IN THE CITY SAFE.
THAT'S YOUR DUTY.
...IT IS, ISN'T IT?
GET DANIEL.
MEET ME AT THE COUNCIL CHAMBER.

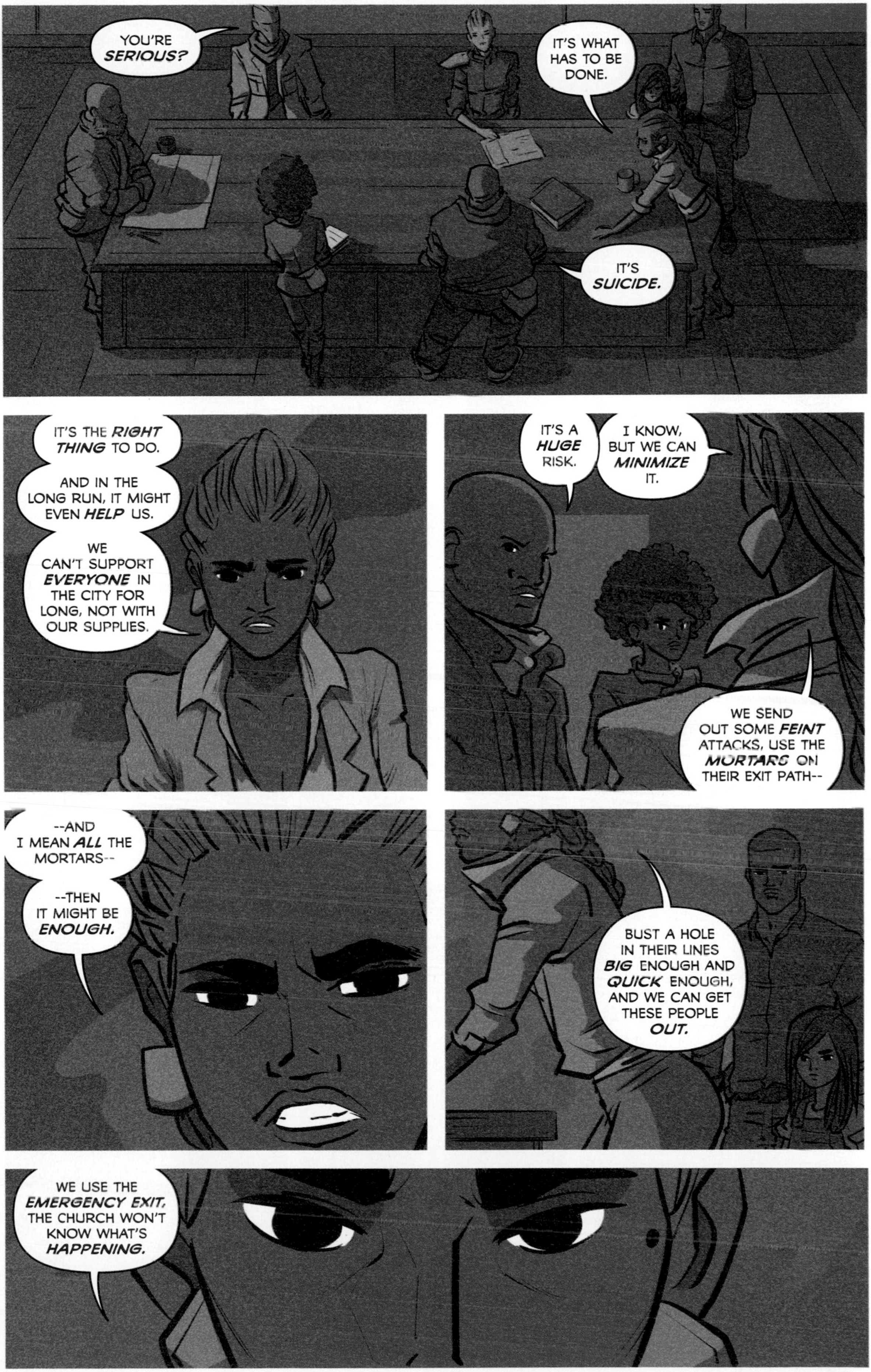
YOU'RE SERIOUS?
IT'S WHAT HAS TO BE DONE.
IT'S SUICIDE.
IT'S THE RIGHT THING TO DO.
AND IN THE LONG RUN, IT MIGHT EVEN HELP US.
WE CAN'T SUPPORT EVERYONE IN THE CITY FOR LONG, NOT WITH OUR SUPPLIES.
IT'S A HUGE RISK.
I KNOW, BUT WE CAN MINIMIZE IT.
WE SEND OUT SOME FEINT ATTACKS, USE THE MORTARS ON THEIR EXIT PATH--
--AND I MEAN ALL THE MORTARS--
--THEN IT MIGHT BE ENOUGH.
BUST A HOLE IN THEIR LINES BIG ENOUGH AND QUICK ENOUGH, AND WE CAN GET THESE PEOPLE OUT.
WE USE THE EMERGENCY EXIT, THE CHURCH WON'T KNOW WHAT'S HAPPENING.

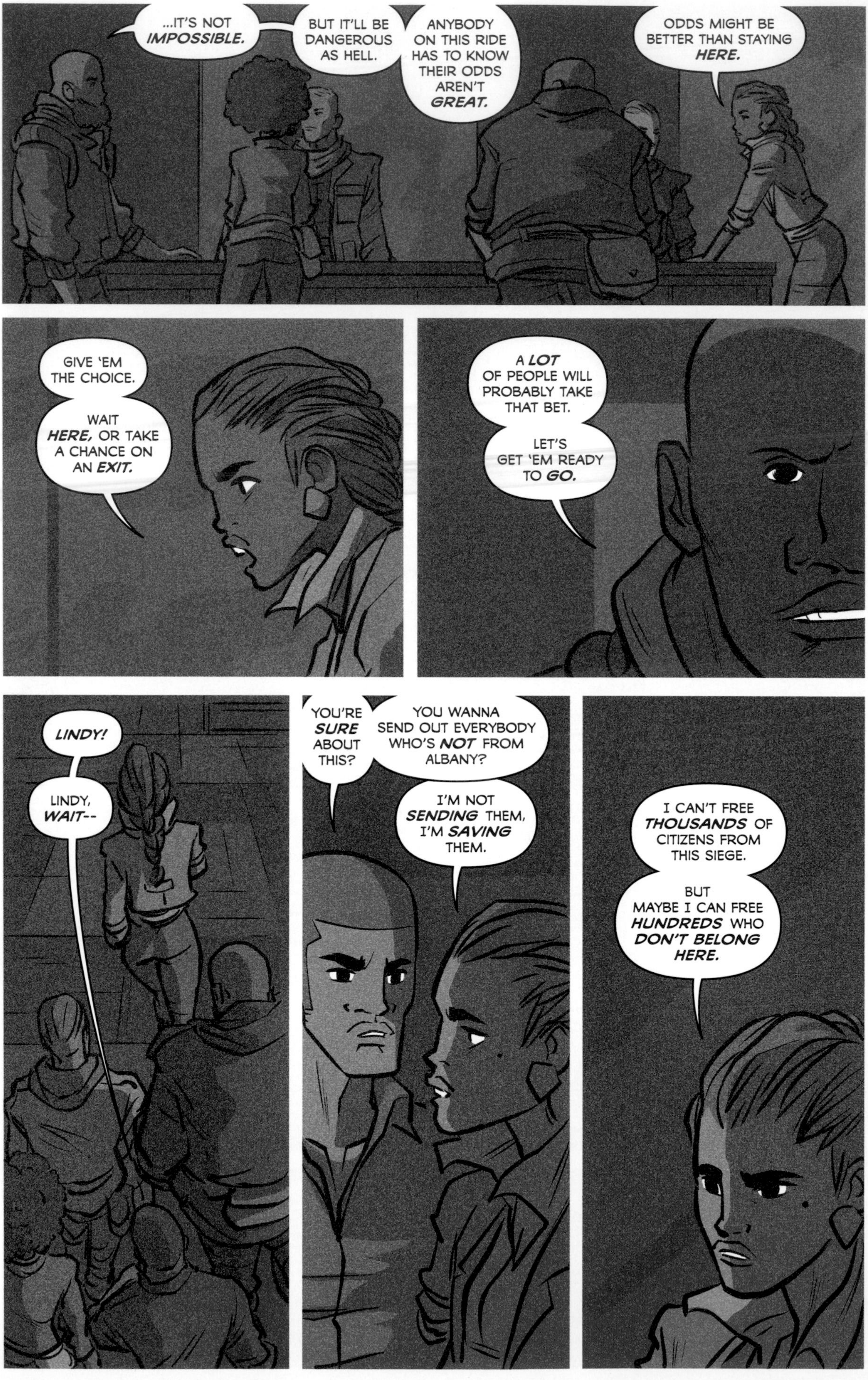
...IT'S NOT IMPOSSIBLE.
BUT IT'LL BE DANGEROUS AS HELL.
ANYBODY ON THIS RIDE HAS TO KNOW THEIR ODDS AREN'T GREAT.
ODDS MIGHT BE BETTER THAN STAYING HERE.
GIVE 'EM THE CHOICE.
WAIT HERE, OR TAKE A CHANCE ON AN EXIT.
A LOT OF PEOPLE WILL PROBABLY TAKE THAT BET.
LET'S GET 'EM READY TO GO.
LINDY!
LINDY, WAIT--
YOU'RE SURE ABOUT THIS?
YOU WANNA SEND OUT EVERYBODY WHO'S NOT FROM ALBANY?
I'M NOT SENDING THEM, I'M SAVING THEM.
I CAN'T FREE THOUSANDS OF CITIZENS FROM THIS SIEGE.
BUT MAYBE I CAN FREE HUNDREDS WHO DON'T BELONG HERE.

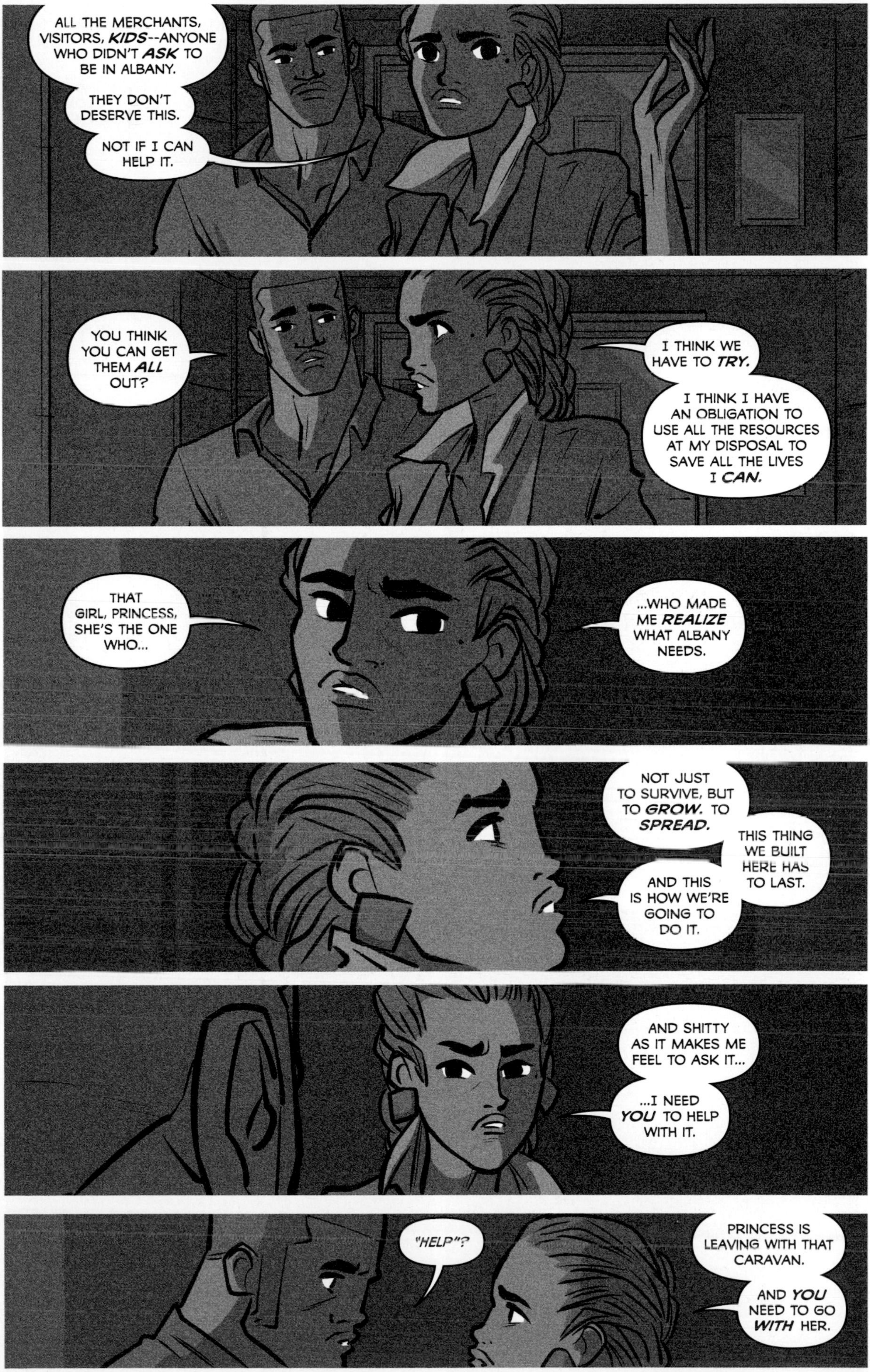
ALL THE MERCHANTS, VISITORS, KIDS--ANYONE WHO DIDN'T ASK TO BE IN ALBANY.
THEY DON'T DESERVE THIS.
NOT IF I CAN HELP IT.
YOU THINK YOU CAN GET THEM ALL OUT?
I THINK WE HAVE TO TRY.
I THINK I HAVE AN OBLIGATION TO USE ALL THE RESOURCES AT MY DISPOSAL TO SAVE ALL THE LIVES I CAN.
THAT GIRL, PRINCESS, SHE'S THE ONE WHO...
...WHO MADE ME REALIZE WHAT ALBANY NEEDS.
NOT JUST TO SURVIVE, BUT TO GROW. TO SPREAD.
THIS THING WE BUILT HERE HAS TO LAST.
AND THIS IS HOW WE'RE GOING TO DO IT.
AND SHITTY AS IT MAKES ME FEEL TO ASK IT...
...I NEED YOU TO HELP WITH IT.
"HELP"?
PRINCESS IS LEAVING WITH THAT CARAVAN.
AND YOU NEED TO GO WITH HER.

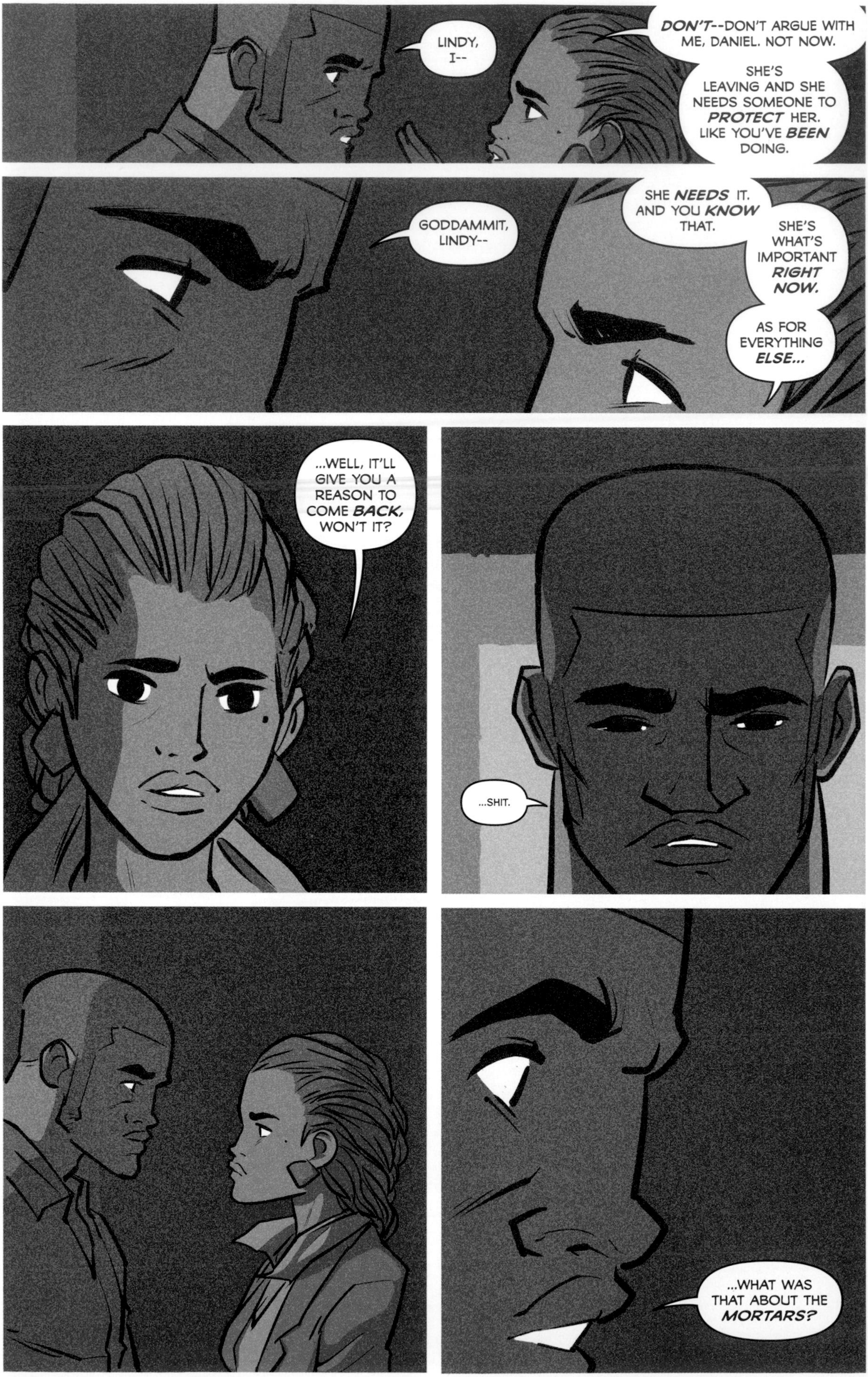
LINDY, I--
DON'T--DON'T ARGUE WITH ME, DANIEL. NOT NOW.
SHE'S LEAVING AND SHE NEEDS SOMEONE TO PROTECT HER. LIKE YOU'VE BEEN DOING.
GODDAMMIT, LINDY--
SHE NEEDS IT. AND YOU KNOW THAT.
SHE'S WHAT'S IMPORTANT RIGHT NOW.
AS FOR EVERYTHING ELSE...
...WELL, IT'LL GIVE YOU A REASON TO COME BACK, WON'T IT?
...SHIT.
...WHAT WAS THAT ABOUT THE MORTARS?

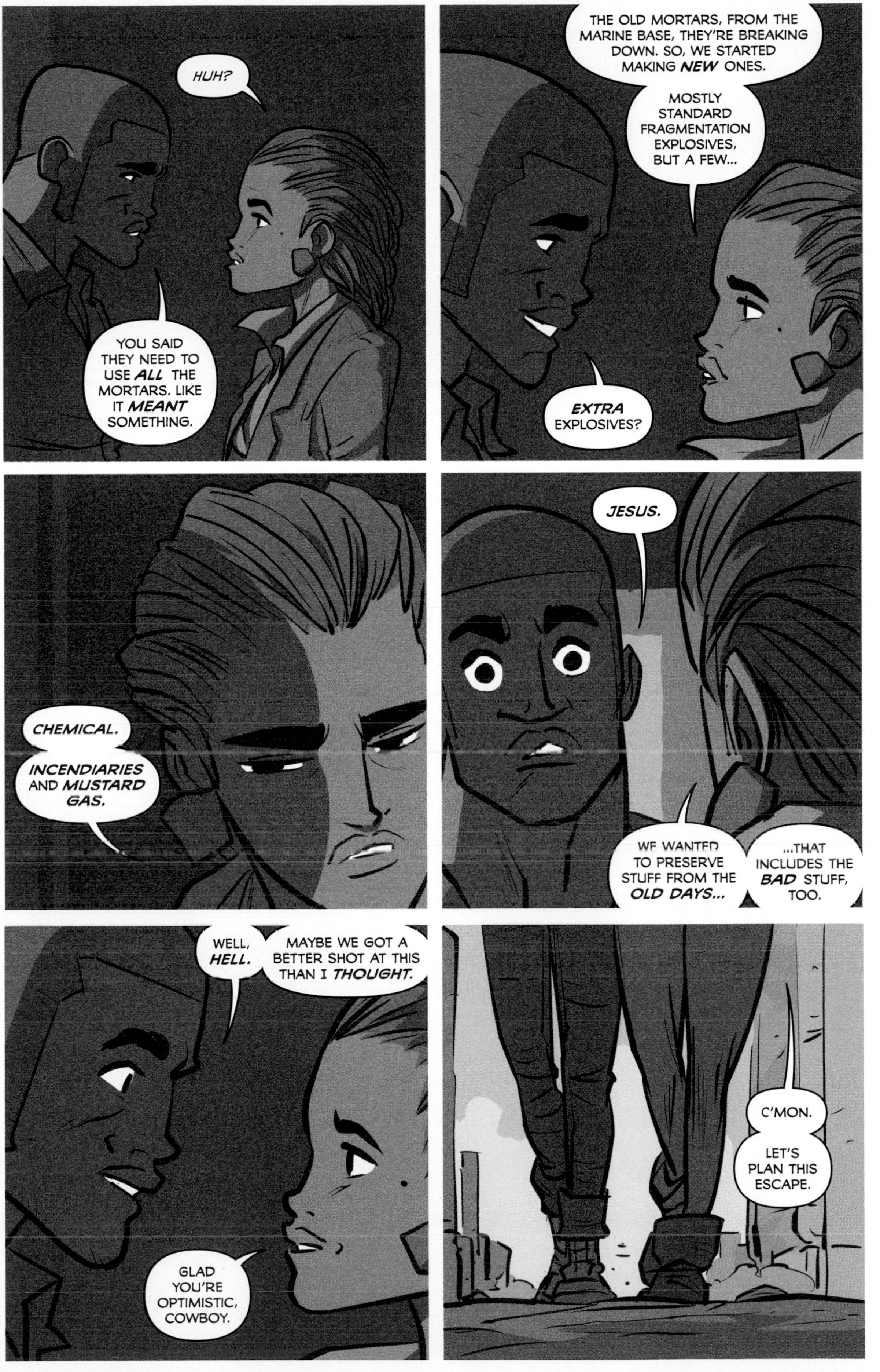
HUH?
YOU SAID THEY NEED TO USE ALL THE MORTARS. LIKE IT MEANT SOMETHING.
THE OLD MORTARS, FROM THE MARINE BASE, THEY'RE BREAKING DOWN. SO, WE STARTED MAKING NEW ONES.
MOSTLY STANDARD FRAGMENTATION EXPLOSIVES, BUT A FEW...
EXTRA EXPLOSIVES?
CHEMICAL.
INCENDIARIES AND MUSTARD GAS.
JESUS.
WE WANTED TO PRESERVE STUFF FROM THE OLD DAYS...
...THAT INCLUDES THE BAD STUFF, TOO.
WELL, HELL.
MAYBE WE GOT A BETTER SHOT AT THIS THAN I THOUGHT.
GLAD YOU'RE OPTIMISTIC, COWBOY.
C'MON.
LET'S PLAN THIS ESCAPE.

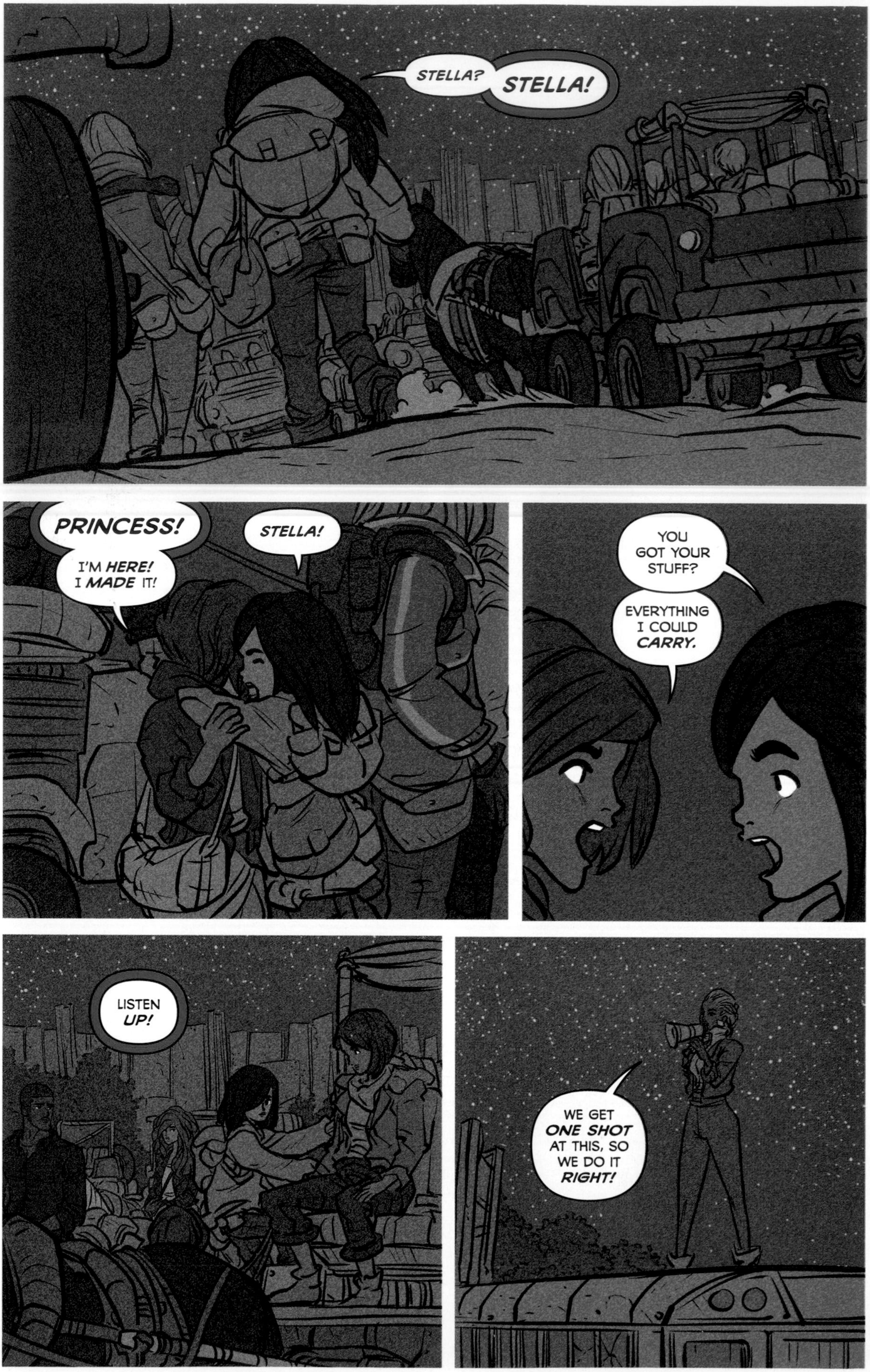
STELLA? STELLA!
PRINCESS!
I'M HERE! I MADE IT!
STELLA!
YOU GOT YOUR STUFF?
EVERYTHING I COULD CARRY.
LISTEN UP!
WE GET ONE SHOT AT THIS, SO WE DO IT RIGHT!

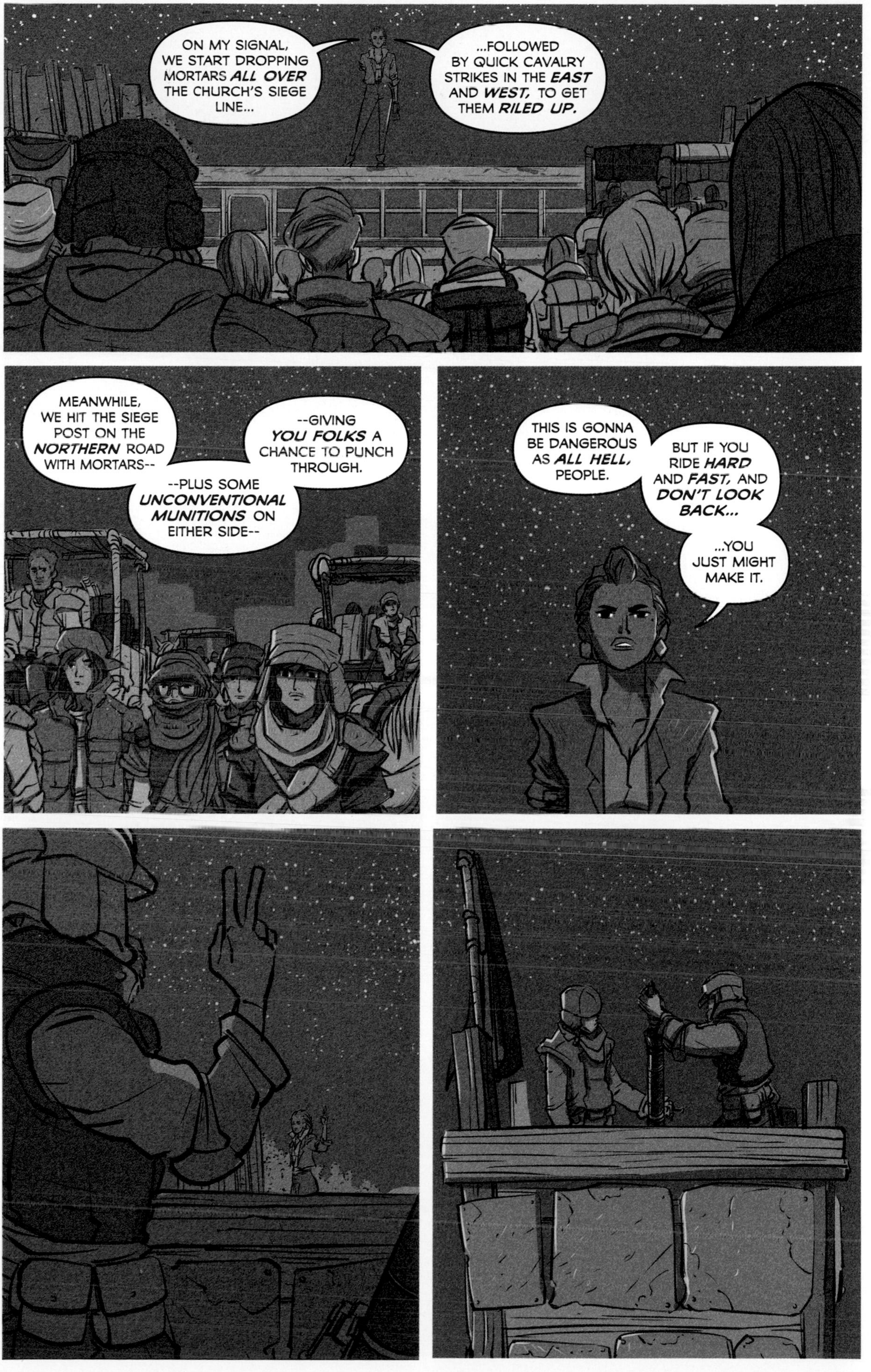
ON MY SIGNAL, WE START DROPPING MORTARS ALL OVER THE CHURCH'S SIEGE LINE...
...FOLLOWED BY QUICK CAVALRY STRIKES IN THE EAST AND WEST, TO GET THEM RILED UP.
MEANWHILE, WE HIT THE SIEGE POST ON THE NORTHERN ROAD WITH MORTARS--
--PLUS SOME UNCONVENTIONAL MUNITIONS ON EITHER SIDE--
--GIVING YOU FOLKS A CHANCE TO PUNCH THROUGH.
THIS IS GONNA BE DANGEROUS AS ALL HELL, PEOPLE.
BUT IF YOU RIDE HARD AND FAST, AND DON'T LOOK BACK...
...YOU JUST MIGHT MAKE IT.

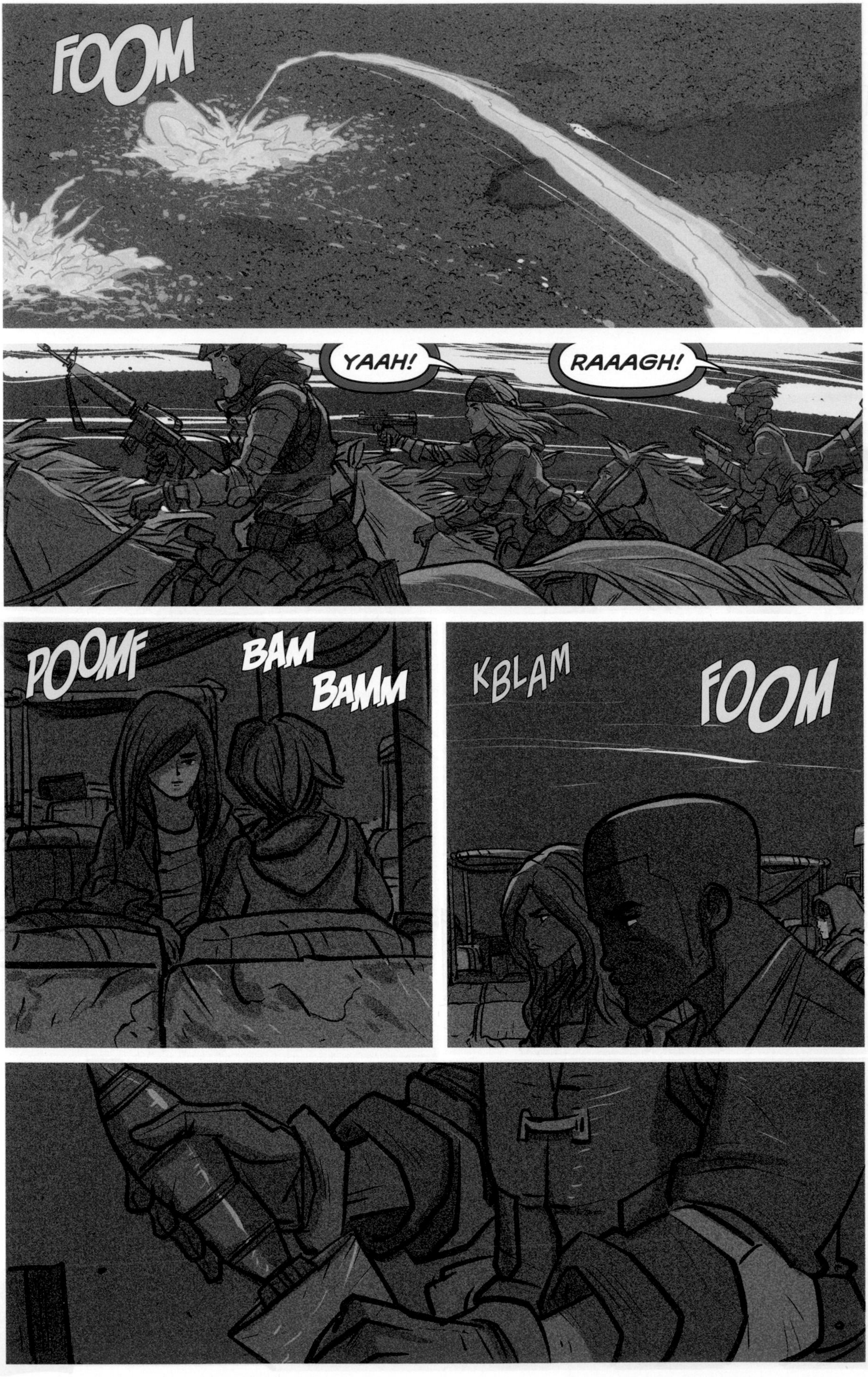
FOOM
YAAH!
RAAAGH!
POOMF
BAM
BAMM
KBLAM
FOOM

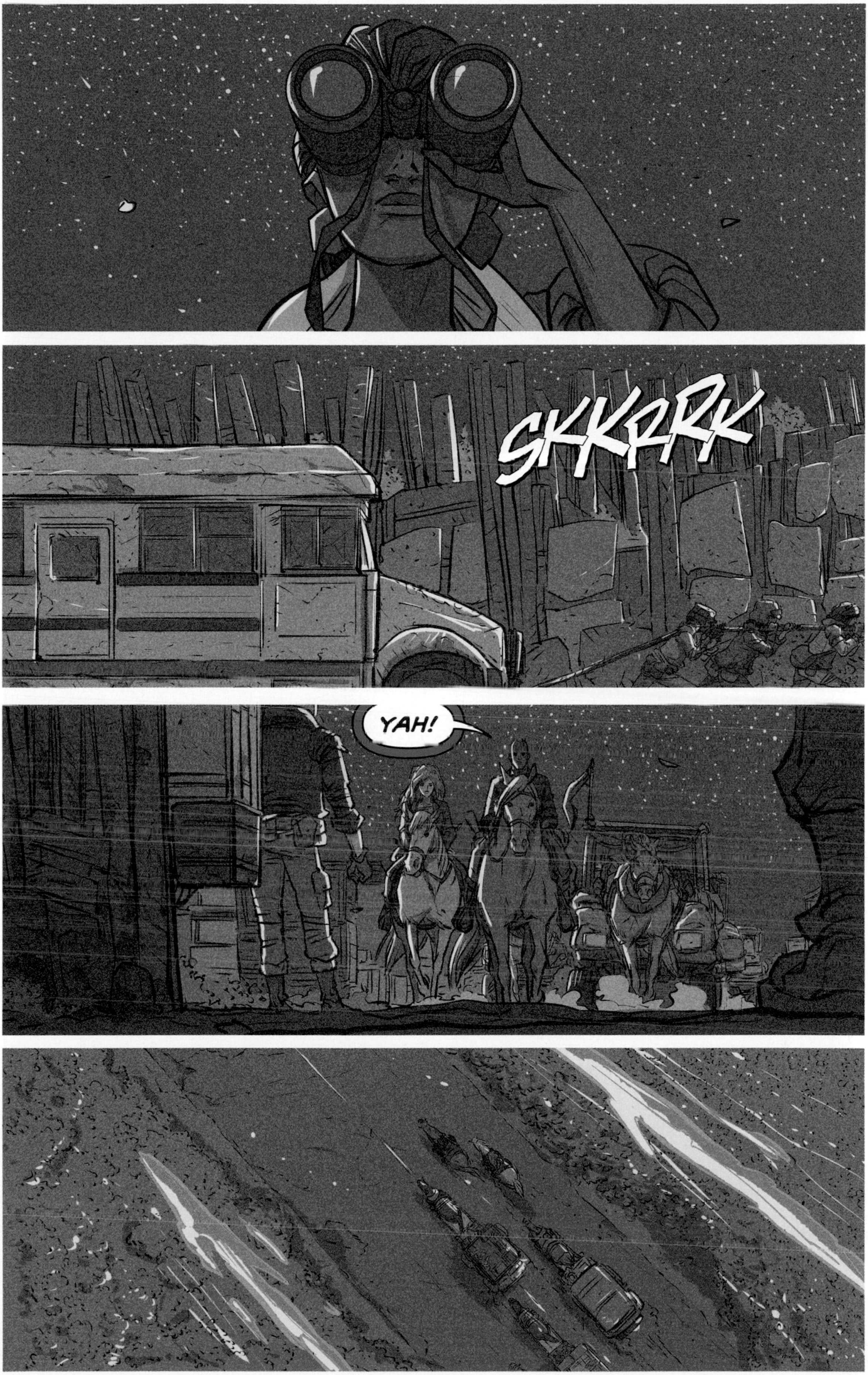
SKKRRK
YAH!

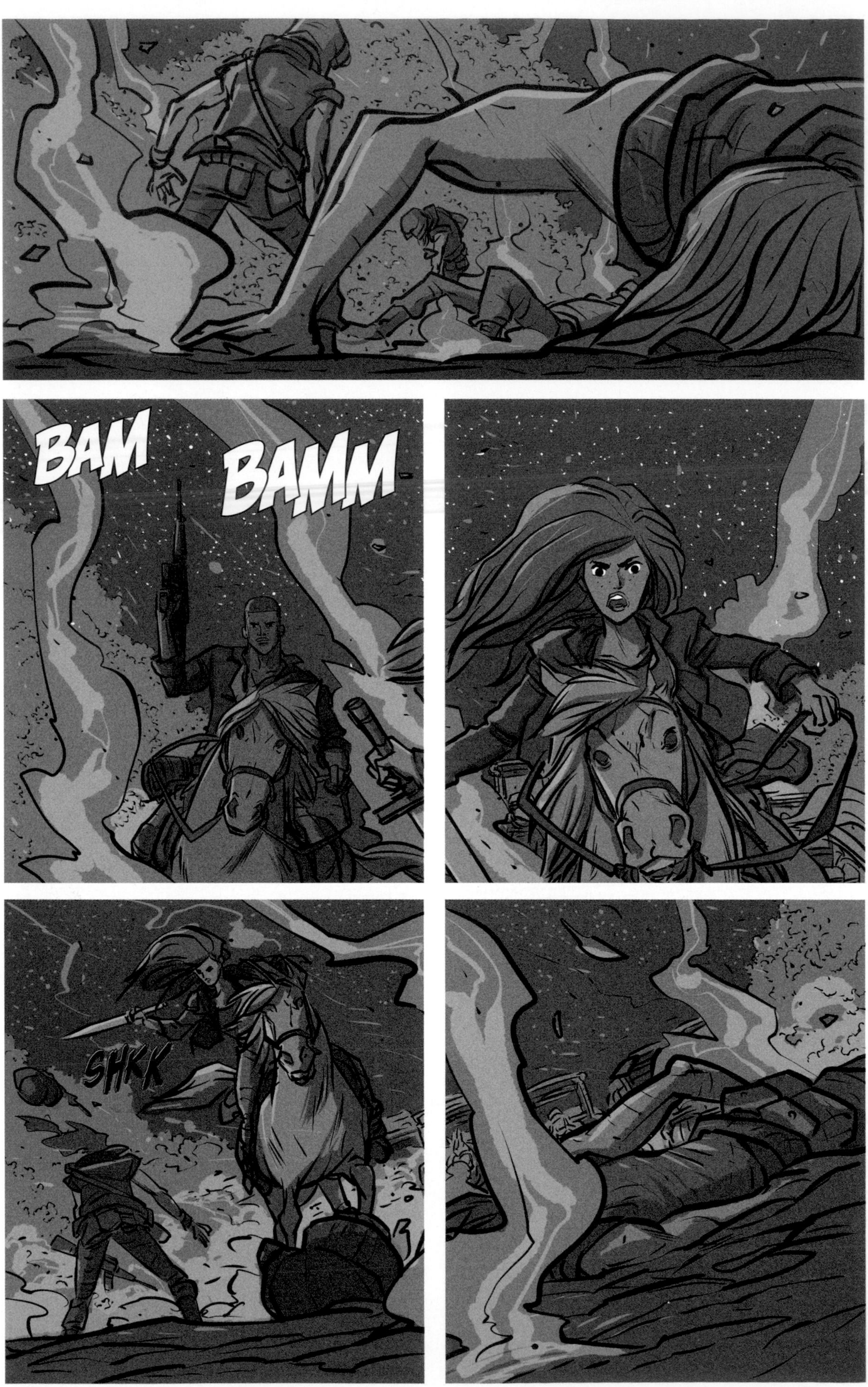
BAM
BAMM
SHKK

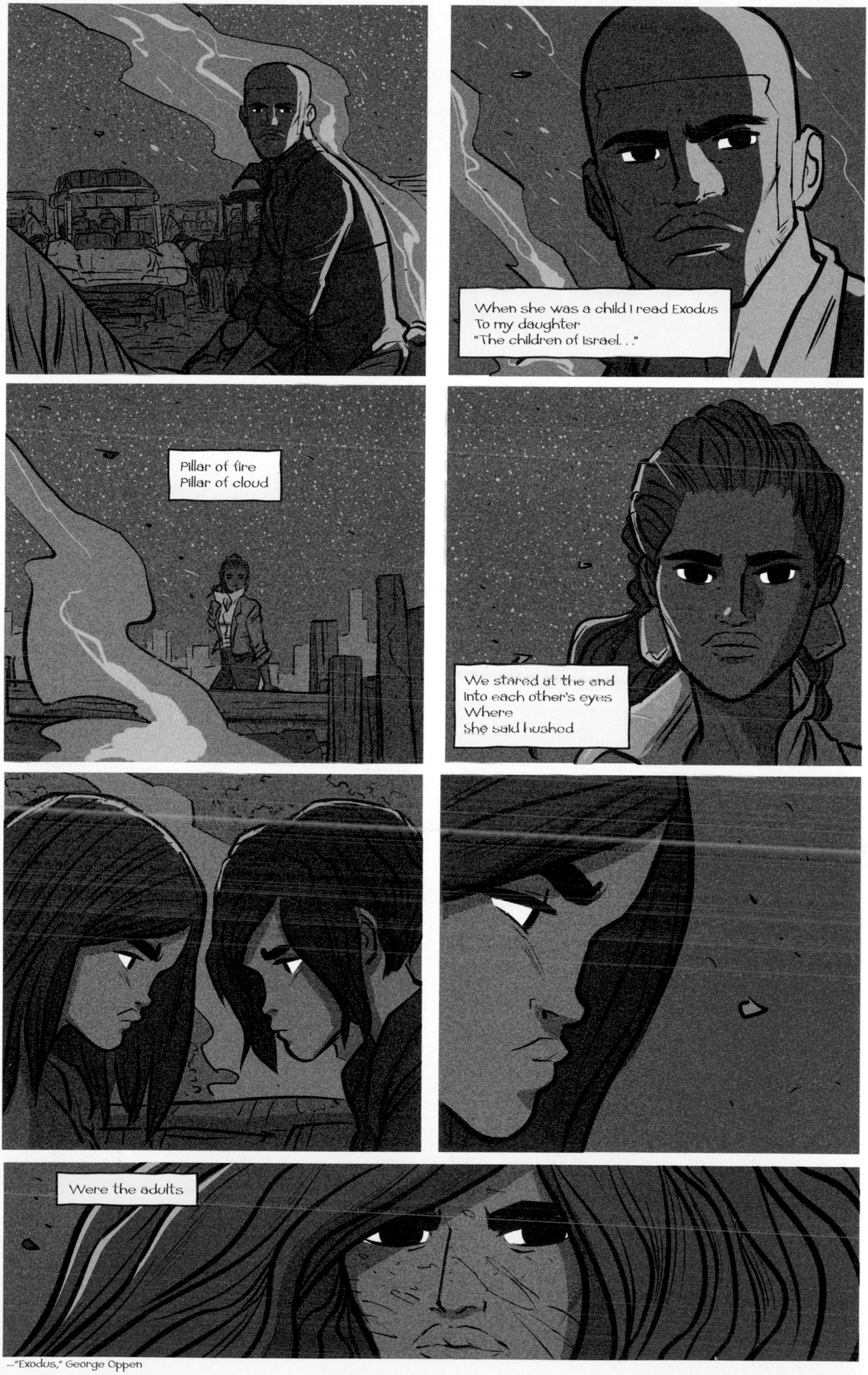
When she was a child I read Exodus
To my daughter
"The children of Israel. . ."
Pillar of fire
Pillar of cloud
We stared at the end
Into each other's eyes
Where
She said hushed
Were the adults

--"Exodus," George Oppen

ORPHAN AGE™

BEHIND THE SCENES

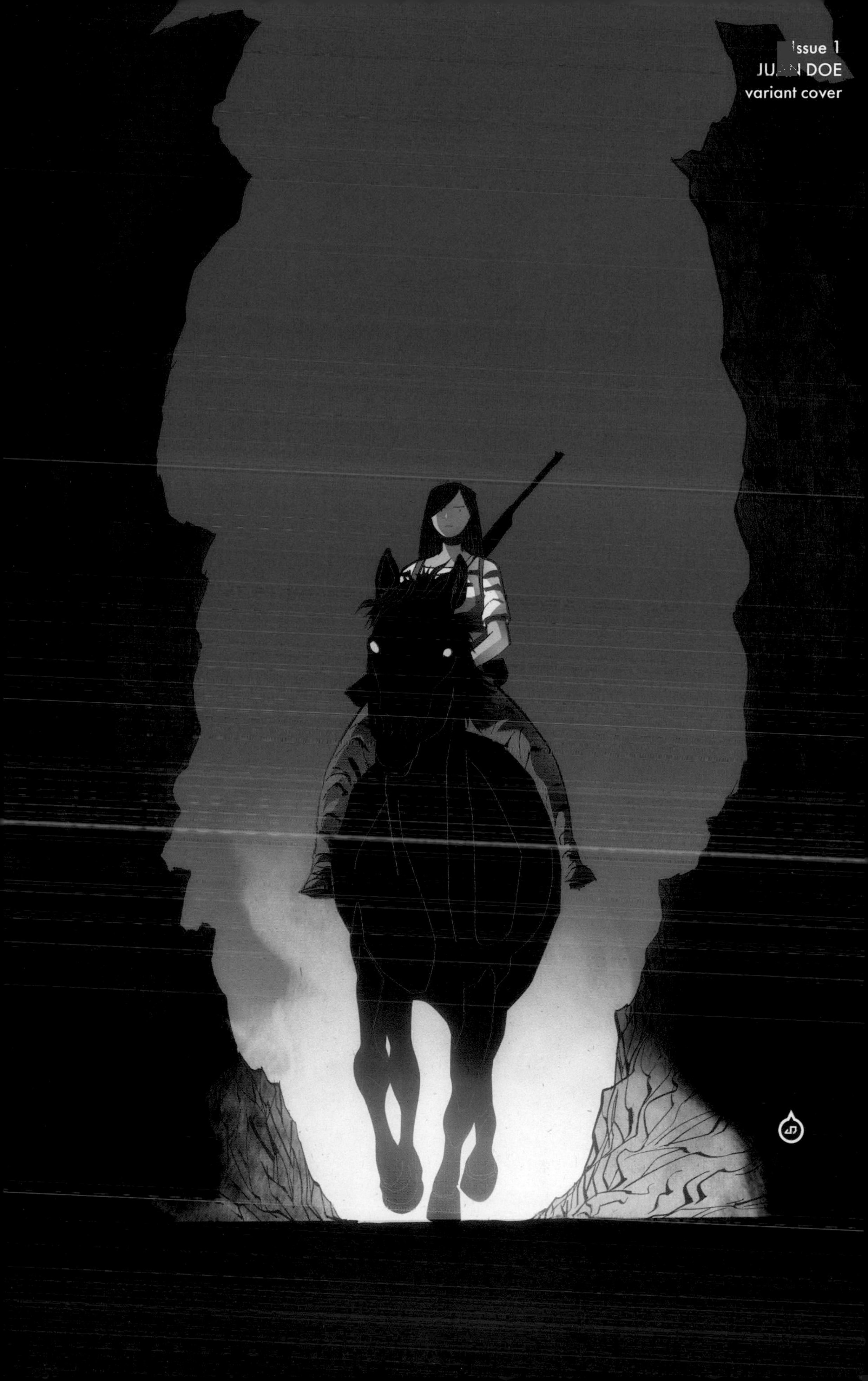
[redacted]ssue 1
JU[redacted] DOE
variant cover

ORPHAN AGE ™

#5

TITLE: Exodus

PAGE ONE

Panel 1. Just inside the gate that our heroes passed through in the previous issue. The gate is completely closed and all the guards are on the inside, trying to hold back a massive crowd of panicked people that are trying to flee the city. This takes place shortly after the end of issue 4; Albany has closed all its gates to hold back the New Church forces. (However, the Church forces aren't advancing; they're staying put in the trees.) So right now it's early morning or mid-morning, around 9 or 10. Stella is in the middle of the crowd, pushing her way up to the gate. Like everybody else, she's trying to leave, but the guards are staying put.

1 STELLA:
Excuse me!

Panel 2. Stella makes her way up to the gate, just in time for one of the guards to yell out over the crowd. The guard prominently holds his rifle as he shouts. He's not going to hurt anyone, but he needs to make sure nobody leaves.

2 STELLA:
Excuse me, please, I need to—

3 GUARD:
Gate's closed!

Panel 3. As the guard continues, a couple desperate-looking people manage to slip behind the guards and out the gate.

4 GUARD:
The Church's got snipers everywhere out there—you go out, you're dead.

5 GUARD:
Council told us to put the city on lockdown.

Panel 4. The guards notice the two people sneaking out! They're not going to shoot the escaping people, but they are very worried about what's going to happen.

6 GUARD:
Head back and—

7 GUARD:
—hey!

Panel 5. As the two people start running across the open road, they're both shot dead! The bullets are coming from the trees—the New Church killed them.

8 SFX (gunshot):
BLAM

9 SFX (gunshot):
Krak

Panel 6. Close on Stella and the guard's faces as they react with horror. Frame this so we're looking through part of the gate at them.

10 CAPTION (Councilman 1):
"Order!"

11 CAPTION (Councilman 1):
"Order, goddammit!"

script by
TED ANDERSON

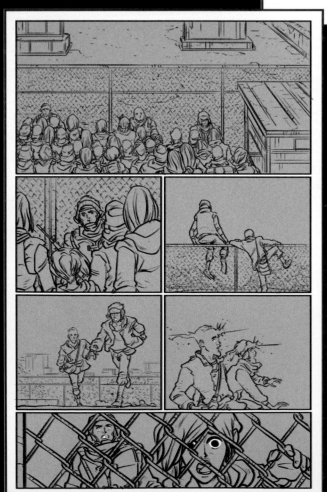

PAGE 1
PROCESS

art by
NUNO PLATI

colors by
JOÃO LEMOS

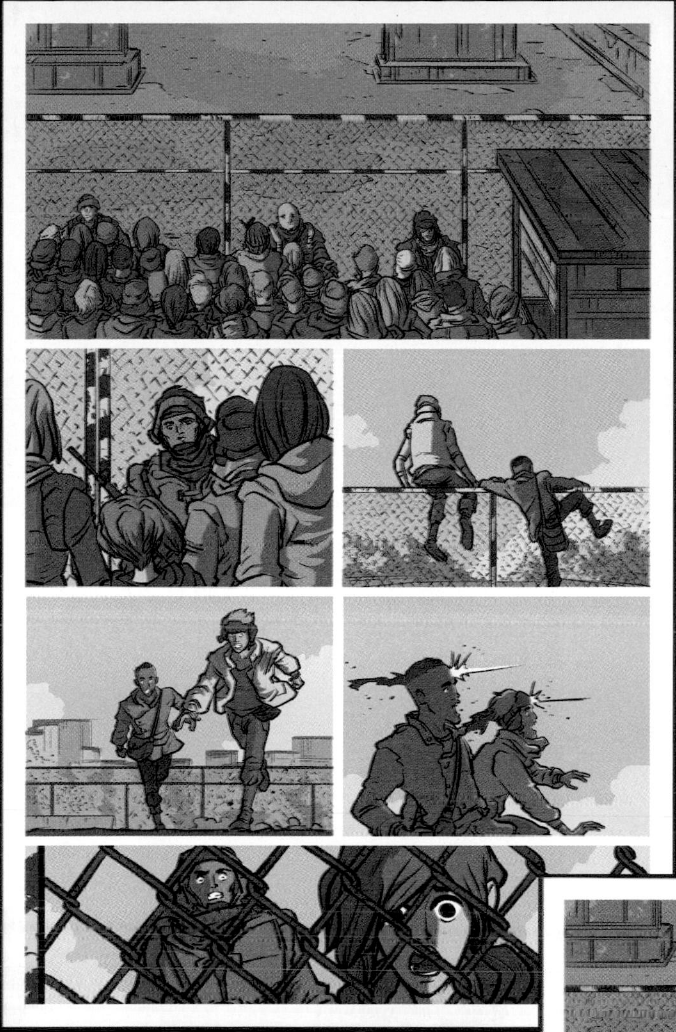

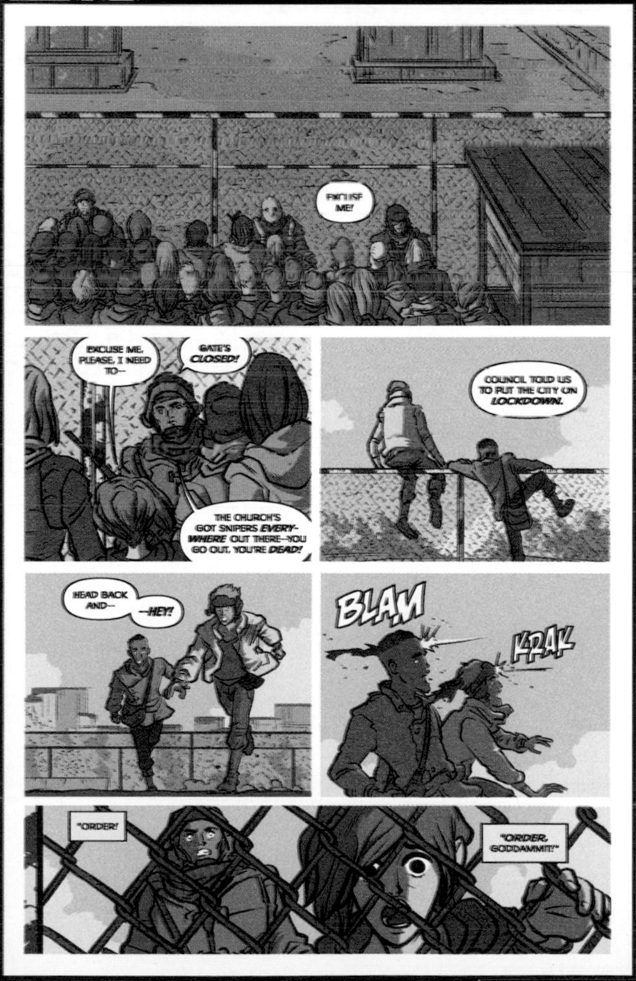
EXCUSE ME!
EXCUSE ME, PLEASE, I NEED TO--
GATE'S CLOSED!
THE CHURCH'S GOT SNIPERS EVERY-WHERE OUT THERE--YOU GO OUT, YOU'RE DEAD!
COUNCIL TOLD US TO PUT THE CITY ON LOCKDOWN.
HEAD BACK AND--
--HEY!
BLAM
KRAK
"ORDER!
"ORDER, GODDAMMIT!"

lettering by
MARSHALL DILLON

ORPHAN AGE

Character Designs
By artist NUNO PLATI

PRINCESS

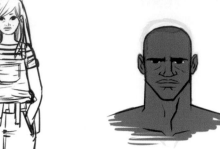

DANIEL

WILLA

AFTERSHOCK
AFTERSHOCKCOMICS.COM

STOCK UP ON THESE GREAT AFTERSHOCK
COLLECTIONS!

A WALK THROUGH HELL VOL 1
GARTH ENNIS / GORAN SUDZUKA
SEP181388

ALTERS VOL 1 & VOL 2
PAUL JENKINS / LEILA LEIZ
MAR171244 & APR181239

AMERICAN MONSTER VOL 1
BRIAN AZZARELLO / JUAN DOE
SEP161213

ANIMOSITY YEAR ONE, VOL 1, VOL 2,
VOL 3 & VOL 4
MARGUERITE BENNETT / RAFAEL DE LATORRE
FEB181034, JAN171219, AUG171130, MAY181314 & FEB191349

ANIMOSITY: EVOLUTION VOL 1 & VOL 2
MARGUERITE BENNETT / ERIC GAPSTUR
MAR181079 & FEB188089

ANIMOSITY: THE RISE HARDCOVER
MARGUERITE BENNETT / JUAN DOE
AUG178324

ART OF JIM STARLIN HARDCOVER
JIM STARLIN
MAR181077

BABYTEETH YEAR ONE, VOL 1 & VOL 2
DONNY CATES / GARRY BROWN
OCT181328, OCT171087 & APR181225

BETROTHED VOL 1
SEAN LEWIS / STEVE UY
DEC181449161115

BEYONDERS VOL 1
PAUL JENKINS / WESLEY ST. CLAIRE
JAN191460

BLACK-EYED KIDS VOL 1, VOL 2 & VOL 3
JOE PRUETT / SZYMON KUDRANSKI
AUG161116, FEB171199 & JAN181163

BROTHERS DRACUL VOL 1
CULLEN BUNN / MIRKO COLAK
SEP181404

CAPTAIN KID VOL 1
MARK WAID / TOM PEYER / WILFREDO TORRES
APR171231

CLAN KILLERS VOL 1
SEAN LEWIS / ANTONIO FUSO
JAN191469

COLD WAR VOL 1
CHRISTOPHER SEBELA / HAYDEN SHERMAN
JUL181518

DARK ARK VOL 1 & VOL 2
CULLEN BUNN / JUAN DOE
FEB181035 & SEP181394

DREAMING EAGLES HARDCOVER
GARTH ENNIS / SIMON COLEBY
AUG161114

ELEANOR & THE EGRET VOL 1
JOHN LAYMAN / SAM KIETH
DEC171041

FU JITSU VOL 1
JAI NITZ / WESLEY ST. CLAIRE
APR181241

HER INFERNAL DESCENT VOL 1
LONNIE NADLER / ZAC THOMPSON /
KYLE CHARLES / EOIN MARRON
OCT181341

HOT LUNCH SPECIAL VOL 1
ELIOT RAHAL / JORGE FORNES
DEC181449

INSEXTS YEAR ONE, VOL 1 & VOL 2
MARGUERITE BENNETT / ARIELA KRISTANTINA
APR181228, JUN161072 & SEP171098

JIMMY'S BASTARDS VOL & VOL 2
GARTH ENNIS / RUSS BRAUN
DEC171040 & JUN181333

LOST CITY EXPLORERS VOL 1
ZACHARY KAPLAN / ALVARO SARRASECA
NOV181434

MONSTRO MECHANICA VOL 1
PAUL ALLOR / CHRIS EVENHUIS
JUL181517

MOTH & WHISPER VOL 1
TED ANDERSON / JEN HICKMAN
FEB191351

NORMALS VOL 1
ADAM GLASS / DENNIS CALERO
SEP181391

OUT OF THE BLUE VOL 1 & VOL 2
GARTH ENNIS / KEITH BURNS
JAN191460 & MAY191310

**PATIENCE! CONVICTION!
REVENGE!** VOL 1
PATRICK KINDLON / MARCO FERRARI
FEB191350

PESTILENCE VOL 1 & VOL 2
FRANK TIERI / OLEG OKUNEV
NOV171154, OCT181340

REPLICA VOL 1
PAUL JENKINS / ANDY CLARKE
MAY161030

ROUGH RIDERS VOL 1, VOL 2 & VOL 3
ADAM GLASS / PATRICK OLLIFFE
OCT161101, SEP171097 & AUG181474

SECOND SIGHT VOL 1
DAVID HINE / ALBERTO PONTICELL
DEC161186

SHIPWRECK VOL 1
WARREN ELLIS / PHIL HESTER
MAR181078

SHOCK VOL 1 HARDCOVER & VOL 2 HARDCOVER
VARIOUS
JAN181139 & APR191300

SUPERZERO VOL 1
AMANDA CONNER / JIMMY PALMIOTTI / RAFAEL DE LATORRE
MAY161029

UNHOLY GRAIL VOL 1
CULLEN BUNN / MIRKO COLAK
JAN181151

WITCH HAMMER OGN
CULLEN BUNN / DALIBOR TALAJIC
SEP181387

WORLD READER VOL 1
JEFF LOVENESS / JUAN DOE
SEP171096

www.aftershockcomics.com/collections

Each series Copyright © 2018 by their respective owner. All rights reserved. AfterShock Comics and its logos are trademarks of AfterShock Comics, LLC.

ABOUT THE CREATORS OF

ORPHAN AGE™

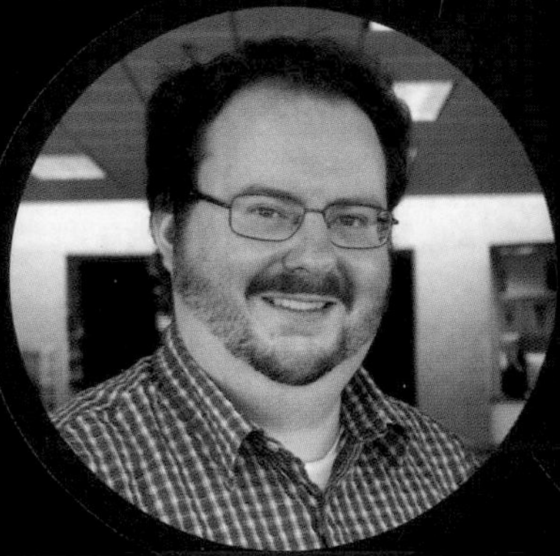

TED ANDERSON writer

@TedlyAnderson

Ted Anderson is a librarian, writer and mammal. He has written for properties including *My Little Pony* and *Adventure Time*, and has never successfully defrauded a major corporation. He lives in Minneapolis with no regrets.

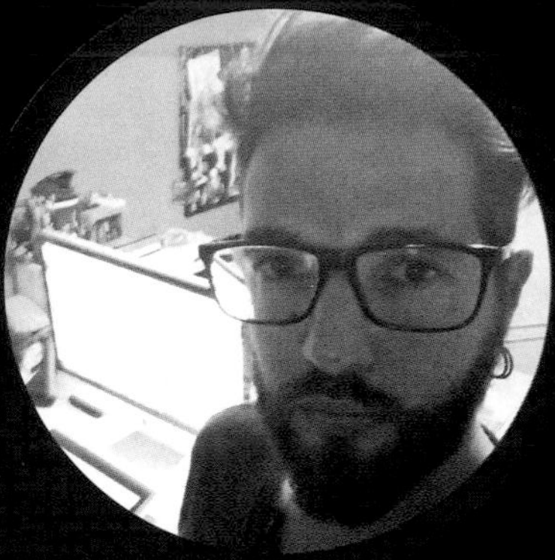

NUNO PLATI artist

Nuno Plati is a Portuguese illustrator and comic book artist. He's worked in videogames, fashion and editorial illustration since 2004 and in comics since 2007. Nuno has worked mostly with Marvel Comics, and has recently finished a graphic novel for the French Publisher, Glenat. He is currently the artist on ORPHAN AGE for AfterShock Comics.

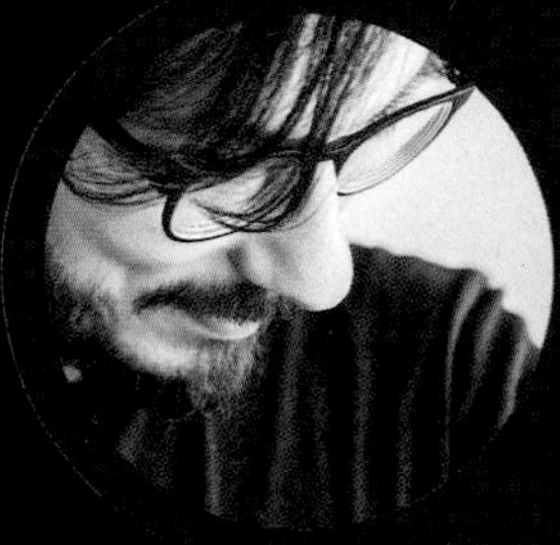

JOÃO LEMOS colorist

João M. P. Lemos is an illustrator and comics author who has drawn and written for Marvel, Vertigo and Archaia. He has also art directed music CDs, designed posters and worked on ABC's *Once Upon A Time* TV series. This is his very first time coloring anyone else's work.

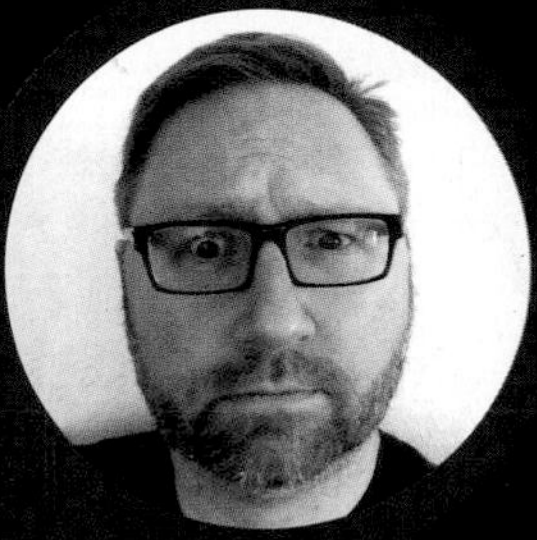

MARSHALL DILLON letterer

@MarshallDillon

A comic book industry veteran, Marshall got his start in 1994, in the midst of the indie comic boom. Over the years, he's been everything from an independent self-published writer to an associate publisher working on properties like *G.I. Joe*, *Voltron*, and *Street Fighter*. He's done just about everything except draw a comic book, and worked for just about every publisher except the "big two." Primarily a father and letterer these days, he also dabbles in old-school paper and dice RPG game design. You can catch up with Marshall at firstdraftpress.net.